Ancient Chronology

Part I

By Olaf Alfred Toffteen

ISBN: 978-1-63923-641-1

All Rights reserved. No part of this book maybe reproduced without written permission from the publishers, except by a reviewer who may quote brief passages in a review to be printed in a newspaper or magazine.

Printed: January 2023

Published and Distributed By:
Lushena Books
607 Country Club Drive, Unit E
Bensenville, IL 60106
www.lushenabks.com

ISBN: 978-1-63923-641-1

TO
EMORY COBB
THE FRIEND OF HIGHER EDUCATION
IN TOKEN OF
GRATITUDE
AND
SINCERE REGARD

PREFACE

Chronology is necessarily a very uninteresting subject. At the same time, it is the skeleton of history, and the essential basis for historical research, without which no trustworthy results in the study of ancient history, civilization, or religion may be attained.

I have, therefore, no excuse to offer for the appearance of this volume. Although I recognize the value of the scholarly efforts which have lately been made in this field, the rapid course of new discoveries in the Orient tends to antiquate any work which attempts to deal adequately with such a broad subject. Whatever has been done hitherto, and however praiseworthy the researches of modern scholars may be, the time is ripe for a new investigation of the whole subject.

The present volume is an expansion of lectures delivered last fall before the Oriental Society of the Western Theological Seminary, Chicago, and is published in response to requests made by several members of that society. It was at first intended to issue it as an introduction to *Side-Lights on Biblical Chronology*, but the material was too extensive, and would have made that volume too bulky. For this reason I decided to publish the more technical matter separately under the present title.

This volume attempts to cover the ancient chronology of Palestine, Assyria, Babylonia, and Egypt, down to 1050 B. C. The period from this date to the Christian era will be treated in a subsequent book.

In the first chapter I have treated biblical chronology solely on the basis of the dates furnished by the Bible, taking them at their face value, and without any inquiry, either into the age of the documents, or into their histor-

PREFACE

icity. These questions will be taken up in a succeeding volume on *Side-Lights on Biblical Chronology*, which will be an expansion of this chapter. But biblical chronology is indissolubly bound up with the chronology of the eastern empires of Egypt, Babylonia, and Assyria.

In the second chapter, on Assyrian and Babylonian chronology, I have entered as fully as is possible under present circumstances into the ancient history of these countries. The results which I have reached differ in many and essential particulars from those of modern scholars who have written on the subject. I feel confident, however, that my conclusions will be found to be within the bounds of legitimate research and high probability. A certain class of Assyriologists seem to be possessed by an idea that Babylonian history, in order to be of any interest at all, must extend several millennia back of Christ, and they have felt supported in this view by Nabonidus' date of Narâm-sin. Several protests have lately been made against this contention, and I have taken one step farther. I believe that the question of Sargon's place in history is settled, so far as certainty may be expected. Since the manuscript of this book was written, new discoveries, bearing on the chronology of Babylonia and Assyria, have been made, and it has been a pleasure to me to find that every one which has come under my notice has sustained the views which were here set forth before the appearance of Vols. VI, XIV, XV, and XX of the publications of the Babylonian Expedition of the University of Pennsylvania, which have entirely dispelled the obscurity surrounding the dates of the dynasties of Ur, Isin, and part of the Kassite period. In the month of May of this year the library of the Seminary came into possession of the latest volumes issued by the Deutsche Orient-Gesellschaft, of the publication of which I was unaware up to that time. Several dates of ancient Assyrian chronology have been made sure by these researches, and I was again sustained in my views. A week ago, Professor R. F. *H*arper kindly sent me King's *Chronicles Concerning Early Assyrian Kings*, and it was a source of satisfaction to me to find my conclusions as to the partial contemporaneity of the Second Dynasty of the Sea-Land with the *H*ammurabi and the Kassite Dynasties confirmed by the documents published in these volumes. Although my book was already in type, and part of it in page form, I felt it my duty to incur the delay necessary to insert these documents, and to add a few comments on them. I am unable to accept some of King's conclusions, but I hope that my reasons for this attitude are legitimate, and may perhaps be found convincing.

In the matter of Egyptian chronology, I am under obligation to the excellent work done in this field by the eminent historian, Dr. Eduard *M*eyer, and by Professor James *H*. Breasted, my former teacher. I wish here to acknowledge my indebtedness to the researches made by these scholars, in spite of the fact that I have felt constrained to differ from them in treating some of the important periods of Egyptian history. This applies especially to the accession of Amenhotep IV, where considerations of Babylonian chronology have convinced me that the reign of this king should be placed thirty years before the time assigned him by these scholars. The same may be said of the Eleventh Dynasty, the lower date of which has led to the result that I have felt obliged to place the accession of *M*enes and the founding of the united Egyptian kingdom more than one hundred years later than Professor Meyer has done, although his date has been regarded by many as too late. My views on the reign of Seti I may be questioned, but I am satisfied that the testimony of the monuments, when read in the light of Manetho, favors my position.

I trust that the several chronological charts and indices may be found helpful to scholars who are pursuing studies in this subject.

I wish to express my gratitude to my friend and former teacher, Dr. R. F. Harper, for allowing me unrestricted access to his valuable library.

It is due to my readers to explain that, writing in a language other than my native tongue, it has been impossible to avoid a certain inaptness of expression, and I hope for their indulgence.

I desire also to express my grateful obligation to the Rev. Erle H. Merriman, B.D., who has helped me in this respect by reading my manuscript, as well as in the correction of the proofs.

For many valuable suggestions offered by my dean, the Rev. W. C. DeWitt, S.T.D., and my colleague, the Rev. Stuart L. Tyson, M.A., I am sincerely grateful.

I cannot refrain from expressing my profound appreciation of the generosity of two friends of our seminary (whose names I am not at liberty to mention) for the financial guarantee which has made this publication possible. My thanks are due to the Rev. William O. Waters, treasurer of the Oriental Society, for many acts of encouragement and assistance in this undertaking.

OLAF A. TOFFTEEN

WESTERN THEOLOGICAL SEMINARY
CHICAGO, ILLINOIS
August 6, 1907

BIBLIOGRAPHY

A. ABBREVIATIONS

ABL., R. F. Harper, *Assyrian and Babylonian Letters*, Vols. I–VIII.
AKA., E. A. Wallis Budge and L. W. King, *Annals of the Kings of Assyria*, Vol. I, 1902.
AJSL., *American Journal of Semitic Languages and Literatures*.
AL., H. Winckler, *The Tell el-Amarna Letters*.
AOF., H. Winckler, *Altorientalische Forschungen*.
ARE., James H. Breasted, *Ancient Records of Egypt*, Vols. I–V, 1906.
BA., *Beiträge zur Assyriologie*.
BE., Babylonian Expedition of the University of Pennsylvania, Ser. A, Vols. I, VI, IX, X, XIV, XV, XX; Ser. D, Vol. III.
BM., British Museum.
HC., Robert F. Harper, *Code of Hammurabi*.
ICC., *International Critical Commentary*.
JRAS., *Journal of the Royal Asiatic Society*.
K., *The Kuyunjik Collection of the British Museum*.
KAT.[3], H. Winckler und H. Zimmern, *Keilinschriften und das Alte Testament*, 3te Aufl.
KB., Eberhard Schrader, *Keilinschriftliche Bibliothek*, Vols. I–VI.
MDOG., *Mittheilungen der deutschen Orient-Gesellschaft*.
MVG., *Mitteilungen der vorderasiatischen Gesellschaft*.
PSBA., *Proceedings of the Society of Biblical Archaeology*.
R., *Cuneiform Inscriptions of Western Asia*. Vols. I–V.
RP., *Records of the Past*.
RT., *Recucil de Travaux*.
SBAW., *Sitzungsberichte der Berlinischen Akademie der Wissenschaften*.
TSBA., *Transactions of the Society of Biblical Archaeology*.
UAG., H. Winckler, *Untersuchungen zur altorientalischen Geschichte*.
ZA., *Zeitschrift für Assyriologie*.
ZÄ., *Zeitschrift für Ägyptische Sprache und Altertumskunde*.

B. BOOKS

James H. Breasted. *Ancient Records of Egypt*, Vols. I–V.
   History of Egypt.
H. Brugsch-Bey. *Egypt under the Pharaohs.*
E. A. Wallis Budge and L. W. King. *Annals of the Kings of Assyria*, Vol. I.
Albert T. Clay. *Temple Documents of the Kassite Period*, BE., Ser. A, Vols. XIV, XV.
Friedrich Delitzsch. "Die Königsliste," *Sitzungsberichte der kgl. sächs. Akademie der Wissenschaften.*
   Zur babylonischen Königslisten.
   Assyriologische Miscellen.
A. von Gutschmid. *Kleine Schriften.*
Robert Francis Harper. *Assyrian and Babylonian Letters (ABL.)*, Vols. I–VII.
   Code of Hammurabi (HC.),
H. V. Hilprecht. *Old Babylonian Inscriptions (BE.*, Vol. I).
   Mathematical and Chronological Tablets (BE., Vol. XX).
Fl. Josephus. *Antiquities.*
   Contra Apionem.
L. W. King. *Chronicles Concerning Early Babylonian Kings*, Vols. I, II.
   Letters of Hammurabi, Vols. I–III.
   Records of Tukulti-Ninib I.
L. W. King and H. R. Hall. *History of Egypt.*
J. A. Knudtzon. *Assyrische Gebete an den Sonnengott*, Vols. I, II.
C. F. Lehmann. *Zwei Hauptprobleme.*
R. Lepsius. *Das Königsbuch.*
Ernst Lindl. *Die Datenlisten der erstern Dynastie von Babylon (BA.*, Vol. IV, pp. 338–402).
J. Marquart. *Chronologische Untersuchungen.*
B. Meissner. *Altbabylonisches Privatrecht.*
Eduard Meyer. *Aegyptische Chronologie.*
   Sumerier und Semiten in Babylonia.
F. G. Moore. *Judges (ICC.).*
Carl Niebuhr. *Die Chronologie der Geschichte Israels, Aegyptens, Babylonians und Assyriens.*

L. B. Paton. *The Early History of Syria and Palestine.*
Pauly-Wissowa. *Real-Encyclopedie.*
W. M. Flanders Petrie. *History of Egypt*, Vols. I–III.
H. Radau. *Early History of Babylonia.*
R. Rogers. *A History of Babylonia and Assyria*, Vols. I, II.
Paul Rost. *Untersuchungen zur altorientalischen Geschichte.*
Eberhard Schrader. *Keilinschriftliche Bibliothek (KB.)*, Vols. I–VI.
    Keilinschriften und die Geschichtsforschung.
    Die keilinschriftliche babylonische Königsliste, SBAW., 1887.
Kurt Sethe. *Untersuchungen zur Geschichte und Altertumskunde Agyptens.*
F. Thurean-Dangin. *Recherches sur l'origine de l'écriture cunéiforme.*
Olaf A. Toffteen. *Researches in Assyrian and Babylonian Geography* (see also, *AJSL.*, XXIII). (In press.)
    Side Lights on Biblical Chronology, I. (In press.)
F. Weissbach. *Babylonische Miscellen.*
Hugo Winckler. *Altorientalische Forschungen*, Reihe I–III, 2
    The Tell el-Amarna Letters.
    Untersuchungen zur altorientalischen Geschichte.
H. Winckler and H. Zimmern. *Keilinschriften und das Alte Testament*, 3te Aufl.

ERRATA

Page 78, line 6 from above, for 2223 read 2233.
Page 80, line 6 from below, exchange the numbers 43 and 55.
Page 203, line 5 from above, for former read latter.
Page 203, line 6 from above, for latter read former.
Page 232, line 11 from below, strike out all before Egypt.
Page 233, line 7 from above, for Mentuhotep II read Mentuhotep I.
Page 234, line 4 from above, for Mentuhotep II read Mentuhotep I.
Page 235, line 15 from below, for monarch read nomarch.
Page 235, line 1 from below for southern read northern.

Bitiliashu II, 70; Seal of Shagarakti-Shuriash, 71; Dynasty A of Babylon, 73; Chronology of Simplicius, 76; Chronology of Berossos, 77; Chronology of Dynasty A, 79; Dynasty B of Uru-kha, 81; Chronology of Dynasty B, 82; Date of Nebuchadrezzar I, 82; Boundary Stone of Bêl-nâdin-aplu, 83; Fall of Dynasty B, 86; Rise of the Kassite Power, 87; Conquest of Babylonia, 90; Original

CONTENTS

	PAGES
CHAPTER I. BIBLICAL CHRONOLOGY	1–19

The Ptolemaic Canon, 1; Assyrian *Limmu-Lists*, 2; *Expedition-Lists*, 2; Shalmaneser II, 3; Ahab and Jehu, 5; Early Kings of Judah and Israel, 6; Building of the Temple of Solomon, 7; Patriarchal Chronology, 8; Genealogy of Shem, 11; The Heroic Age, 12; Book of Judges, 12–17; Chronology of the Judges, 18.

CHAPTER II. BABYLONIAN AND ASSYRIAN CHRONOLOGY   20–148

A. The Chronological Material, 20–59; Biblical References, 20; Egyptian Inscriptions, 20; Classical Authors, 21; Assyrian and Babylonian Inscriptions, 22; the *King-Lists*, 22; *King-List B*, 22–24; *King-List A*, 24–28; the *Date-Lists*, 29–31; Minimum Dates, 31; *Amarna Letters*, 32; Synchronistic History, 33; Babylonian Chronicles, 38; *Chronicle P*, 40; *Chronicle A*, 44; *Chronicle K¹*, 47; *Chronicle K²*, 51; *Chronicle K³*, 53; Genealogical References, 57.

B. Babylonian Chronology, 60; Dynasty D of Pashe, 60; the Bavian Inscription, 60; Boundary Stone of Marduk-nâdin-akhê, 62; Dynasty E of of Sea-Land, 63; Dynasty C of the Kassites, 63; Chronology of the Kassite Dynasty, 65; Date of Shagarakti-Shuriash, 67; Kara-Khardash, 69; Bitiliashu II, 70; Seal of Shagarakti-Shuriash, 71; Dynasty A of Babylon, 73; Chronology of Simplicius, 76; Chronology of Berossos, 77; Chronology of Dynasty A, 79; Dynasty B of Uru-kha, 81; Chronology of Dynasty B, 82; Date of Nebuchadrezzar I, 82; Boundary Stone of Bêl-nâdin-aplu, 83; Fall of Dynasty B, 86; Rise of the Kassite Power, 87; Conquest of Babylonia, 90; Original

Home of the Babylonians, 100; Dynasty of Isin, 107; Dynasty of Ur, 108; Dynasty of Agade, 108; Kingdom of Shumir and Akkad, 116; Kingdom of the Four Regions, 117; Kings of Larsa, 120; Dynasty of Erech, 120; Gishkhu, 121; Dynasty of Telloh, 122; Dynasty of Kish, 123; Dynasty of Ki-en-gi, 124; Sumerians, 124–130.

C. Assyrian Chronology, 130–148; Early Assyrian Kings, 130; Ashur-nirara III, 131; Ashur-bêl-nishêshu, 131; Ashur-nâdin-akhê, 131; Bêl-nirari, 132; Shalmaneser I, 133; Tukulti-Ninib I, 133; Ashur-dân I, 134; Pateses of Assyria, 136; Shamshi-Adad II, 136; Shamshi-Adad I, 136; Igurkabkabu, 137; Bêl-tâbi, 139; Erishu and Ilushûma, 139; Founding of the Assyrian Kingdom, 144–148.

CHAPTER III. EGYPTIAN CHRONOLOGY 149–266

A. The Chronological Material, 149–175; Cuneiform Data, 151; Biblical References, 151; Classical Authors, 152; Manetho, 152; Josephus, 153; History of the Hyksos, 153; Settlement of Hyksos, 153; Salatis, 154; Successors of Salatis, 154; meaning of the Hyksos' Name, 155; Expulsion of the Hyksos, 155; Josephus' Epitome of Manetho, 156; Manetho's History of the Nineteenth Dynasty, 157; Josephus' Chronology of the Hyksos Period, 158; Josephus' Account of Osarsiph, 159; Manetho's Account of Osarsiph, 161; the Epitomes of Manetho, 165; Sothis-Book, 165; Theban Kings of Eratosthenes, 167; Egyptian Inscriptions, 168; King-Lists, 169; Karnak-List, 169; Abydos-List, 169; Sakkara-List, 171; Palermo Stone, 172; Turin Papyrus, 173; Minimum Dates, 174.

B. Astronomical Dates, 175–184; Sirius Star, 175; Sothic Cycles, 176; Censorinus, 176; Era of Menophris, 177; Clement of Alexandria, 178; Era of Year 2781, 179; First Sothic Date, 179;

Second Sothic Date, 180; Third Sothic Date, 180; New Moon Festivals, 182.

C. Egyptian Chronology, 184–250; Dynasty XVIII, 185; the Feud of the Thutmosids, 188; Ahmose, 191; Amenhotep I, 192; Thutmose I, 192; Thutmose II, 193; Hatshepsut, 193; Thutmose III, 194; Amenhotep II, 196; Thutmose IV, 197; Amenhotep III, 198; Amenhotep IV, 199; Dynasty XIX, 200; Haremhab, 203; Ramses I, 204; Seti I, 205; Ramses II, 206; Merneptah, 207; Amenmeses, 207; Osarsiph, 208; Thouoris, 209; Dynasty XX, 210; Dynasty XII, 211; the Hyksos, 217; Era of Opeh(ti)set, 221; Dynasties XIII–XVII, 223; Dynasty XI, 230; Dynasty X, 237; Dynasties VII–IX, 238; Dynasty VI, 241; Dynasty V, 244; Dynasties I–IV, 245.

D. Predynastic and Prehistoric Kings of Egypt, 250–66; Syncellus, 251; Eusebius, 252; Manetho and Panodorus, 252; *Turin Papyrus*, 253; the Horus Period, 254; the Two Goddesses, 254; Followers of Horus, 255; Archaeological Discoveries, 255; the Palaeolithic age, 256; the Neolithic Age, 257; the Chalcolithic Age, 258; Legends of Egyptian Settlements, 259; Egyptian Royal Titles, 259; the Horus Period, 261; the Period of the Two Goddesses, 262; the Period of the Demigods, 263; the Invasion of the Sunworshipers, 265.

SYNCHRONISTIC TABLE 268–283

INDICES 285–302
    A. Classical Authors, 287.
    B. Biblical References, 287.
    C. Inscriptions, 288.
    D. Miscellaneous, 288–302.

CHAPTER I
BIBLICAL CHRONOLOGY

The chronological data for determining the dates of the patriarchs are fully given in the Bible. The only difficulty is to find an unchallenged date, from which we can begin our reckoning. As such a date is not at our disposal in the time of the patriarchs, nor for a thousand years later, we must go down to the kings of Israel and Judah, when they had transactions with other lands, the chronology of which is settled and accepted. From this period we can then work backward. We possess at present two such chronologies, the Ptolemaic Canon and the *Limmu-Lists*.

The Ptolemaic Canon

The Ptolemaic Canon is a work by Claudius Ptolemaeus, an eminent Egyptian astronomer, who lived in the second century A. D., and who furnishes in his *Canon of Kings*[1] a list of Babylonian, Persian, and Greek monarchs. His catalogue, beginning with *Nabonassar* of Babylon and extending to Alexander the Great, gives the length of reign of each king of that period. It has been tested by scholars from every point of view, and has in every case stood the test. It is therefore regarded as one of the most accurate chronological works bequeathed to us by antiquity.

Originally, however, it was not intended for chronological purposes. It omits all kings who reigned less than one year, or rather who were not reigning on the first New-

[1] Κανὼν βασιλέων.

Year's Day following their accession to the throne. The reign of each king is therefore reckoned from the first New-Year's Day celebrated after his accession. This fact stamps it as primarily an astronomical work.

This is corroborated by another fact. *Nabonassar* was not the first king of a new dynasty, nor was he a particularly great or important king. The selection of this king to begin the Canon must therefore depend on some other reason than that of chronology. Winckler[1] has pointed out that a calendar reform took place in Babylonia under the reign of this king. The reform was called forth by the fact that about this time the sun rose in the zodiacal sign of *Aries* at the vernal equinox. This means that about 747 B. C., when *Nabonassar* came to the throne, a new era began, in which the New Year began on the twenty-first day of *Nisan*, the first month of the Babylonian year.

Assyrian Limmu-Lists

In Assyria each year was named after a *Limmu*-officer, who held a position analogous to that of the Greek first *archon*,[2] or the Roman *consul*. We have lists of such *Limmu*-officers in unbroken succession from 893 to 667 B. C.

The Expedition-Lists

In some of these lists, commonly called *Expedition-Lists*, the chief event of each year is also recorded. The king himself held the *Limmu*-office during the second[3] full year that he reigned, and each reign is generally indicated on the tablet by a deep line at its beginning and end.

---

[1] *KAT.*³, pp. 317, 324.   [2] Ἄρχων ἐπώνυμος.

[3] Before 747 B. C., i. e., before the *Nabonassar-era*, the king held this office the first full year that he reigned.

From the Ptolemaic Canon we know that *Sargon* of Assyria became king of Babylon in 710 B. C. We know likewise from the inscriptions of *Sargon*, that his conquest of Babylon took place in the thirteenth year of his reign. Applying these data to the Assyrian *Limmu-Lists*, their dates are easily arranged accordingly.

We are, furthermore, in a position to test the accuracy of this arrangement. In the *Expedition-Lists* for the year 763, when the *Limmu*-office was held by *Pur-ⁿSagali*, a great eclipse of the sun is recorded as having occurred in Assyria in the month of *Sivan* (= June). Astronomers[1] have verified this statement by calculations and have found that an eclipse, total for Nineveh, occurred on June 15, 763 B. C., lasting two hours and forty-three minutes, the middle of the eclipse being at 10:05 A. M. The accuracy of Assyrian chronology is thus astronomically established.

While the Ptolemaic Canon furnishes us with certain dates from 331 B. C. back to 747 B. C., the Assyrian *Limmu-Lists* carry these dates back to 893 B. C., up to which year Assyrian chronology is absolutely reliable.

Shalmaneser II

On the basis of this chronology we have two certain dates in the reign of *Shalmaneser II* (860–825 B. C.), dates which have an important bearing on biblical chronology.

In 854 B. C. *Shalmaneser* fought the battle at Qarqar against the kings of Syria and Palestine, among whom was also *Ahab*, king of Israel, whose name appears upon an inscription of *Shalmaneser II*, reading as follows:[2]

---
[1] See Schrader, *Keilinschriften und die Geschichtsforschung*, pp. 338 ff.
[2] Monolith, col. II, 91 f.

" .... *2,000 chariots, 10,000 soldiers of A-kha-ab-bu¹ of the land of Sir-²-la-ai²* - - - - *came against me.*"

Again we read in his inscriptions for his eighteenth year, i. e., 842 B. C., as follows:³

"*In my eighteenth year of reign I crossed the river Euphrates for the sixteenth time. Hazael of the land of Damascus trusted in his great army and mustered his numerous soldiers. Mount Saniru,⁴ a mountain-peak opposite Mount Lebanon, he made his citadel. I fought with him, (and) accomplished his overthrow. Eighteen thousand picked men of his army I slew. One thousand, one hundred and twenty-one chariots, four hundred and seventy of his cavalry horses, together with his camp, I captured from him. In order to save his life he fled, (but) I pursued him. In the city of Damascus, his capital, I besieged him and cut down its gardens. To the mountains of Hauran I went. Innumerable cities I destroyed, devastated, burnt with fire, (and) carried away their booty without number. To the mountain Ba᾽ alira᾽ si, at the head of the sea, I went, (and) erected there my royal image. At that time I received presents from the land of Tyre, from the land of Sidon, (and) from Ja-u-a, son of Khu-um-ri.*"

Ja-u-a represents king *Jehu* of Israel, and *Khu-um-ri* is King *Omri*, founder of the dynasty of *Omri*. *Jehu* was not a "son," nor a "descendant" of *Omri*, and *Shalmaneser's* expression means only that *Jehu* occupied the throne of *Omri*, i. e., Samaria.

The two inscriptions certify that *Ahab* was still on the throne in the year 854 B. C., and that *Jehu* was king as early as 842 B. C.

¹ =*Ahab*.   ³ Obelisk, ll. 97–99; III R. 5, No. 6, 40–65.
² *Israel*.   ⁴ Mount Shenir of the Anti-Lebanon.

Ahab and Jehu

From the Bible we know that *Ahab* died in a war against Syria,[1] and was succeeded by his son *Ahaziah*,[2] who reigned two years.[3]

Ahaziah was succeeded by his brother *Jehoram* or *Joram*, who reigned twelve years,[4] when he was murdered by *Jehu*.

Ahab's war against Syria was probably undertaken in the fall of the year of the battle of Qarqar, 854 B. C., *Ahab* counting upon the exhausted condition in which both the land and army of Syria were then placed. This was, however, a miscalculation which cost him his life, his death occurring in the winter of the same year.

Jehu, on the contrary, seeing the king and army of Assyria besieging the city of Damascus and approaching his own land, was eager to head off an unwelcome visit of the Assyrians, and probably also anxious to secure the protection of the Assyrian king both against enemies within his own land, the throne of which he had usurped, as well as against Damascus (Syria), the hereditary foe of Israel. His tribute or "gift" to *Shalmaneser II* in 842 B. C. would therefore naturally be one of his first acts after obtaining the throne of Israel, and we are safe in regarding this year as his accession year. We shall presently find that these two dates are correct.

The space between 854 and 842 is, however, only twelve years, while the combined reigns of *Ahaziah* and *Jehoram* are stated in the Bible to amount to fourteen years. This discrepancy can be explained by the fact

---

[1] I Kings 22:1–37; for Syria the Hebrew text has Aram or Aram Dameseq, which corresponds to the land or city of Damascus in the Assyrian inscriptions.

[2] I Kings 22:40.   [3] I Kings 22:51.   [4] II Kings 3:1.

that the *H*ebrew annalists counted both the accession year and the death year of a king among his regnal years. On this principle one year should be subtracted from the regnal year of each king in order to find the actual length of his reign. *Ahaziah* would then have reigned from 854 to 853 B. C. and *Jehoram* from 853 to 842 B. C.

This principle of counting regnal years in the Books of Kings can be tested and proved. In the same year that *Jehu* became king of Israel, *Athaliah* ascended the throne of Jerusalem. The year 842 B. C. is therefore admirably fitted for a starting-point and a test of this principle.

Early Kings of Judah and Israel

From the year of *Solomon's* death and the division of the kingdom to the year 842, there had reigned in Israel nine kings, for a period of ninety-eight regnal years, while six kings, reigning in all ninety-five years, had ruled during the same time in Jerusalem:

Kings of Judah		Kings of Israel	
Rehoboam	17 years	*Jeroboam*	22 years
Abijah	3 years	*Nadab*	2 years
Asa	41 years	*Baasha*	24 years
Jehoshaphat	25 years	*Zimri*	7 days
Joram	8 years	*Elah*	2 years
Ahaziah	1 year	*Omri*	12 years
Total	95 years	*Ahab*	22 years
		Ahaziah	2 years
		Joram	12 years
		Total	98 years

This discrepancy can be overcome only by remembering that in the case of Israel there had been eight changes of rulers within this period, and that we therefore should

THE BUILDING OF THE TEMPLE OF SOLOMON 7

subtract eight from the total of ninety-eight, leaving ninety years as the real length of time from the accession of *Jeroboam I* to that of *Jehu*. In Jerusalem there had been, in this space of time, five changes of succession, and we should therefore subtract five from the total of ninety-five regnal years, leaving in this case also ninety years.[1] The death of *Solomon* and the division of the kingdom must therefore be placed at 932 B. C.

The Building of the Temple of Solomon

This date enables us to take another step. *Solomon* reigned forty years.[2] His accession therefore occurred in 971 B. C. Some modern scholars doubt this, because they regard the number *forty* as a round number, denoting a lifetime. This doubt is not well founded, for we can show that he actually reigned forty years, *forty* being interpreted according to the principle established above by subtracting one year from it.

The annalist records that he began to build the temple in his fourth year.[3] That brings us to the year 968 B. C. This last date can be verified from other sources. Josephus[4] states, on the authority of *Menander of Ephesus*, that the building of the temple began 143 years, 8 months before the founding of Carthage. Trogus[5] assigns the founding of Carthage to 72 years before the founding of Rome in 753 B. C. Carthage would then have been founded in 825 B. C., and the beginning of the building of the temple being 143 years before this, we arrive at the

---

[1] Rost reaches practically the same result. See *KAT.*³, pp. 319 f., and especially note 1, according to which Rost argues that the first year of *Jeroboam I* is the year of his rebellion, and should therefore not be counted.

[2] I Kings 11:42.
[3] I Kings 6:1.
[4] *Contra Apion.* 1:17.
[5] Justin, 18:6.

year 968 B. C. This was in the twelfth year of *Hiram*, who consequently ascended the throne of Tyre in 979 B. C.

Trogus[1] also states that the building of the temple of *Solomon* began 240 years after the founding of the new city of Tyre, which happened one year before the fall of Troy. Ephorus, followed by the Parian Chronicle, assigns 1208 B. C. as the year of the fall of Troy.[2] The new city of Tyre was accordingly founded in 1209 B. C., and 240 years from that date gives us the year 969/968 B. C. as the date for the beginning of the building of the temple.

This date is thus certified from three sources and we have no cogent reason to doubt its correctness.

Patriarchal Chronology

By these researches we have thus far gained two important results:

1. The principle of *H*ebrew chronology in the Books of Kings.[3]
2. The date of the building of *Solomon's* temple.

Let us then apply this same principle of subtracting one year from each period mentioned in the Bible, and reckon backward from the year 968 B. C.

The building of the temple was begun 480 years after

---

[1] Justin, 18:3.

[2] The actual date of the fall of Troy was probably 1183 B. C. (see below, p. 201), but Ephorus and Menander seem to have followed the Asianic calendar (as employed by Herodotus in giving Lydian dates), according to which the year consisted of only 254 days (12 months of $29\frac{1}{2}$ days each). This would make a difference of about 25 Lydian years from the fall of Troy to the time of Herodotus.

[3] The same chronological principle seems to underlie all biblical documents of Hebrew origin. In other documents, the origin of which points to Babylonia or Egypt, the chronological principle employed seems to be that of those lands, i. e., the number indicates full calendar years.

the exodus from Egypt.[1] The Exodus falls therefore in 1447 B. C.

The stay in Egypt lasted 430 *full* years,[2] and *Jacob* must accordingly have entered Egypt in 1877 B. C.

Jacob was one hundred and thirty years old[3] when he entered Egypt, and he was consequently born in 2006 B. C.

Isaac was sixty years old[4] at the birth of *Jacob*. Hence he was born in 2065 B. C.

Abram was one hundred years old[5] at the birth of *Isaac*, and was therefore born in 2164 B. C. This year may be regarded as the beginning of the history of Israel. From this year we may commence and count downward, and *H*ebrew chronology offers us the following dates:

2164, Birth of *Abram.*
2154, Birth of *Sarai.*[6]
2090, Arrival of *Abram* in Canaan at the age of 75.[7]
2078, Birth of *Ishmael.*[8]
2066, Institution of circumcision.[9] *Abraham* was then ninety-nine years old and *Ishmael* thirteen years.
2065, Birth of *Isaac* in the one hundredth year of *Abraham.*[10]
2046, Marriage of *Isaac.*[11]
2022, Death of *Sarah* at the age of one hundred and twenty-seven years.[12]
2006, Birth of *Esau* and *Jacob*, *Isaac* being sixty years old.[13]

---

[1] I Kings 6:1.
[2] Exod. 12:40, 41.
[3] Gen. 47:9.
[4] Gen. 25:26.
[5] Gen. 21:5.
[6] Gen. 17:17.
[7] Gen. 12:4.
[8] Gen. 16:16.
[9] Gen. 17:24.
[10] Gen. 21:5.
[11] Gen. 25:20.
[12] Gen. 23:1.
[13] Gen. 25:26.

1990, Death of *Abraham* at the age of one hundred and seventy-five years.[1]
1967, Marriage of E*sau* at the age of forty.[2]
1943, Death of *Ishmael*.[3]
1931, Removal of *Jacob* to Paddan-Aram.[4]
1924, Marriage of *Jacob*.[5]
1917, Birth of *Joseph*.[6]
1911, Return of *Jacob* to Canaan.[7]
1901, *Joseph* sold into Egypt in his seventeenth year.[8]
1887, *Joseph* governor of Egypt in his thirtieth year.[9]
1887, Death of *Isaac*.[10]
1877, Migration of *Jacob* to Egypt.[11]
1860, Death of *Jacob* at the age of one hundred and forty-seven years, and his burial in Canaan.[12]
1807, Death of *Joseph* at the age of one hundred and ten years.[13]
1526, Birth of *Moses*.[14]
1486, Flight of *Moses* to Midian.[15]

[1] Gen. 25:7.   [2] Gen. 26:34.   [3] Gen. 25:17.

[4] Fourteen years before the birth of *Joseph*; Gen. 30:25.

[5] Seven years before the birth of *Joseph*.

[6] Thirty years before he became governor of Egypt. See note 5 and cf. Gen. 30:25.

[7] Six years after the birth of *Joseph*; Gen. 31:41.

[8] Gen. 37:2.

[9] Gen. 41:46; this happened ten years before the migration by *Jacob* into Egypt. The chronology of the events in the life of *Joseph* depend on this date. The seven years of plenty, the two visits of *Joseph's* brothers, and finally *Jacob's* removal to Egypt must have occupied ten years. But the date of *Jacob's* removal to Eygpt, 1877 B. C., is assured. The year 1887 B. C. is therefore the most likely date for the appointment of *Joseph* as governor of Egypt.

[10] Gen. 35:28.   [12] Gen. 47:28.   [14] Deut. 34:7.

[11] Gen. 47:9.   [13] Gen. 50:26.   [15] At the age of forty.

1447, Exodus.[1]
1407, Death of *Moses.*[2]
1407, Joshua succeeds *Moses.*[3]
1355(?), Death of *Joshua* (about).[4]

Genealogy of Shem

The period between the "Flood" and *Abram* is covered by the genealogy of Gen. 11:10–26, i. e., from *Shem* to *Terah* inclusive. The dates differ greatly between the Hebrew and the Samaritan texts. The Septuagint agrees practically with the Samaritan texts, except that it adds the name of *Cainan* after *Arpachshad*, and also that the best manuscripts have one hundred and seventy-nine years instead of seventy-nine years for the age of *Nahor* at the birth of *Terah*. The following table presents the three variations of this genealogy:

	HEBREW		SAMARITAN		SEPTUAGINT	
	Age at Birth of Successor	Rest of Life	Age at Birth of Successor	Rest of Life	Age at Birth of Successor	Rest of Life
Shem............	100	500	100	500	100	500
Arpachshad.....	35	403	135	303	135	430
Cainan..........	..	...	...	...	130	330
Shelah..........	30	403	130	303	130	330
Eber............	34	430	134	270	134	370
Peleg...........	30	209	130	109	130	209
Reu.............	32	207	132	107	132	207
Serug...........	30	200	130	100	130	200
Nahor...........	29	119	79	69	179	129
Terah...........	70	135	70	75	70	135

Assuming that the Septuagint represents an older and more trustworthy text, I shall take it as a basis for constructing the chronology of the period from *Shem* to *Abram*, a period, which I shall designate as the

---

[1] Exod. 7:7; 12:40; I Kings 6:1. [3] Deut. 34:9; Josh. 1:1.
[2] Deut. 34:7. [4] Josh. 24:29; Judg. 2:8.

Heroic Age[1]

NAME	BEFORE BIRTH OF SUCCESSOR		AFTER BIRTH OF SUCCESSOR	
	Age	Period B. C.	Age	Period B. C.
Shem....................	100	3424–3325	500	3325–2826
Arpachshad..............	135	3325–3191	430	3191–2762
Cainan...................	130	3191–3062	330	3062–2733
Shelah...................	130	3062–2933	330	2933–2604
Eber.....................	134	2933–2800	370	2800–2431
Peleg....................	130	2800–2671	209	2671–2463
Reu......................	132	2671–2540	207	2540–2334
Serug....................	130	2540–2411	200	2411–2212
Nahor....................	179	2411–2233	129	2233–2106
Terah....................	70	2233–2164	75	2164–2090

The Judges

The period between the Exodus and the building of *Solomon's* temple is stated definitely to be 480 years.[2] There is no cogent reason for doubting the accuracy of this figure; on the contrary, I believe it can be shown to be reasonable.

There is, however, another chronology, given in the book of Judges and intended to comprise this period, but it does not conform to the figures given above. The Book of Judges covers, namely, a period of 410 years. To that must be added: (1) The 40 years of the wandering in the wilderness; (2) the period of *Joshua's* leadership, which can hardly have been less than fifteen years, and more likely was at least forty-five years. These two dates precede the period of the Judges. After the Judges we must add:

---

[1] I have chosen this name, because to the Hebrew mind this age corresponds with similar heroic ages of other peoples. It seems evident, however, that we are dealing here not with individuals but with dynasties or nationalities, that succeeded each other in the government of Babylonia, Mesopotamia, or Syria.

[2] I Kings 6:1.

1. 40 years of *Eli's* judgeship.
2. About 12 years of *Samuel's* judgeship.
3. 40 years of *Saul's* reign.
4. 40 years of *David's* reign.
5. 3 years of *Solomon's* reign.

If we assume that *Joshua's* leadership lasted only fifteen years, the total of all these data amounts to 600 years, which should correspond to the 480 years in I Kings 6:1, being the period from the Exodus to the building of the temple. These two totals are so conflicting that biblical scholars have been forced to assume either that the figure in I Kings 6:1 is wrong, or that the figures in the Book of Judges are confused, or else that both documents give misleading figures. The difficulty is serious. It is possible that we may never be able to explain these discrepancies.

As the Book of Judges now stands, it is evident that its author regarded[1] it as a continuation of the history of the Israelites after the death of *Joshua*. A careful study suggests that the chronological error should be looked for chiefly in this book, and that its dates are confused. In order to evade this, certain scholars have suggested that some of the Judges were contemporary, one set ruling in the North, another set in the South, and a third over the East-Jordanic tribes. This is contradicted, however, by the chronology itself, which evidently was intended to be taken as consecutive. So far as I am aware, no adequate solution has as yet been offered in regard to these chronological difficulties.

Far from being able myself to give anything like an adequate explanation of the phenomena presented in this

[1] Judg. 2:8.

book, I would nevertheless offer the following tentative suggestions:

1. A close study of the Book of Judges reveals the fact that not only in chronology but in other historical data, as well as in its religious problems, it differs widely from a large part of the Pentateuch, from the Book of Joshua, and the Books of Kings. In the Book of Judges the conquest is carried out, so that each tribe has to fight alone in order to secure its possession, except that Judah and Simeon combine in their conquest of southern Palestine. In the Book of Joshua, on the other hand, the conquest of the land is carried out by all the tribes, acting in unison. There seems, therefore, to be a plain contradiction between these two books in regard to the manner in which the conquest was carried out.

2. In the Book of Judges the people worship at a number of sanctuaries. This is entirely contrary to the Levitical and Deuteronomic codes. The critical theory meets this by assuming that these codes were compiled long after the period of the Judges. But the critical theory assumes also that the Elohistic code was compiled long after this period. Yet this last code is in perfect harmony with the religious practices[1] of this time.

It has therefore occurred to me that we might have in these stories traces of some ancient *H*ebrews, who had settled in the land of Canaan before the time of the conquest by *Joshua*. These *H*ebrews might have possessed in substance, at least, the laws of the Elohistic code, Exod. 20:23—23:33. This code is strikingly similar to the *Code of Hammurabi*. It does not mention the Isra-

---

[1] Cf. Exod. 20:24: *In every place where I record my name I will come unto thee, and I will bless thee.*

elites in a single instance, but refers to the Hebrews,[1] or the "people," Hebr. ᶜam, which is the name of the inhabitants of Palestine, by which the Egyptians generally knew them. While in the other codes the motive for keeping the Sabbath is based upon an appeal to the bondage in Egypt, this code knows of no bondage in Egypt. On the other hand it affirms that the people had been "strangers"[2] —*Ger*—in the land of Egypt. The other codes also mention the "strangers," not as wanderers, but as a people that had affiliated with the *H*ebrews. Now there was a Benjamite clan *Gera*, which I presume to be identical with the land of *Gare* in the *Amarna Letters*, and it is not unlikely that this name signifies "the land of the strangers." In the Levitical code the "stranger" stands practically on an equal footing with the Israelite, enjoying the same rights,[3] bound by the same laws,[4] civil,[5] moral, religious,[6] and ceremonial.[7] It is possible that these "strangers" lived in Palestine before the time of the first *H*ebrew settlement, but it seems equally probable that they joined themselves to the *H*ebrews, and that both became allied afterward with the Israelites.

In the *Amarna Letters* a people, called *Khabire*, are often mentioned, and it seems certain that these *Khabire* were a "*H*ebrew" people. They appear in these letters at the time when, according to the chronology of the Bible, *Joshua* carried out the conquest of Canaan. But it is also possible that some of these letters antedate the conquest, and in that case we must assume that these

---

[1] Exod. 21:2.   [2] Exod. 23:9.   [3] Num. 35:15.
[4] Exod. 12:49; Lev. 24:22; Num. 9:14; 15:15, 16, 29.
[5] Lev. 24:22.   [6] Lev. 18:26; 20:2; 24:16.
[7] Exod. 12:19; Lev. 16:29; 17:8, 10, 12, 13, 15; 22:18; Num. 15:14, 26, 30; 19:10.

Khabire or *H*ebrews were in Canaan before the time of *Joshua.*

This is supported by an old biblical fragment telling of a raid upon the men of Gath by some Ephraimites long before the Exodus.[1]

Then again we find that in the conquest of *Joshua* cities in Issachar and Asher were allotted to *Manasseh*,[2] which would suggest that *Asher* and *Issachar* had lived in this region before the conquest.

These and similar passages seem to indicate that there lived a *H*ebrew people in Canaan before *Joshua's* conquest. My assumption, therefore, is that there were old documents, preserved by this people, giving the history of some former judges, like *Othniel, Ehud, Shamgar, Deborah,* and *Barak.* These documents were then collected with those giving the history of the later judges. When the author of the Book of Judges compiled them into a history, he placed all of them after *Joshua.* Moore[3] assigns the fifth or fourth century B. C. for the composition of the Book of Judges, and if this date be correct, we should perhaps not be surprised that the editor confused the dates by placing *all* the judges, instead of *the larger part* of them after *Joshua.*

On this hypothesis we can account for the divergent stories of the conquest: the one in Judges as that of the old *H*ebrews, settling in Canaan before the conquest, while the Book of Joshua presents the history of the conquest as carried out by *Joshua.* The "irregular" forms of worship, presented in the Book of Judges, are then not really irregular nor illegal, but pre-*M*osaic, inherited by

[1] I Chron. 7:21, 22.   [2] Josh. 17:11.
[3] Judges, *Int. Crit. Com.*, pp. xxxiii–xxxv.

this people and carried on in Canaan even after the conquest.

Inasmuch as there exists a wide discrepancy in chronology between the Book of Judges and I Kings 6:1, and as no adequate solution has as yet appeared, this tentative suggestion is offered, which may be found valuable for the time being, until an adequate explanation of *all* the problems in the Book of Judges has been found.

It is singularly interesting that Josephus[1] identified the Exodus with the expulsion of the *Hyksos*. Equally interesting is the fact that the chronology of the Book of Judges carries the period of the Judges close to this time. For while the expulsion of the *Hyksos* took place about 1566 B. C.,[2] the oppression by *Cushan-Rishathaim*, which is the first item in the chronology of the Book of Judges, began about 1531 B. C. The intervening period, 35 years, is reasonable for the wandering in the wilderness and the conquest of Canaan.

There is, however, one difficulty in this chronology which impairs its accuracy. The Bible nowhere mentions the number of years that *Samuel* was judge, i. e., the period from the convocation of *Mizpeh*,[3] to the anointing of *Saul*.[4] The only guide we have is the statement that *Samuel* became old[5] in the meantime. Josephus[6] states that it was 12 years. He probably followed a trustworthy tradition, and his figure is reasonable. To avoid a new conjecture, I shall assume that Josephus' figure is correct, and build the chronology of the Judges upon it.

---

[1] *Contra Apion*, 1:16: "*These shepherds, as they are here called, who were no other than our forefathers, were delivered out of Egypt.*"

[2] See below, p. 192.

[3] I Sam. 7:6.

[4] I Sam. 10:1.

[5] I Sam. 8:1, 5.

[6] Ant. VI, 13:5.

Another difficulty is that the Old Testament does not state the length of Saul's reign. St. Paul[1] claims, probably following a good tradition, that he reigned forty years. As Josephus[2] affirms this number, we have no reason to doubt its accuracy.

Starting with the accession year of *Solomon*, 971 B. C., we obtain the following

Chronology of the Judges

Name	Term of Office	Date
The Elders[3]	35(?) years	(1566)–1531 B. C.
Cushan-Rishathaim[4]	8 years	1531–1523 B. C.
Othniel[5]	40 years	1523–1483 B. C.
Eglon of *Moab*[6]	18 years	1483–1465 B. C.
Ehud[7]	80 years	1465–1385 B. C.
Jabin[8]	20 years	1385–1365 B. C.
Deborah and *Barak*[9]	40 years	1365–1325 B. C.
Midian Occupation[10]	7 years	1325–1318 B. C.
Gideon[11]	40 years	1318–1278 B. C.
Abimelech[12]	3 years	1278–1275 B. C.
Tola[13]	23 years	1275–1252 B. C.
Jair[14]	22 years	1252–1230 B. C.
Philistine Occupation[15]	18 years	1230–1212 B. C.
Jephthah[16]	6 years	1212–1206 B. C.
Ibzan[17]	7 years	1206–1199 B. C.
Elon[18]	10 years	1199–1189 B. C.

[1] Acts 13:21.
[2] Ant. VI, 14:9.
[3] Judg. 2:7.
[4] *Ibid.*, 3:8.
[5] *Ibid.*, 3:11.
[6] *Ibid.*, 3:14.
[7] *Ibid.*, 3:30, 31.
[8] *Ibid.*, 4:3.
[9] *Ibid.*, 5:31.
[10] *Ibid.*, 6:1.
[11] *Ibid.*, 8:28.
[12] *Ibid.*, 9:22.
[13] *Ibid.*, 10:1, 2.
[14] *Ibid.*, 10:3.
[15] *Ibid.*, 10:8.
[16] *Ibid.*, 12:7.
[17] *Ibid.*, 12:9, 10.
[18] *Ibid.*, 12:11.

Abdon[1]	8 years	1189–1181 B. C.
Philistine Occupation[2]	40 years	1181–1141 B. C.
Samson[3]	20 years	1141–1121 B. C.
Eli[4]	40 years	1121–1081 B. C.
Philistine Occupation[5]	20 years	1081–1061 B. C.
Samuel[6]	12 years	1061–1049 B. C.
Saul[7]	40 years	1049–1010 B. C.
David[8]	40 years	1010– 971 B. C.
Solomon[9]	40 years	971– 932 B. C.

This chronology is corroborated by other biblical writers. St. Paul[10] says that Israel was governed by judges for a space of 450 years. The Book of Judges covers 410 years, and if we add to this the 40 years of *Eli*, who was styled a judge, we get 450 years. *Jephthah*[11] avers that Israel had been under judges for 300 years up to his time. The period from the oppression by *Cushan-Rishathaim* to the death of *Jair* is 301 years, which virtually covers the date given by *Jephthah*.

[1] *Ibid.*, 12:14.
[2] *Ibid.*, 13:1.
[3] *Ibid.*, 15:20.
[4] I Sam. 4:18.
[5] *Ibid.*, 7:2.
[6] Josephus, Ant. VI, 13:5.
[7] Acts 13:21.
[8] I Kings 2:11.
[9] *Ibid.*, 11:42.
[10] Acts 13:19, 20.
[11] Judg. 11:26.

CHAPTER II
BABYLONIAN AND ASSYRIAN CHRONOLOGY
A. BABYLONIAN CHRONOLOGICAL MATERIAL

The sources to which we must turn for the material needed in reconstructing the chronologies of Assyria and Babylonia[1] consist chiefly of the Assyro-Babylonian inscriptions, and of references in the Bible, in the Egyptian inscriptions, and in the works of classical authors.

Biblical References

For the period under consideration in this book, ending about 1050 B. C., the Bible has only one direct reference to Babylonian chronology, viz., the contemporaneity of *Abram* and *Amraphel*.[2] No light is thrown by the Bible on Assyrian history in this period.

Egyptian Inscriptions

The Egyptian inscriptions of the Eighteenth and Nineteenth Dynasties refer to transactions between the kings of Egypt and the kings of Assyria and Babylonia,[3] but

---

[1] For modern works on Assyrian and Babylonian chronology cf.: Lehmann, *Zwei Hauptprobleme*, 1898; Marquart, *Chronologische Untersuchungen*, 1900; Niebuhr, *Die Chronologie der Geschichte Israels, Aegyptens, Babyloniens und Assyriens*, 1896; Rogers, *History of Babylonia and Assyria*, Vol. I, pp. 312-48, 1900; Rost, *Untersuchungen zur altorientalischen Geschichte*, *MVG.*, 1897, Vol. II, pp. 105-74; Winckler, *Untersuchungen zur altorientalischen Geschichte*, 1889, pp. 1-46. For early Babylonian history see Radau, *Early History of Babylonia*, 1900.

[2] Gen. 14:1, 9.

[3] So Breasted (*ARE.*, Vol II, pp. 484, 859; Vol. III, p. 479), who identifies S'-n-g-r' with Shinar=Babylonia. This is highly uncertain. This *Sangarạ* is more probably the kingdom of that name in Mesopotamia.

the names of these latter are not given, and we have therefore no direct help from these inscriptions. In the *Amarna Letters* two Assyrian and four Babylonian kings[1] are mentioned as contemporary with two Egyptian kings, *Amenhotep III* and *Ikhnaton*, and as we are able to calculate the dates of the reigns of these kings with tolerable certainty, Egyptian chronology becomes of great value for this period of Assyrian and Babylonian history.[2]

Classical Authors

Classical authors frequently refer to the kings of Assyria and Babylonia. We have pointed out above the value of the Ptolemaic Canon,[3] but as it only goes back to 747 B. C., it has no direct bearing on our period except that it furnishes us with an absolutely certain date, 731 B. C.,[4] from which we can reckon backward by applying the data given in the Babylonian inscriptions.

The quotations from Berossos, a Chaldean priest living in Greece in the time of Alexander the Great and the first Seleucidae, as given by Alexander Polyhistor and from him by Eusebius, Syncellus, and others, are of particular interest for our work and will be considered later on.[5] Of equal importance is a quotation by Porphyry from Simplicius' treatise on Aristotle, to which reference will also be made.[6] Of other classical authors who have written on the history of Assyria and Babylonia, we shall have occasion to refer to the works of Ktesias, Herodotos, Calisthenes, Diodorus, Agathias, and Castor.

[1] See below, pp. 32 f.
[2] See below, pp. 198 ff.
[3] See p. 1.
[4] Rise of *Dynasty* K in Babylon.
[5] Below, p. 144–48.
[6] Below, p. 76.

Assyrian and Babylonian Inscriptions

The preponderance of material for the reconstruction of Babylonian and Assyrian chronology comes from the cuneiform inscriptions. In this material there is, however, no complete chronology, and it is only by careful analysis of all data at hand, that we are able to construct an approximately trustworthy chronology of Babylonia. This material consists of: (1) the *King-Lists;* (2) the *Date-Lists;* (3) maximum dates on legal documents; (4) the *Amarna Letters;* (5) the *Synchronistic History;* (6) the Babylonian *Chronicles;* (7) genealogies of Assyrian and Babylonian kings, and (8) isolated historical references.

I. The King-Lists

Two tablets have been discovered, giving partial lists of the kings of Babylonia. They are now generally known as *King-Lists A* and *B*.

King-List B[1]

King-List B gives only the names of the kings of the first two dynasties, and in the case of the First Dynasty it gives also the number of years of each reign. Besides this it gives the total number of kings in each dynasty. On the *obverse* of the tablet is given the dynasty of Babylon, which we shall call *Dynasty A of Babylon*, and it reads as follows:

Dynasty A of Babylon

1. 15 years, *Sumu-abi*.
2. 35 years, *Sumu-la-ilu*.

---

[1] For the text, see Rost, *MVG.*, 1897, Vol. II, p. 240; Pinches, *PSBA.*, 1880, pp. 21 f.; Schrader, "Die keilinschriftliche babylonische Königsliste," *SBAW.*, 1887, pp. 582 f., and Table XI; Winckler, *UAG.*, p. 145.

Obverse

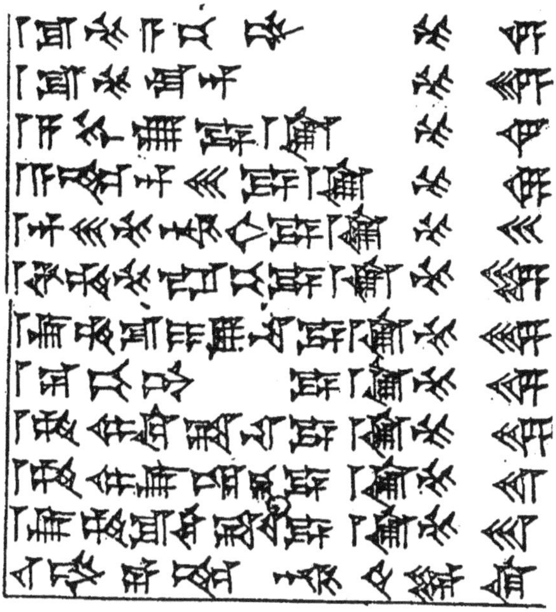

[cuneiform text]

Reverse

[cuneiform text]

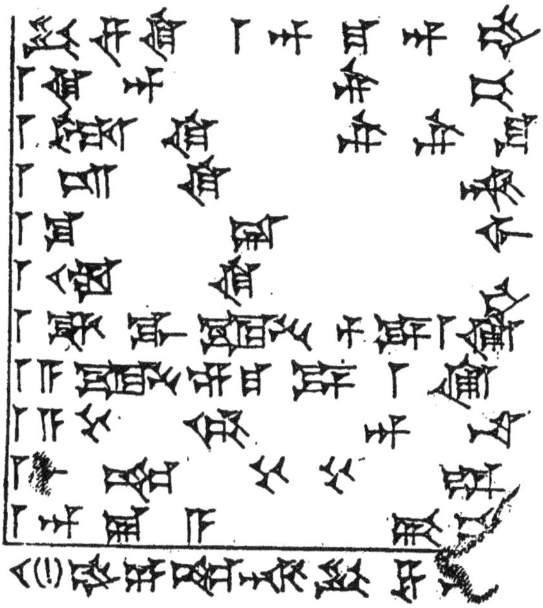

Fig. 1

KING-LIST B

3. 14 years, *Zabu.*
4. 18 years, *Apil-Sin.*
. 30 years, *Sin-muballit.*
6̄. 55 years, *Khammurabi.*
7. 35 years, *Samsu-iluna.*
8. 25 years, *Abeshu.*
9. 25 years, *Ammi-ditana.*
10. 21 years, *Ammi-sadugga.*
11. 31 years, *Samsu-ditana.*

11 kings of the *Dynasty of Babylon.*

The *reverse* of this tablet gives the kings of the *Dynasty of Uru-kha,*[1] known also as the *Dynasty of the Sea-Land,* and here designated as

Dynasty B of Uru-kha

1. *Ilu-ma-ilu.*
2. *Ki-an-ni-bi.*
3. *Damqi-ili-shu.*
4. *Mil-ki-pal.*
5. *Qad-ush-shi.*
6. *Gul-ki-shar(?).*
7. *Kir-gal-dara-bar.*
8. *A-dara-kalama.*
9. *A-kur-ul-an-na.*
10. *Melam-kur-kur-ra.*
11. *Ea-ga-mil.*

11 kings of the *Dynasty of Uru-kha.*

King-List A

King-List A[2] is contained on a tablet, badly mutilated, but once giving all the kings of Babylonia down to the

[1] Instead of the former reading *Uru-azag.*

[2] For editions of the text see Peiser, *PSBA.,* 1884, pp. 194 ff.; Winckler, *UAG.,* pp. 146 f.; Delitzsch, *Sitzungsberichte der kgl., sächs. Akad. der Wis*

PLATE I

Obverse

KING-LIST A

(From Lehmann, *Zwei Hauptprobleme.*)

Obverse

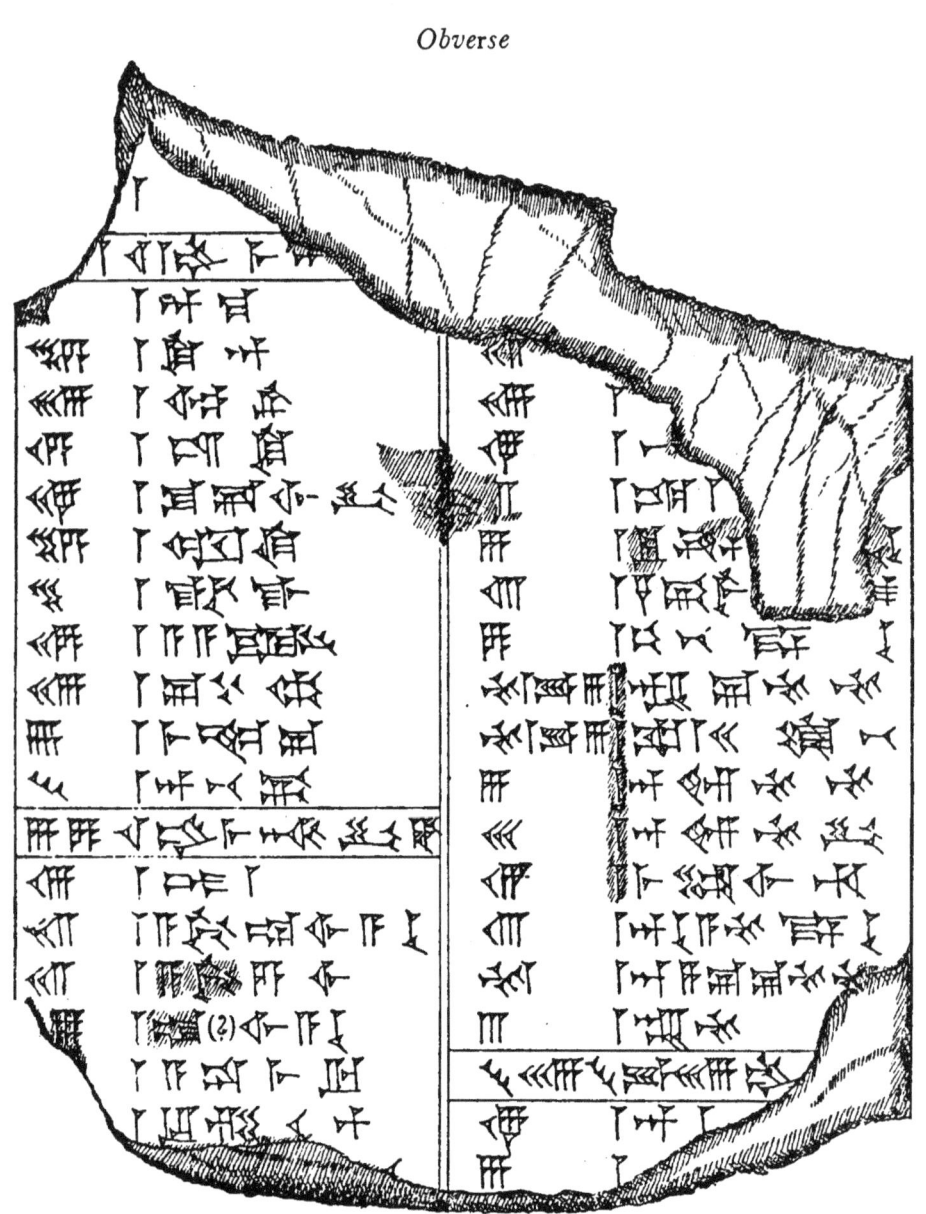

Fig 2

KING-LIST A

(From Rost, *Untersuchungen, MYG.*, 1897, 2, pp. 241-242.)

Persian conquest. The first part, containing *Dynasty A* has been broken off. For the six succeeding dynasties, the following remains:

Dynasty B of Uru-kha

1. 60 years, *Ilu-ma[-ilu]*.
2. 56 years, *Ki-ni- - -*.
3. 26 years, *Damqi- - -*.
4. 15 years, *Qad-ush-shi-sis*.
5. 24 years, *Mil-ki- -*.
6. 55 years, *Gul(?)-ki-ash(?)- -*.
7. 50 years, *Kir-gal- - -*.
8. 28 years, *A-dara - - -*.
9. 26 years, *Ê-kur-ul - - -*.
10. 8 years, *Me-lam-má - - -*.
11. 20 years, *Ea-ga - -*.

368 years, 11 kings of the *Dynasty of Uru-kha*.

Dynasty C, the Kassite Dynasty

1. 16 years, *Gan-dish*.
2. 22 years, *A-gu-um-shi - -*.
3. 22 years, *Bi-til-ia-shi*.
4. (1)9 years, *Du-shi-a-shu*.
5. - - - - *A-du-me-tash*.
6. - - - *Tash-zi-gur-mash*.

(Fifteen lines broken away.)

22. 24 years, - - - - - - - -.
23. 26 years, - - - - - - -.
24. 17 years, - - - - - - - -.
25. 6 years, *Ka-[dash-ma-an-Bêl]*.
26. 8 years, *Kudur-Bêl*.

senschaften, 1893, pp. 183 ff.; idem, Zur babylonischen Königsliste; idem, Assyriologische Miscellen, I; Schrader, KB., Vol. II, pp. 286 ff.; Lehmann, Zwei Hauptprobleme, pp. 13 ff., and Tafel 2; Rost. MVG., 1897, 2, pp. 241 f, Knudtzon, Gebete an den Sonnengott, Vol. I, p. 60; Vol. II, p. 277.

PLATE II

Reverse

KING-LIST A

(From Lehmann, *Zwei Hauptprobleme*.)

Reverse

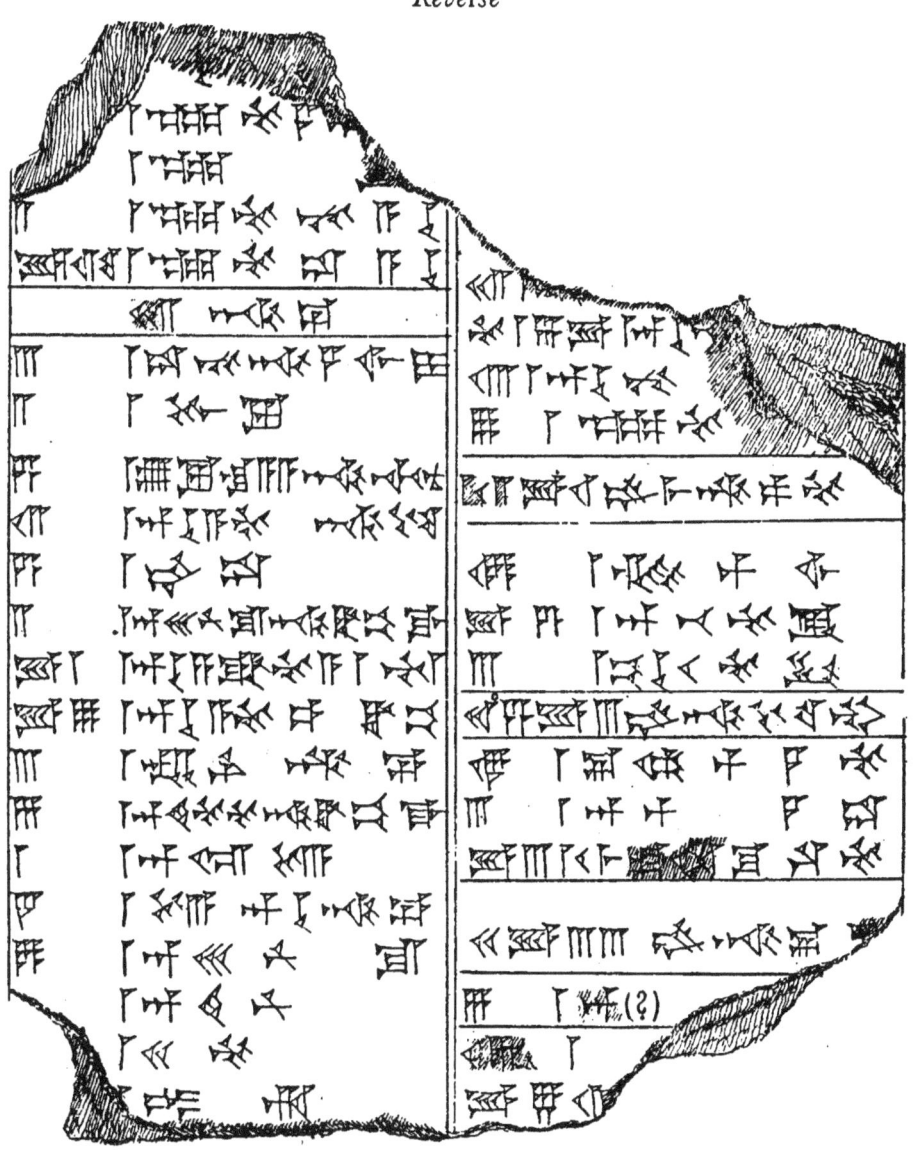

Fig. 3

KING-LIST A

27. 13 years, *Sha-ga-rak[-ti-Shuriash]*.
28. 8 years, *Bi-til*.
29. 1 year, 6 months, *Bêl-shum-iddin*.
30. 1 year, 6 months, *Ka-dish-man-khar-be*.
31. 6 years, *Adad-shum-iddin*.
32. 30 years, *Adad-shum-uzur*.
33. 15 years, *Me-li-shi-pak*.
34. 13 years, *Marduk-apil-iddin*.
35. 1 year, *Za-ma-ma-shum-iddin*.
36. 2 (?) years, *Bêl-shum-iddin*.
   576 years, 9 months, 36 kings [of the *Dynasty of the Kassites*].

Dynasty D of Pashe
1. 18 years, *Marduk* [- -].
2. 6 years, - - - - -.

- -
- -
- -
- -
- -

8. 22 years, *Marduk-nâdin-akhê*.
9. 1 year, 6 months, *Marduk-akhê-irba*.
10. 12 years, *Marduk-[shâpik]-zêr[-mâti]*.
11. 8 years, *Nabû-nâdin*.
   132 years, 6 months, 11 kings of the *Dynasty of Pashe*.

Dynasty E of the Sea-Land
1. 18 years, *Sim-mash-shi - -*.
2. 5 months, *Bêl-mu-kin - -*.
3. 3 years, 5 months, *Kash-shu-u-nâdin-akhê*.
   21 years, 6 months, 3 kings of the *Dynasty of the Sea-Land*.

II. The Date-Lists

Besides the *King-Lists* we have also four chronological inscriptions from the time of *Dynasty A*, called *Date-Lists*.[1] These lists record the chief event of each year; or, rather, the year was named, probably by royal proclamation, after the chief event of the preceding year, and all legal documents of this dynasty were dated according to this cumbersome method.[2] After each reign is a line stating the number of years of that reign. While lists *A* and *B* begin with the name of the first known king of *Dynasty A*, *Sumu-abi*, *List A* stops with the name of *Abeshu*, but *List B*, although very mutilated, carries us down to the tenth year of *Ammi-sadugga*. Each document allows one line for each year, and the order of events is clear.

There are, however, such serious discrepancies between *King-List B* and these *Date-Lists*, that scholars have felt warranted in declining to ascribe to them any real chronological value. Serious differences appear in the length of some of these reigns, particularly those of *Sin-muballit* and *Hammurabi*, and a solution of this difficulty must be found before we can erect a trustworthy chronology upon these documents. The importance of the differences between these two classes of documents may be seen by placing a synopsis of them side by side.

[1] *Date-Lists A* and *C*, published in transliteration, and translation, with notes, by Lindl, *BA.*, Vol. IV, pp. 338-402, and notes by Delitzsch, *ibid.*, pp. 403-9; *Date-Lists A and B* published in transcription, transliteration, and translation, with notes by L. W. King; *Letters of Hammurabi*, Vol. II, pl. 228, No. 102, and Vol. III, pp. 212-53; *Date-List D* published by King. *Chronicles Concerning Early Babylonian Kings*, Vol. II, pp. 97-109, 183-193.

[2] This method was in use in the dynasties of *Agade*, *Ur*, and *Isin*, and was a Semitic institution. In the *Kassite Dynasty* dating was done after the regnal years of the king, in conformity with Egyptian usage. The *Dynasty of Uru-kha* followed the older order of dating.

Kings	King-Lists	Date-Lists
Sumu-abi	15 years	14 years
Sumu-la-ilu	35 years	36 years
Zabu	14 years	14 years
Apil-Sin	18 years	18 years
Sin-muballit	30 years	20 years
Khammurabi	55 years	43 years
Samsu-iluna	35 years	38 years
Abeshu	25 years	28 years
Ammi-ditana	25 years	37 years
Ammi-sadugga	21 years	17 years
Samsu-ditana	31 years	

It should be noted that the *Date-Lists* never record any reverses suffered by the Babylonian kings. We know, however, from other documents, that the Babylonians did sustain such reverses, especially in the time of *Sin-muballit*. His foe was *Eri-Aku* of the Sea-Land, and as we have legal documents, bearing the oath customarily made in the name of the gods of Northern and Middle Babylonia and in that of King *Eri-Aku*, this must mean that *Eri-Aku* had ruled some time over Northern and Middle Babylonia, which can only have been the case in the latter part of the reign of *Sin-muballit* and the first part of *Hammurabi's* reign.

I believe, therefore, that *Eri-Aku* overpowered *Sin-muballit* in the twentieth year of the latter's reign, and the fact that the *Date-List* ceases just here to record events of *Sin-muballit's* time would fail to excite comment, because he was no longer supreme king. He would perhaps reign as vassal king for some years more (i. e., ten), and so we find that the *King-List* accords him thirty years. This subjection of Babylonia to *Eri-Aku* lasted for twelve years after *Sin-muballit's* death, when *Hammurabi* succeeded in driving out *Eri-Aku* from Northern and Middle Babylonia.

The discrepancy in the two records of the reigns of *Samsu-iluna*, *Abeshu*, and *Ammi-ditana* I regard as due to coregencies, in the same manner as coregencies occur at this time in the Twelfth Dynasty of Egypt.

III. Minimum Dates

Dr. Clay's admirable edition of legal documents of the Kassite period[1] enables us to establish a number of minimum dates. These documents were dated in such and such year of a certain king, and the highest year indicates that a a king lived at least into that year of his reign, mentioned on the tablet. These documents are quite numerous for the period from *Burna-Buriash* to *Bitiliashu II*. In the period which they cover, the highest dates on these tablets agree perfectly with *King-List A*, and we have thus every reason to believe that this list is correct. The following kings, with their highest dates, occur:

King	Date on Tablets	Date on King-List
Burna-Buriash	year 25	year ?
Kuri-Galzu	year 23	year 24
Nazi-Maraddash	year 24	year 26
Kadashman-Turgu	year 16	year 17
Kadashman-Bêl	year 6	year 6(?)
Kudur-Bêl	year 9	year 8(?)
Shagarakti-Shuriash	year 12	year 13
Bitiliashu	year 6	year 8

This indicates that all the dates on *King-List A* are practically correct, and we learn further that *Burna-Buri-*

[1] *BE.*, Ser. A, Vol. XIV, pp 3-5 ff.

ash reigned at least twenty-five years. On the other hand, we are struck by the entire absence of any monuments from the king or kings reigning between *Burna-Buriash* and *Kuri-Galzu II*. The *Synchronistic History* mentions here a king, *Kara-Khardash*, son of *Burna-Buriash*, and a usurper, *Nazibugash*. *Chronicle P* mentions a king, *Kadashman-Kharbe*, son of *Kara-Khardash*, and a usurper, *Shuzigash*. The absence of any monuments of this period indicates that it must have been very short, hardly more than three years.

IV. The "Amarna Letters"

By means of the *Amarna Letters*[1] we are enabled to fix approximately the dates of two Assyrian and four Babylonian kings. These letters were addressed to *Amenhotep III*[2] and *Ikhnaton*, kings of Egypt, and as the dates of the Egyptian kings are tolerably certain, the reigns of the Assyrian and Babylonian kings can be estimated. The most probable[3] dates of these Egyptian kings are:

Amenhotep III, 1438–1402 B. C.

Ikhnaton, 1407–1371 B. C.

Ikhnaton was coregent with his father, *Amenhotep III*, for five years, 1407–1402 B. C.

Ashur-uballit, king of Assyria, wrote a letter (*A. L.*, No. 15) to *Ikhnaton*, in which he refers to the gold, which *Amenhotep III* had sent to *Ashur-nâdin-akhê*, father of *Ashur-uballit*. This proves that there was at least a partial contemporaneity of *Ashur-nâdin-akhê* and *Amenhotep III*, and also of *Ashur-uballit* and *Ikhnaton*.

---

[1] Winckler, *The Tell-el-Amarna Letters*, 1896, Nos. 1–15, pp. 2–31.

[2] The first of these letters was written by *Amenhotep III* and addressed to *Kadashman-Bêl*.

[3] See below, pp. 191, 198 ff.

Kadashman-Bêl wrote a letter (*A. L.*, No. 2) to *Amenhotep III*, in which he refers to some messengers, whom his father *Kara-Indash* had sent to *Amenhotep III*. From this it follows that *Kara-Indash* was the father of *Kadashman-Bêl*, and that at least a part of the reign of *Kara-Indash* must have fallen within the reign of *Amenhotep III*, and also that at least a part of the reign of *Kadashman-Bêl* must have fallen within the reign of *Amenhotep III*.

Burna-Buriash writes to *Ikhnaton* (*A. L.*, No. 6), that *Kuri-Galzu I*, father of *Burna-Buriash*, had been on friendly terms with *Ikhnaton*. *Burna-Buriash* adds in another letter (*A. L.*, No. 7), that *Kuri-Galzu I* and *Amenhotep III* also had been good friends. In a third letter (*A. L.*, No. 8), *Burna-Buriash* refers to the messengers sent between *Kara-Indash* and *Amenhotep III*, and also to the fact that *Amenhotep III* had sent gold to *Kuri-Galzu I*. From this it appears that:

Kara-Indash	was contemporary with	*Amenhotep III*.
Kadashman-Bêl	" "	" *Amenhotep III*.
Kuri-Galzu I	" "	" *Amenhotep III*.
Kuri-Galzu I		" *Ikhnaton*.
Burna-Buriash	" ..	" *Ikhnaton*.

Kuri-Galzu I was therefore reigning at the time of the death of *Amenhotep III* and the accession of *Ikhnaton*.

V. The "Synchronistic History"[1]

This document was compiled in the time of *Adad-nirari III* (811–783 B. C.), of Assyria. The original is

---
[1] Schrader, *KB.*, I, pp. 194 ff.; *AKA.*, Vol. I, pp. xxii ff.; Winckler, *UAG.*, pp. 148–51.

lost, but a copy of it was made for the library of *Ashurbanipal*. This copy, badly mutilated, is now in the British Museum. It gives an account of the conflicts between the kings of Assyria and Babylonia, from the time of *Kara-Indash* onward, mentioning only those kings between whom wars were carried on or alliances made. While, therefore, it does not present a complete list of kings in either land, it establishes the contemporaneity of the kings mentioned. The transactions between the kings of Assyria and Babylonia recorded in this *History* follow:

Ashur-bêl-nishêshu and Kara-Indash[1]

"*Kara-Indash*, king of Kâr-Duniash, and *Ashur-bêl-nishêshu*, king of Assyria, made a covenant with one another, and in brotherly agreement each took an oath of the other in regard to the boundaries.'

Buzur-Ashur and Burna-Buriash

"*Buzur-Ashur*, king of Assyria, and *Burna-Buriash*, king of Kâr-Duniash, took an oath, and in a brotherly agreement established the boundaries."

Ashur-uballit and Kara-Khardash

"In the time of *Ashur-uballit*, king of Assyria, the *Kassites* revolted against *Kara-Khardash*, king of Kâr-Duniash, the son of *Muballitat-Sherûa*, daughter of *Ashur-uballit*, and slew him, and they raised up *Nazi-bugash*, [a *Kassite*] and a man of lowly birth, to be king over them. [- - - -] *Ashur-uballit* invaded Kâr-Duniash in order to take vengeance [for *Ka*]*ra-Indash* [his grandson], and he slew [*Naz*]*i-bugash*, king of Babylonia, and made [*Ku*]*ri-Galzu*, the younger, the son of *Burna-Buriash*, king, and seated him upon his father's throne."

Bêl-nirari and Kuri-Galzu II

"In the time of *Bêl-nirari*, king of Assyria, *Kuri-Galzu*, the younger, [invaded Assyria]. At the city of Sugagi, which is by the Up[per Zâb] river, *Bêl-nirari*, king of Assyria, joined battle with him and defeated him, and slew his hosts. From the [- - -] of the land of

[1] K., 4401 u+R., 854   The first eleven lines are lost.

Col. I

SYNCHRONISTIC HISTORY
K. 4401a + R. 854
(From Winckler, *UAG*, pp. 148–9.)

Shubarî, even unto the land of Kâr-Duniash they divided the territory between them and established the boundaries."

Adad-nirari and Nazi-Maraddash[1]

"[*Adad-nirari*, king of Assyria], and *Nazi-Maraddash*, king of Kâr-Duniash, fought [with one another at] Kâr-Ishtar of Akarsallu. [*Adad-nirari*] defeated *Nazi-Maraddash* [and he smote him], and his camp and his priests he captured. [Concerning] the boundary (they agreed) as follows: [Their boundary] from the land of Pilasqi [which is on the farther side of] the Tigris, (from) the city of Arman-akar-sali as far as Lulu-mê they established, and (thus) they divided it."

Tukulti-Ninib (I) and Bitiliashu

"[*Tukulti-Ninib*, king of Assyria, smote] *Bitiliashu*, king of Kâr-Duniash, [- - - -] in the midst of the fight [- - - - - -][2] his slaves he made [- - - - - -] as far as the city of Kullar [- - - - - -]."

Bêl-kudur-uzur and Adad-shum-uzur

"*Bêl-kudur-uzur*, king of Assyria, and [*Adad-shum-uzu*r, king of Kâr-Duniash], fought. *Adad* [*-shum-uzu*r, king of Kâr-Duniash] slew *Bêl-kudur-uzur* in the battle, and *Ninib-apil-Ê*[*kur*, his son] returned unto his own land. His [numerous] forces [he(=*Adad-shum-uzur*) summoned], and he marched against the city of Ashur to conquer it [- - - -], and he fought therein, and turned, and [went back unto his own land]."

Ashur-dân I and Zamama-shum-iddin

"In the time of *Zamama-shum-iddin*, king of [Kâr-Duniash], *Ashurdân*, king of Assyria, [invaded] Kâr-Duniash, and [captured] the cities of Zaban, Irria, and Akarsallu, and [he carried away] their heavy [spoil] to Assyria."

Ashur-rêsh-ishi and Nebuchadrezzar I[3]

"In pursuit of him (=*Ashur-rêsh-ishi*) *Nebuchadrezzar* took his siege-engines and marched against Zanqi, a fortress of As[syria], to take it. But *Ashur-rêsh-ishi*, king of Assyria, summoned his chariots

---

[1] *S*, 2106.   [2] *K.*, 4401 *b*.
[3] *K*, 4401|*a*+*R.*, 854. The first seventeen lines are lost.

Col. 2

SYNCHRONISTIC HISTORY
K. 4401a + R. 854

to march against him. Then *Nebuchadrezzar*, because the siege-engines impeded (him), burned his siege-train with fire, and he turned and went back unto his own land. And *Nebuchadrezzar*, together with chariots and foot-soldiers, marched against the Assyrian fortress to take it. But *Ashur-rêsh-ishi* sent chariots and foot-soldiers to its help, and he fought with him (= *Nebuchadrezzar*), and defeated him, and slew his host, and plundered his camp. And forty chariots with the trappings thereof they brought back with them and they took captive *Karashtu*, the leader of his forces."

Tiglath-pileser I and Marduk-nâidn-akhê

"*Tiglath-pileser*, king of Assyria, and *Marduk-nâdin-akhê*, king of Kâr-Duniash, a second time set in array for battle (their) chariots that were (assembled) above the Lower Zâb, over against the city of Arzukhina. In the second year they fought in Marriti, which is above the land of Akkadî, and (*Tiglath-pileser*) captured the cities of Dûr-Kurigalzu, and Sippara of *S*hamash, and *S*ippar of An'unitum, and Babylon, and Opis, the great cities, together with their fortifications. At the same time he plundered Akarsallu, even to the city of Lupdi, and [he subdued] all the land of Sukhi, even to the city of Rapiqi."

Ashur-bêl-kala and Marduk-shâpik-zêr-mâti

"In the time of *Ashur-bêl-kala*, king of [Assyria], *Marduk-shâ-pik-zêr-mâti* was king of Kâr-Duniash, and they formed a treaty of complete alliance with one another. At the time of *Ashur-bêl-kala*, king of Assyria, *Marduk-shâpik-zêr-mâti* [fled from (?)] Kâr-Duniash, his land, and *Adad-apil-iddina*, the son of *Esagil-Shaduni*, a man of humble origin, they appointed as king over them. *Ashur-bêl-kala*, king of Assyria, married the daughter of *Adad-apil-iddina*, king of Kâr-Duniash, and he took her together with her rich dowry to Assyria, and the peoples of Assyria and Kâr-Duniash were [allied] with one another."

VI. "Babylonian Chronicles"

Six *Babylonian Chronicles* have been discovered. Three of these are in a very fragmentary condition, and

Col. I

CHRONICLE P

82-7-4, 38

(From Winckler, *AOE*, I, pp. 298-303.)

only four of them have references to the period under consideration in this volume.

Chronicle P[1]

This chronicle contained the records of war-expeditions by early Babylonian kings. About one-fourth of the text is preserved, beginning with the reign of *Kadashman-Kharbe*, son of *Kara-Khardash* of the *Kassite Dynasty*.

Ashur-uballit and Kara-Khardash

"[- - - - - - - - - - - - -] king of Kâr-Duniash and [- - - - - - -] divided they, and fixed the boundary between themselves in a friendly manner, [- - - - - -] to his place he restored. [*Kadashman-kh*]*ar-be*, son of *Ka-ra-khar-dash*, son of *Muballitat-Sherûa*, [daughter] of *Ashur-uballit*, king of Assyria, accomplished the overthrow of the plundering *Sutu* from east to west, even to the annihilation of their power. The city of *Birutu* in the land of *Kharkhar*(?) he fortified [- - - - -]. In order to strengthen the fortifications he settled people therein. Afterward the Kassites rebelled against him, killed him, and set up *Shuzigash*, a Kassite of unknown antecedents, as king over themselves. *Ashur-uballit*, [king] of Assyria, marched to Kâr-Duniash in order to take vengeance for *Kadashman-Kharbe*, the son of his daughter *Shuzigash*, the Kassite, [he killed. *Kuri-Galzu*, son of *Ka*]*dashman-Kharbe* he placed on the throne."

Adad-nirari and Kuri-Galzu II

"Against *Adad-nirari*, king of Assyria, to the land of [- - - -] he marched. In the city of Sugaga, by the river Zalzallat he joined battle with him and slew him [- - - - -], his people he slew, his noblemen [he took captives]."

Adad-Nirari I and Nazi-Maraddash

"*Nazi-Maraddash*, son of *Ku*[*ri-Galzu* fought against *Adad-nirari*], king of Assyria."

[1] Pinches, *JRAS*., 1894, pp. 807 ff.; *Records of the Past*, New Series, Vol. V pp. 106 ff.; Winckler, *AOF*., Vol. I, pp. 115 ff.; 297 ff.

Col. 2

CHRONICLE P

Col. 3

CHRONICLE P

Tukulti-Ninib I and Bitiliashu

"[*Tukulti-Ninib* accomplished] the defeat of *Bitil*[*iashu* and] before the god *Ninib* he set [up *Bêl-shum-iddin*. On his revolt *Tukul*]*ti-Ninib* returned to Babylon and drew nigh [against *Bêl-shum-iddin*]. He destroyed the wall of Babylon, and the men of Babylon he slew with the sword. The treasures of Esagil and of Babylon he profanely brought forth, and the great lord *Marduk* he removed from his dwelling-place, and he carried him away into Assyria. The administration of governors he set up in the land of Kâr-Duniash. For seven years did *Tukulti-Ninib* rule over Kâr-Duniash. Afterward the nobles of Akkadî and of Kâr-Duniash revolted, and they set *Adad-shum-usur* upon his father's throne. Against *Tukulti-Ninib*, who had brought evil upon Babylon, *Ashur-nâzir-pal*, his son, and the nobles of Assyria revolted, and from his throne they cast him and they besieged him in a house in the city of Kâr-Tukulti-Ninib, and they slew him with the sword. For [- -]+6 years, until the time of *Tukulti-Ashur*, *Bêl*(=*Marduk*) dwelt in Assyria; in the time of *Tukulti-Ashur* did *Bêl* go unto Babylon."

Bêl-shum-iddin

"[- - -] *Bêl-shum-iddin*, the king, went out. *Kidinkhutrash*, king of Elam, [- - - - - - - -] his hand to *Nippur*. Its inhabitants he destroyed. *Dûr-ili* and *Kharsagkalama* [- - - -] its inhabitants he captured, he drove away. *Bêl-shum-iddin*, the king [- - - - -]."

Adad-shum-iddin

"[- - - -] *Adad-shum-iddin* returned. When *Kidinkhutrash*, attacked *Akkadî* the second time, the [- - - - - -] he marched into Isin; the river Tigris entirely [- - - - - - - -] the overthrow of many people he carried out."

Chronicle A[1]

Only a little part of this important document has been preserved. On the obverse was a list of very early

---

[1] K. 8532+K. 8533+K. 8534; also known as *Chronicle S;* published by George Smith in *TSBA.*, Vol. III, pp. 371 ff.; Winckler, *Untersuchungen zur altorientalischen Geschichte*, p. 153; King, *Chronicles Concerning Early Babylonian Kings*, Vol. II, pp. 46–56, 143–45.

CHRONICLE A 45

Babylonian kings, preceding *Dynasty A*, but only the following names are preserved:

Col. I: - - - - - - - - - *he reigned*
- - - - - - - *total.*
- - - - - - - - - - - - - - -
Col. II: - - - - - - - - - - - - -
Ilu-illati, son of the same - - - - - -
En-men-nun-na - - - - - - - - -
Apil-Kishshu, son of - - - - - -

The reverse began with *Dynasty A* and gave the history of Babylonia, but only the following is preserved:

Col. I: [- - - - - - - - - - -]
Babylon [- - - - - - - - - -]
Sumu-[*la-ilu* - - - - -]
Zabû [- - - - - -]
Apil-[*Sin* - - - - - -]
Sin-[*muballit* - - - - - -]
[*Hammurabi* - - - - - - - - -
[*Samsu-iluna* - - - - - - - - -]
[*Abeshu* - - - - - - - - -]
[*Ammi-ditana* - - - - -]
[*Ammi-sadugga* - - - - -]
[*Samsu-ditana* - - - - - - -]
[- - - - - - - - -]
El[*even kings* - - - - - - -]

[- - - - - - - -]
Ki-[*an-ni-bi* - - - - - - -]
[- - - - - - - - -]
[- - - - - - - - -]

(Here the tablet is broken off.)

Col. II: [- - - - - - - - - - - -]
[- - - - - - -] *of the Sea-Land* [- - -]

The ruler of the Sea-L[*and*], *Simmashshipak, the son of Erba-Sin,*

Obverse

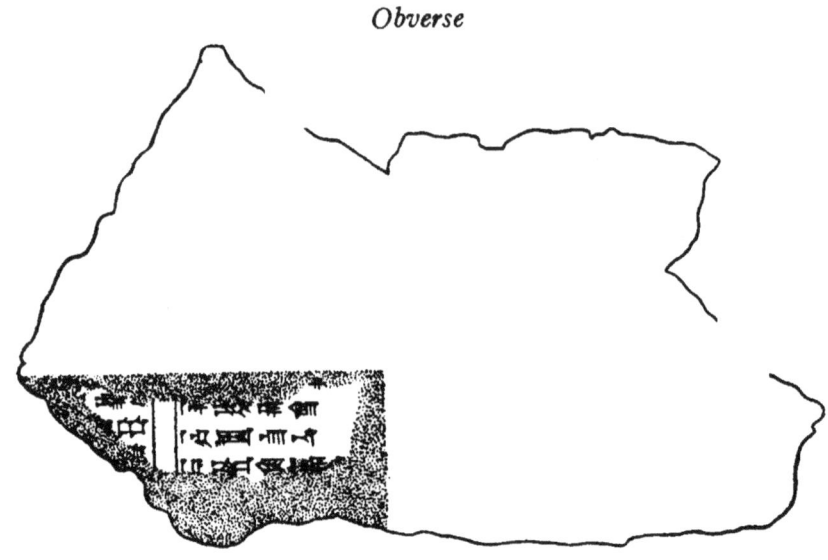

Reverse

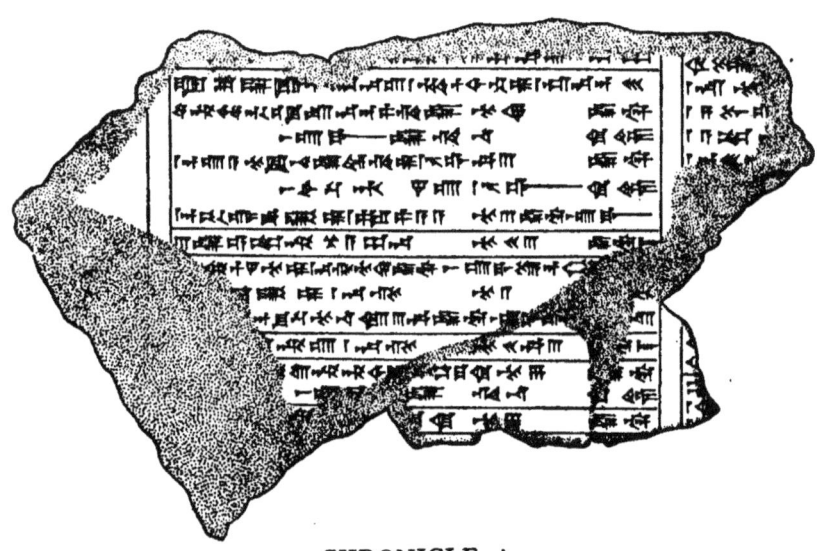

CHRONICLE A
K. 8532.
(From King, *Chronicles Concerning Early Babylonian Kings*.)

a man of the Dynasty of Dâmiq-ilishu, was slain with the sword. He reigned for 17 years.
He was buried in the Palace of Sargon.
Ea-mukîn-zêr, the usurping king, the son of Khashmar, reigned for three months.
He was buried in the swamp of Bêl-Khashmar.
Kashshû-nâdin-akhi, the son of Sippâ, reigned for three years. [He was buried] in the palace.

Three kings of the Dynasty of the Sea-Land. They reigned for twenty-three years.

[Ê]-ulbar-shâkin-shum, the son of Bazi, reigned for fifteen years. [He was buried] in the palace of Êtir-Marduk.
[Ninib-ku]durri-uzur, the son of Bazi, reigned for two years.
[Shilanum]-Shuqamuna, the son of the same, reigned for three months. [He was buried] in the palace.
[- - - - - -]
[Three kings] of the Dynasty of the house of Bazi. They reigned for twenty years and three months.

[- - - - -] descendant of [- - - -] of Elam, reigned for six years.
He was buried in the palace of Sargon.

(One king) of the Dynasty of [El]am. He reigned for six years.

[- - - - - - - - - - - - - - - - -]

Chronicle K 1[1]

King has lately published the inscriptions of three very interesting Chronicles, dealing with the reigns of the early Semitic rulers of Babylonia. I shall designate them as *K 1*, *K 2*, and *K 3*. The first of these reads:

---

[1] B. M., No. 26,472. Published by L. W. King, *Chronicles Concerning Early Babylonian Kings*, Vol. II, pp. 3 ff.

Sargon

"*Sargon, king of Agade, was exalted through the insignia of royalty bestowed by Ishtar, and he possessed no foe nor rival. His glory over the lands he poured out. The Sea in the East he crossed, and in the eleventh year the Country of the West in its full extent his hand subdued. He united them under one control; he set up his images in the West. Their booty he brought over into the Sea-Land.[1] The sons of his palace for five kasbu he settled, and over the hosts of the lands he ruled together with (them). Against Kazalla he marched and he turned Kazalla into mounds and heaps of ruins; he destroyed therein even the resting place for a bird. Afterwards, in his old age, all the lands revolted against him, and they besieged him in Agade. But Sargon went forth to battle and defeated them; he accomplished their overthrow, and their widespreading hosts he destroyed. Afterward he attacked the land of Su-edin in his might, and it submitted to his arms, and Sargon settled that revolt, and defeated them; he accomplished their overthrow, and their widespreading hosts he destroyed, and he brought their possessions into Agade. The soil from the trenches of Babylon he removed, and the boundaries of Agade he made like those of Babylon. But because of the evil which he had committed the great lord Marduk was angry, and he destroyed his people by famine. From the rising of the Sun unto the setting of the Sun they opposed him and gave [him] no rest.*"

Narâm-Sin

"*Narâm-Sin, the son of Sargon, [marched] against the city of Apirak and he constructed mines [against it], and Rêsh-Adad, the king of Apirak, and the governor of Apirak, his hand sub[dued]. He marched against Magan, and Mannu-dannu, the king of Magan, [his hand subdued].*"

Dungi

"*Dungi, the son of Ur-Engur, cared greatly for the city of Eridu, which was on the shore of the sea. But he sought after evil, and the treasure of Esagila and of Babylon he brought out as spoil. And Bêl was [- - - -], and body and - - - - he made an end of him.*"

---

[1] The *Omens* of *Sargon* read *Sea-Land*, but the *Chronicle* has "at the words," *ina a-ma-a-ti*, the meaning of which is not clear, and is evidently a corruption of the original text.

Obverse

CHRONICLE K 1
B. M., No. 26,472
(From King, *Chronicles Concerning Early Babylonian Kings*.)

Reverse

CHRONICLE K 1
B. M., No. 26,472
(From King, *Chronicles Concerning Early Babylonian Kings*.

Bêl-ibni

"*Ura-imitti, the* king, *set Bêl-ibni, the* gardener, *upon his throne that* [*the dynasty*] *might not come to an end; and the crown of his sovereignty he placed upon his head; Ura-imitti in his palace* - - - - [- - - *died*]. *Bêl-ibni, who sat upon the throne, did not arise* (*therefrom*), *but as king he was established.*"

Ilu-shûma

"*Ilu-shûma, king of Assyria, against Su-abu.*"

Chronicle K 2[1]

This chronicle seems to be a continuation of the preceding, mentioning the more important events from the latter part of the *Dynasty of Isin* to the fall of *Dynasty B of Uru-kha*. The interesting text of this monument reads:

Bêl-ibni

"[*Ura-imitti, the king*], *set Bêl- ibni, the* gardener, *upon his throne,* [*that* (*the dynasty*) *might not come to an end*], *and the crown of his sovereignty he placed upon his head. Ura-imitti in his palace* - - - - - - - - - - - - - *died. Bêl-ibni sat upon the throne, and did not arise* [*therefrom*], *and was established as king.*"

Hammurabi

"*Hammurabi, king of Babylon, summoned his forces, and against Eri-Aku, king of Ur, he marched. The cities of Ur and of Larsa his hand conquered, and he brought their possessions unto Babylon.* [- - - - -] *he overthrew* [- - - - - -] *he carried away.*"

Samsu-iluna

"[*Samsu-il*]*una, king of Babylon, the son of Hammurabi, the king,* [- - - - - - -], *and* [- - - - - - -] *Eri-Aku unto* [- - - - - -] *marched,* [- - - - -] *his hand conquered.* [- - - -] *him alive in the palace* [*he burnt*]. [- - - - - - -] *he marched and besieged* [- - - - -] *his peoples* [- - - - - - - - - - - - - - - - -].*"

---

[1] B. M., No. 96,152. Published by L. W. King, *Chronicles Concerning Early Babylonian Kings*, Vol. II, pp. 15 ff.

Obverse

CHRONICLE K 2
B. M., No. 96,152
(From King, *Chronicles Concerning Early Babylonian Kings*.)

Ilu-ma-ilu

"[*Ilu-ma*]-*ilu*[- - - - -] he made [- - - -] he waged war against him and [- - - - -] *their dead bodies the sea* [- - - - -]. Samsu-iluna again marched [against -. - - - -]. Ilu-ma-ilu advanced to the attack, and the defeat of the forces of [- - - - - - he accomplished]."

Abeshu

"Abishi, the son of Samsu-iluna, to conquer Ilu-ma-ilu [- - -], and his heart prompted him to dam the Tigris. And he dammed the Tigris, but he caught not Ilu-ma-ilu."

Samsu-ditana

"Against[1] Shamash-ditana the men of the land of Khatti [marched] against the land of Akkadî."

Ea-gâmil

"Ea-gâmil, king of the Sea-Land, [set out] against the land of Elam; and in pursuit of him Ulam-Buriash, the brother of Bitiliash, the Kassite, summoned his forces, and he conquered the Sea-Land, and he exercised dominion over the land."

Agum

"Agum, the son of Bitiliash, summoned his forces, and marched against the Sea-Land. He conquered the city of Dûr-Ea, and Ê- - - - *uruna*, the temple of Ea in the city of Dûr-Ea, he razed to the ground."

Chronicle K 3[2]

The mutilated text of this tablet begins with the reigns in the middle of *Dynasty D* and reads:

Obv. 1. [- - - - - - - - - - - - - - - -]
2. [- - - - - - - - - - - -]
3. [- - - - -] *heavy* [*spoil*] *he carried away.*

4. Marduk-shâpik-zêr-mâ[ti - - - - - - -] *made.*

---

[1] The text reads *ana | arṣi,* "against," but the meaning is evidently *ina | arṣi,* "in the time of."

[2] B. M., No. 27,859. Published by King, *Chronicles Concerning Early Babylonian Kings*, Vol. II, pp. 57–69, 147–55.

Reverse

CHRONICLE K 2
B. M., No. 96,152
(From King, *Chronicles Concerning Early Babylonian Kings*.)

5. [- - - - -] *and forty-four kings of the lands of
   [- - - -] and they beheld abundance.*
6. *He established peace and friendly relations with Ashur-
   bêl-kala, king of Assyria.*
7. *At that time the king went from Assyria unto Sippara.*

8. *Adad-aplu-iddina, the son of ·Itti-Marduk-balatu, the
   Aramaean, the usurping king.*
9. [- - - -] *the town, all that* [- - - -] *the city of
   Dûr-ili.*
10. [- - - - -] *they cast down. The* [*men of the land
    of*] *Sutû made attack and the spoil of Sumer and
    A*[*kkadî*].
11. *They brought out unto their own land. The shrine
    of Marduk* [- - - -] *in the midst* [- - - -]
    the god [- - *he*] *completed.*

12. *Simmashshipak, the son of Erba-Sin, the ruler of
    [- - - - -].*
13. *Made the throne of "the Lord of All" in the temple of
    Êkurigigal.*

14. *Within the shrine the fifth year of Ê-ulbar-shâkin-shum,
    the king.*
15.   *the fourteenth year.*

16.   *the fourth year of Ae-aplu-uzur.*
17.   *the first year of Nabû-mukîn-ap*[*li, the ki*]*ng.*

18. [- - - -. - - - - *the* - - - - *year*].
Edge 1. [*the* - - - *year*].
2. [*the* - - - - *year*].

3. [*the* - - - *year of* [- - -
   akh]*ê-iddina.*

Rev. 1. [- - - - *Adad-nirar*]*i, king of Assyria, against*
   [*Shamash-mudammi*]*q.*

2. [*In the time of Nabû-sh*]*um-ukîn Tiglath* [-*pileser,
   king of*] *Assyria.*

3. [- - - *ap*]*lu-iddina, the son of Nabû-shum* [- - - -].

Edge

CHRONICLE K 3

GENEALOGICAL REFERENCES

4. *Marduk-zâkir-shum, the son of* [- - - -].
5. *Marduk-bêl-ushe* [- - - - - -].
6. *Against Marduk-balatsu-*[- - - - -] *Marduk-zâkir-shum.*
7. *For* [- - -] *years there was no king in the land.*
8. *Erba-Marduk, the son of Marduk-shâkin-shum,*
9. *in the second year grasped the hand of Bêl and the son of Bêl.*
10. *Now the Aramaeans who were in Shigiltu and Subartu seized the fields of them that dwelt in Babylon and B*[*orsî*]*ppa;*
11. *but (Erba-Marduk) smote them with the sword and defeated them,*
12. *and he took the fields and the gardens from them, and gave them unto the men of Babylon and Borsippa.*
13. *In the same year in Esagila and Ezida* [- - - - *the thr*]*one of Bêl he set up.*
14. [- - - - -] *Erba-Marduk unto Babylon* [- - - -].
15. [- - - - *Erba*]-*Marduk fr*[*om* - - - - -] *went forth.*
16. [- - - - - *n*]*âzir.*
17. [- - - - - - - - - - -].
18. [- - -], *the king of Assyria sat upon the throne.*
19. [- - - -] *sat* [*upon the thr*]*one.*
20. [- - - - - - - - - - - - -].

Genealogical References

These relate mostly to the Assyrian kings, who in their inscriptions refer to their predecessors. Thus we find genealogies given by the following Assyrian kings:

Ârik-dîn-ili:[1]   Ashur-uballit, father of
   Bêl-nirari, father of
   Arik-dîn-ili.

[1] *AKA.*, Vol. I, p. 3, and n. 2.

Reverse

CHRONICLE K 3
B. M., No. 27,859
(From King, *Chronicles Concerning Early Babylonian Kings*.)

GENEALOGICAL REFERENCES

Adad-nirari I:[1]   Ashur-uballit, father of Bêl-nirari, father of Ârik-dîn-ili, father of Adad-nirari I.

Shalmaneser I:[2]   Ârik-dîn-ili, father of Adad-nirari I, father of Shalmaneser I.

Tukulti-Ninib:[3]   Shalmaneser I, father of Tukulti-Ninib I.

Ashur-rêsh-ishi:[4]   Ashur-dân I, father of Mutakkil-Nusku, father of Ashur-rêsh-ishi.

Tiglath-pileser I:[5]   Ninib-apil-Êkur, father of Ashur-dân I, father of Mutakkil-Nusku, father of Ashur-rêsh-ishi, father of Tiglath-pileser I.

Shamshi-Adad III:[6]   Ashur-rêsh-ishi, father of Tiglath-pileser I, father of Shamshi-Adad III.

Ashur-bêl-kala:[7]   Ashur-rêsh-ishi, father of Tiglath-pileser I, father of Ashur-bêl-kala.

Adad-nirari II:[8]   Tiglath-pileser II, father of Ashur-dân II, father of Adad-nirari II.

---

[1] *Ibid.*, pp. 5-7.   [2] *Ibid.*, p. 13; King, *Tukulti-Ninib I*, pp. 130 f.
[3] *AKA.*, Vol. I, p. 16.; King, *Tukulti-Ninib I*, p. 141.
[4] *AKA.*, Vol. I, pp. 20, 24, 25.
[5] *Ibid.*, pp. 93, 94.   [7] *Ibid.*, p. 152.
[6] *Ibid.*, p. 150.   [8] *Ibid.*, p. 154.

B. BABYLONIAN CHRONOLOGY.

In the Assyrian and Babylonian inscriptions appears here and there a chronological reference stating the number of years that had elapsed between two given events. If the date of one of these events is known and certain, such a reference becomes of immense value for the history of the time, but even if we are not able to locate with certainty any of its dates, such a reference is still of great value in indicating the distance of these events. I shall therefore enumerate the more important of these references that concern the period treated in this volume.

Dynasty D of Pashe

We are now fortunate in being able to fix a date in the *Dynasty of Pashe*, by which a number of dates in Babylonian chronology become tolerably certain, if not quite accurate.

The Bavian Inscription

Sennacherib, king of Assyria (705–681 B. C.), inscribed on the rocks of Bavian, a few miles north of Nineveh, three identical inscriptions, relating his capture of the city of Babylon in 689 B. C. In this inscription we read:

"*Adad and Shala, the gods of the city of Êkallâte, whom Marduk-nâdin-akhê, king of Akkadî, in the time of Tiglath-pileser I, king of Assyria, had taken and had brought unto Babylon, after four hundred and eighteen years I brought forth from Babylon, and I restored them to their places in the city of Ê[kallâte].*"[1]

This number, *418* years, occurs on all three panels of this inscription. The reading must therefore be regarded as certain, nor have we any reason to question its correctness. Lehmann[2] proposes indeed to change it to *318* and

[1] *III R*, 14, ll. 48–50.   [2] *Zwei Hauptprobleme*, pp. 98 ff.

Rost[1] to 478, one taking away 100 years, the other adding 60 years, but the procedure is unscholarly and, in this case at least, not only unnecessary, but wrong.

THE BAVIAN INSCRIPTION, LL. 48-50
(From King, *Records of Tukulti-Ninib I.*)

This date on the *Bavian Inscription* brings us back to the year 1107 B.C.[2] In that year, then, both *Marduk-*

[1] *Untersuchungen*, MVG., 1897, 2, p. 120.

[2] Rost, *Untersuchungen MVG.*, 1897, 2, p. 120, assumes that Babylon was captured in 690 B.C., and adding 418 thereto he reaches 1118 (*sic!*) B.C. which he then changes to 1178 B.C.

nâdin-akhê of Babylon and *Tiglath-pileser I* of Assyria were reigning. This date has an important bearing on the chronologies both of Assyria and of Babylonia. It helps us to fix approximately the chronology of the kings of Assyria, and it enables us to settle the chronology of *Dynasties C–E of Babylonia*.

The Boundary-Stone of Marduk-nâdin-akhê

From the time of *Marduk-nâdin-akhê*, king of Babylonia, we have a boundary-stone,[1] on which is recorded a victory over Assyria in his tenth year. This victory is also referred to in the *Synchronistic History*, for it mentions a second war[2] between these kings, lasting for two years, in which *Tiglath-pileser I* won. It must therefore have been the first war (not mentioned for patriotic reasons by the Assyrian historiographer), in which *Marduk-nâdin-akhê* of Babylonia conquered. This happened in 1107 B. C. as stated above in the *Bavian Inscription*.

Marduk-nâdin-akhê, therefore, became king in 1116 B. C. According to *King-List A*,[3] he reigned twenty-two years, and hence died in 1094 B. C. His successors in this dynasty reigned, accordingly, as follows:

Marduk-akhê-irba, 1 year, 6 months, 1094–1093 B. C.
Marduk-shâpik-zêr-mâti, 12 years, 1093–1081 B. C.
Nabû-nâdin, 8 years, 1081–1073 B. C.

The *Dynasty D of Pashe* collapsed in 1073 B. C., and as it lasted for 132 years and 6 months, it came into power in 1205 B. C.

Two more kings of this dynasty, *Nebuchadrezzar I* and his son *Bêl-nâdin-aplu*, are known. They were most

---
[1] III R , 43, col. I, 5, 27, 28.
[2] See p. 38.   [3] See above, p. 28.

probably the immediate predecessors of *Marduk-nâdin-akhê*, and their dates will be considered below.[1] Of the first five kings of this dynasty nothing is known, beyond what the *King-List* records.[2] This dynasty reigned for 132 years and 6 months, i. e., from 1205–1073 B. C. Its first king, whose name began with *Marduk* - - - -, reigned 18 years, 1205–1187 B. C., and his successor reigned 6 years, 1187–1181 B. C.

Dynasty E of the Sea-Land

After the fall of the *Dynasty of Pashe* in 1073 B. C., *Dynasty* E of the *Sea-Land* came to power. It lasted only 21 years, 6 months, and according to *King-List A*, its three kings reigned as follows:

1. *Simmashshipak*, 18 years,   1073–1055 B. C.
2. *Bêl-mukîn*, 5 months,   1055–1054 B. C.
3. *Kashshû-nâdin-akhê*, 3 years,   1054–1051 B. C.

Dynasty C of the Kassites

From *King-List A* we know that this dynasty lasted 576 years, 9 months, i. e., from 1782–1205 B. C. Only the first six and the last fifteen names are preserved on this list,[3] and their dates can accordingly be determined.

To these names we can now add the names mentioned in the *Amarna Letters*, *Chronicle P*, the *Synchronistic History*, and the legal tablets of the *Kassite period*, and by these means we are also able to assign to these kings approximate dates.

The great lacuna in the middle of the *Kassite Dynasty* of *King-List A* is thus partially remedied. Eleven names are, however, still lacking, but of these one name, *Agum-*

---

[1] Pp. 82 ff.   [2] See above, p. 28.   [3] See above p. 26, 28.

kakrime, can now be restored with certainty; another, *Zibir*, belongs in all probability to this dynasty; and a third *Adad-shum-nâzir*, belongs possibly here also.

1. *Agum-kakrime*.—In the British Museum are two fragments of an inscription[1] by a Kassite king, *Agum-kakrime*, who calls himself a son of *Tash-shi-gu-ru-mash*, who is undoubtedly identical with *Tashzigurmash*, the sixth king of the *Kassite Dynasty*. *Agum-kakrime* should then be set down as the seventh king of this dynasty.

2. *Zibir*.—In the annals of *Ashurnazirpal III* (885–860 B. C.), we read:

"*At that time in the land of Zamua the city of Attila, which Zibir, king of Kâr-Duniash, had taken for a habitation, had decayed and was turned into mounds and heaps of ruins.*"[2]

This *Zibir* is then another Kassite king who came to the throne some time after *Agum-kakrime*.

3. *Adad-shum-nâzir I*.—In the British Museum is a fragment of a late Assyrian copy of a letter,[3] written by a king *Adad-shum-nâzir*, and addressed to two Assyrian kings, *Ashur-nirara* and *Nabû-dâni*. It has been suggested that this *Adad-shum-nâzir* is identical with the Babylonian king of the same name, who expelled *Tukulti-Ninib I* in 1267 B. C. This may be possible, so far as it concerns the Babylonian king, but it is impossible to find room for two Assyrian kings between *Ashurnazirpal I* and *Tukulti-Ashur*, and we must therefore assign these two Assyrian kings either to a period preceding *Ashur-bêl-nishêshu*, i. e., to some time prior to 1450 B. C., or else to the unknown period of *Dynasty H*, i. e., to some time

---

[1] *VR.*, 64.   [2] *AKA.*, Vol. I, p. 325.
[3] *AKA.*, Vol I, p. xxii.

DYNASTY C OF THE KASSITES

in the tenth or eleventh centuries B. C. It is impossible at present to decide to which of the two unknown periods we should assign this king, and it is only provisionally that I assign this king to the lacuna of the *Kassite Dynasty*.

On the basis of the above-mentioned data we are thus able to reconstruct the chronology of the *Kassite Dynasty*.

	Name	Length of Reign	Date
1.	*Gandish,*	16 years,	1782–1766 B. C.
2.	*Agum-shi,*	22 years,	1766–1744 B. C.
3.	*Bitiliashu I,*	22 years,	1744–1722 B. C.
4.	*Dushi-ashu,*	8 years,	1722–1714 B. C.
5.	*Adumetash,*	....	1714
6.	*Tashzi-gurmash,*	....	
7.	*Agum-kakrime,*		

Zibir

Adad-shum-nâzir,

17.	*Kara-Indash, ca.*	25 years,	*circa* 1460–1435 B. C.
18.	*Kadashman-Bêl I,*	15 years,	*circa* 1435–1420 B. C.
19.	*Kuri-Galzu I,*	15 years,	*circa* 1420–1405 B. C.
20.	*Burna-Buriash,*	25 years,	1405–1380 B. C.
21.	*Kara-Khardash,* 3 (?) years, *Kadashman-Kharbe I,*		1380–1377 B. C.
	Nazibugash, (*Shuzigash*), (Usurper) 1 (?) year,		1377

22. *Kuri-Galzu II*,	24 years,	1377–1353 B. C.
23. *Nazi-Maraddash*,	26 years,	1353–1327 B. C.
24. *Kadashman-Turgu*,	17 years,	1327–1310 B. C.
25. *Kadashman-Bêl II*,	6 years,	1310–1304 B. C.
26. *Kudur-Bêl*,	8 years,	1304–1296 B. C.
27. *Shagarakti-Shuriash*,	13 years,	1296–1283 B. C.
28. *Bitiliashu II*,	8 years,	1283–1275 B. C.
29. *Bêl-shum-iddin*,	1 year, 6 mo.,	1275–1273 B. C.
30. *Kadashman-Kharbe II*,	1 year, 6 mo.,	1273–1272 B. C.
31. *Adad-shum-iddin*,	6 years,	1272–1266 B. C.
32. *Adad-shum-uzur*,	30 years,	1266–1236 B. C.
33. *Meli-Shipak*,	15 years,	1236–1221 B. C.
34. *Marduk-apil-iddin*,	13 years,	1221–1208 B. C.
35. *Zamama-shum-iddin*,	1 year,	1208–1207 B. C.
36. *Bêl-shum-iddin*,	2 years,	1207–1205 B. C.

This reconstruction of the chronology of the *Kassite Dynasty* will be found to conform to almost all the data, so far as now known, on the Babylonian monuments. They agree also with the contemporary Assyrian and Egyptian dates, and should therefore be regarded as approximately correct. The dates are the lowest possible, even after full allowance has been made for any doubtful reading of the *King-List*, for I have chosen the lowest date that the other monuments permit. On the other hand, these dates could not be very much earlier, and in no case more than three years, for *Kuri-Galzu I* was still reigning when *Ikhnaton* became king, and I see no possible way to date *Ikhnaton's* accession earlier than 1407 B. C.

With this reconstruction, as I said above, almost all data agree. The only exception to this, so far as I know now, is the

Building-Inscription of Nabonidus at Sippara

On a building-inscription at Sippara King *Nabonidus* has recorded the following:

"*Ê-Ulmash, his temple in Sippara-Anunit, which no king had built for eight hundred years, since Shagarakti-Buriash, king of Babylon, son of Kudur-Bêl. His foundation-inscription I sought, found, and read.*[1]

INSCRIPTION OF NABONIDUS
GIVING THE DATE OF SHAGARAKTI-BURIASH
(From *VR.*, 64, ca. 27-33.)

This has been taken to mean that *Shagarakti-Buriash* reigned 800 years before *Nabonidus*. The latter king reigned from 555-538 B. C., and *Shagarakti-Buriash* should then have reigned some time between 1355 and 1338 B. C. This name does not occur on the *King-List*. The name most like it is *Shagarakti-Shuriash*, and I believe that the two names are identical and both should be read *Shagarakti-Shuriash*, for the sign *bur* is undoubtedly a

[1] *VR.*, 64, c, ll. 27-33.

miswriting for *Shur*, the two Babylonian signs being very similar. This king reigned, however, from 1296–1283, which is about fifty years later than *Nabonidus*' date indicates. I am unable to explain this discrepancy otherwise than by assuming that *Nabonidus* used an even number, and as such it comes sufficiently near.

The name of the father and predecessor of this *Shagarakti-Shuriash* on *King-List A* has been read by Lehmann and others as *Gish-am-me(?) - - - - ti*. It should, however, be noted that not a single sign in this line is clear, and that the reading must therefore be regarded as very doubtful. Notwithstanding this fact, Lehmann built upon it his theory of the Kassite kings, according to which hardly a single date on the monuments would be correct.

If *Shagarakti-shur-ia-ash* and *Shagarakti-shu-ri-ash* are identical (and of this there can be hardly any doubt), we would expect that *King-List A* should in the preceding line have had the name *Kudur-Bêl*. This I believe stood there also originally, instead of Lehmann's supposed *Gish-am-me-ti - - -* for the mutilated signs of this line can readily be restored to *Ku-dur-ᶦˡᵘBêl*, so that instead of

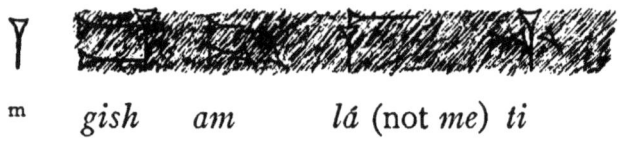

^m   *gish*   *am*   *lá* (not *me*) *ti*

we should read:

^m   *Ku-*   *dur-*   ᶦˡᵘ *Bêl.*¹

---

¹ After this was written and my manuscript was sent to press, Vol. XX, Part I, of *BE.*, Series A, appeared in which Hilprecht states, p. 52, note 1, that

BUILDING-INSCRIPTION OF NABONIDUS AT SIPPARA 69

Clay[1] has shown that a *Kadashman-Bêl II* must be placed between *Kadashman-Turgu* and *Kudur-Bêl*. A real difficulty seems to exist in the apparent contradiction between *Chronicle P* and the *Synchronistic History* in regard to *Kara-Khardash* and *Kadashman-Kharbe I*. *Chronicle P* makes *Kuri-Galzu II* a son of *Kadashman-Kharbe I*, and this king is here a son of *Kara-Khardash*, son of *Muballitat-Sherûa*, the daughter of *Ashur-uballit* of Assyria. *Chronicle P* also calls the usurper by the name *Shuzigash*. The *Synchronistic History*, on the other hand, claims that the revolt was directed against *Kara-Khardash*, son of *Muballitat-Sherûa*, and that the name of the usurper was *Nazi-bugash*. *Kuri-Galzu II* is here mentioned as the son of *Burna-Buriash*. In the case of the usurper, it can be assumed that he had two names, one being his throne-name, the other his birth-name. In regard to the Babylonian kings, both documents agree that *Kara-Khardash* was the son of *Muballitat-Sherûa*, and this Assyrian princess was evidently the queen of *Kara-Khardash*, who was therefore the father of *Kadashman-Kharbe I*, and we must assume that the father had associated his son with him as coregent, and that both father and son were killed in this rebellion. The succession in the line of the elder brother became therefore extinct, and the younger brother, *Kuri-Galzu II*, a son of

he and Mr. King have again carefully gone over this tablet, containing *King-List A*, and both these experts in reading difficult cuneiform texts agree that the signs on the tablets are those of *Kudur-Bêl*, and my assumption has therefore been substantiated in a very satisfactory way. The date of *Kudur-Bêl* on *King-List A* should undoubtedly be restored to 8, and with this agrees his highest date, year 9, on the legal documents. For this date indicates that he had reigned 8 years and begun his ninth. He may have died soon after he began his ninth year, and the chronographer would then have set down his date as 8 years.

[1] *EB.*, Series A, Vol. XIV, pp. 4 f.

Kara-Khardash, was elevated to the throne.[1] The reign of *Kara-Khardash* and his son was evidently very short and the three years that I have suggested for it is ample, even considering the acts that *Chronicle P* assigns to *Kadash-man-Kharbe I*, for these may very well have been carried out in two or three years.

The monuments do not know of two kings, named *Kadashman-Bêl*, one as the predecessor of *Burna-Buriash I*, and the other as the predecessor of *Burna-Buriash II*, for the very simple reason, that they record not two, but only one *Burna-Buriash*, son of *Kuri-Galzu I* and father of *Kara-Khardash*. Lehmann's[2] hypothesis of a *Burna-Buriash I*, son of *Kadashman-Bêl I*, based on BE., Vol. I, No. 68, cannot be relied upon, for, in face of the mutilated condition of that text, his restorations are extremely uncertain and very improbable.

Finally, it should be noted that Lehmann's[3] hypothesis of two kings, *Bitiliashu II* and *III* (Lehmann reads "*Bibeiashu*"), the former the son of *Shagarakti-Buriash*, the latter son of *Shagarakti-shu-ri-ash*, is not borne out by the monuments. As I have said above, *Shagarakti-Buriash* should be read *Shagarakti-shur-ia-ash*, and is identical with *Shagarakti-*SHU-*ri-ash*, and the two alleged *Bitiliashu* are one and the same person, *Bitiliashu II*.

Our date of this *Shagarakti-Shuriash*, given above as 1296–1283 B. C., can be proved from an inscription on a

[1] The *Synchronistic History* is therefore incorrect in making *Kuri-Galzu II* a son and *Muballitat-Sherûa* queen of *Burna-Buriash*. That the author of *Chronicle P* was here better informed has been shown by Dr. Luckenbill who in his admirable essay on the "Temple Documents of the Kassite Dynasty" (*AJSL.*, XXIII, p. 281) calls attention to a tablet published by Clay (*BE.*, Ser. A, Vol. XIV, No. 39), where *Kuri-Galzu* (*II*), father of *Nazi-Maraddash*, is called a son of *Kadashman-Kharbe* (*I*).

[2] *Zwei Hauptprobleme*, pp. 132 ff.   [3] *Ibid.*, p. 143.

Seal of Shagarakti-Shuriash

When *Sennacherib* conquered Babylon in 689 B. C., he found there a seal which had once belonged to *Shagarakti-Shuriash*, and had been taken from Babylon by *Tukulti-Ninib*. Later on it was restored to Babylon, and now at last it was recovered by *Sennacherib*, who brought it back to Assyria and made a copy of it, on which he recorded in duplicate the original inscriptions which it bore, and added thereto its history. The inscription on *Sennacherib's* copy of this seal reads:

"*Tukulti-Ninib I, king of hosts, son of Shalmaneser I, king of Assyria. Booty from the land of Kâr-Duniash. Whosoever altereth my inscription or my name, may Ashur and Adad destroy his name and his land.*"

2. "*This seal the enemy carried away from Assyria to Akkadî, but I, Sennacherib, king of Assyria, after 600 years, conquered Babylon, and from the spoil of Babylon I brought it forth.*"

3. "*Property of Shagarakti-Shuriash, king of hosts.*"

4. "*Tukulti-Ninib (I), king of hosts, son of Shalmaneser (I), king of Assyria. [Booty] from the land of Kâr-Duniash. Whosoever altereth my inscription or my name, may Ashur and Adad destroy his name and his land.*"

5. "*Property of Shagarakti-Shuriash, king of hosts.*"

6. "*This is that which is written upon the seal of Lapis-lazuli.*"[1]

The story of this seal seems to be as follows: *Shagarakti-Shuriash* (1297–1284 B. C.) had made a seal of lapis-lazuli, and engraved sections 3 and 5, one upon the edge and the other upon the side of the seal. When *Tukulti-Ninib I* carried it away in 1289 B. C., he placed his record

[1] King, *Records of Tukulti-Ninib I*, pp. 106–09.

of the capture on both sides of the seal (sections 1 and 4). It was then recovered and taken back to Babylon, but

Obverse

Edge

Reverse

Copy of *Seal-inscription of Shagarakti-Shuriash*, made by *Sennacherib*. (From King, *Records of Takulti-Ninib I*, pp. 163, 165.)

when *Sennacherib* found it, he made a copy of it and added on this copy section 2. The scribe who carried out this copying then added section 6.

The date, 600 years, brings us to 1289 B. C., which falls within the reign of *Shagarakti-Shuriash*, who was king 1296–1283 B. C. It also indicates that *Tukulti-Ninib* was king at that time, and from his annals we know that he had then been king for a considerable period. *Tukulti-Ninib's* victory over *Shagarakti-Shuriash* was only temporary. The Babylonian king died five years later and was succeeded by his son *Bitiliashu II*. In the eighth year of this king, *Tukulti-Ninib* again attacked Babylon, slew *Bitiliashu*, captured the city, and made *Bêl-shum-iddin* king. On his revolt in 1277 B. C. *Tukulti-Ninib* once more invaded Babylon, slew the king, carried away the treasures of the city and of *Marduk's* temple *Esagil*, brought the statue of *Marduk* to Ashur, and ruled the city for 7 years, appointing viceroys under him. The first of these viceroys was *Kadashman-Kharbe II*, who ruled for 1 year, 6 months, and then followed *Adad-shum-iddin*, for 6 years. This is the period of 7 years, of which *Chronicle P* says that *Tukulti-Ninib I* ruled Babylon. The Babylonians then revolted, drove away *Tukulti-Ninib*, and made *Adad-shum-uzur* king of Babylonia. This happened in 1267. *Tukulti-Ninib I* now returned to Assyria, but a revolt, headed by his son *Ashur-nâzir-pal I*, awaited him there, and he was killed, probably in the following year, 1266 B. C.

The inscription on the seal of *Shagarakti-Shuriash* thus confirms the chronology built on the *Bavian inscription* and *King-List A*.

Dynasty A of Babylon

*H*aving ascertained the dates in the *Kassite Dynasty* of Babylonia, we are enabled to take another step and inquire for the dates of *Dynasty A*, the great *Hammu-*

rabi Dynasty. An indication as to the date of *Hammurabi's* reign is given by *Nabonidus* in his *Sippara Inscription.*

"*The name of Khammurabi, one of the old kings, who seven hundred years before Burna-Buriash had built Ê-Barra and the temple towers on the old foundation, I saw therein and worshipped.*"[1]

BUILDING INSCRIPTION OF NABONIDUS, GIVING THE DATE OF HAMMURABI
85-4-30, 2, Col. II, ll. 20-26
(From *IR.*, 69, b, 4-10.)

That *Hammurabi* rebuilt the sun-temple of Sippara is recorded by himself in the prologue to his *code*, where he says:

"*(I am Khammurabi), the diplomatic king, obedient to the mighty Shamash; who refounded Sippara; who clothed with green(?) the shrines of Ai; who decorated the temple of Ê-Barra, which is like a heavenly dwelling.*"[2]

This date has been taken as a round number, and although dates given by *Nabonidus* may be such, it is not necessary that this number be so. But even if it be only approximate, it will still indicate that it is somewhere

[1] *IR.*, 69, b, ll. 4-10.
[2] *Code of Hammurabi*, col. ii, ll. 22-32.

about 2100 B. C., that we should look for the date of this great king. From the biblical chronology we must presume, if that chronology be correct, that *Hammurabi* should have lived about that time.[1] We have also seen that *Burna-Buriash* reigned from 1405–1380 B. C., and we noticed then that this date cannot possibly be more than three years too late and hardly too early. *Hammurabi* would then have restored the sun-temple at Sippara some time between 2105 and 2080 B. C.

This date differs, however, so radically from the dates commonly assigned to *Hammurabi* by the Assyriologists, that it will be necessary to find some other support for it and possibly also to define exactly the dates of *Dynasty A* of Babylon, i. e., the *Hammurabi Dynasty*. At the same time, while I recognize the fact that this date differs radically from those dates usually assigned to *Hammurabi's* reign, it should be borne in mind that scarcely two Assyriologists have as yet been able to agree on the dates of this king's reign. This will readily be admitted after a glance at a partial list of dates, proposed by scholars, who have given their attention to this subject: Rogers[2] has proposed 2342–2288; Paton,[3] 2239–2196; Radau[4] 2288–2233; Lehmann,[5] 2248–2194; Niebuhr,[6] 2081–2026.

This difference of more than 250 years for the accession of *Hammurabi* seems suspicious, and indicates that there

---

[1] If *Hammurabi* is identical with the biblical *Amraphel* (Gen. 14:1, 9), then *Hammurabi* was a contemporary of Abram, and the war mentioned in Gen., chap. 14, was carried on between 2090 and 2080 B. C.

[2] *History of Babylonia*, Vol. I, p. 338.

[3] *Early History of Syria*, p. xiv.

[4] *Early Babylonian History*, p. 30.

[5] *Zwei Hauptprobleme.* Tabelle II.

[6] *Chronologie*, p. 74.

must be something essentially wrong in these calculations, and that a reconsideration of this subject is a necessity.

The best and most exact data for the beginning of the *Hammurabi Dynasty* come to us from two Greek sources, which we shall now consider.

Chronology of Simplicius

Simplicius in his commentary on Aristotle's treatise "About *H*eaven," claims, on the authority of Porphyry, that Aristotle requested Calisthenes, an officer in the army of Alexander the Great, to send him any records of astronomical observations that he might find in Babylon. When Alexander the Great entered that city, Calisthenes complied with this request, and sent Aristotle some Babylonian records. According to the present manuscripts, these records covered a period of 31,000 years, but *M*oerbeka wrote a Latin translation about 1271 A. D. in which the text read 1903 years. Diels and Lehmann[1] have verified this date and have shown that the 31,000 depends on a misreading of the Greek cipher signs, which originally must have read 1903. This date 1903 extends "to the time of Alexander the *M*acedonian,"[2] i. e., to 331 B. C., the year, when Alexander the Great captured Babylon.

If we now add these two dates together, we obtain the year 2233 B. C. This date must designate the beginning of the First Dynasty of Babylon, when it became a Semitic capital. It is entirely out of the question to assign to this date some hypothetical event in the reign of

[1] *Zwei Hauptprobleme*, p. 110. The original ΑΠΓ (=Χιλίων καὶ ἐνακοσίων τριῶν=1903) was read read as ΑΜΓ (=χιλίων καὶ μυριάδων τριῶν= 31,000!.

[2] ἕως τῶν Ἀλεξάνδρου τοῦ Μακεδόνος χρόνων. It includes the year 331 B. C. but it cannot include, however, the reign of Alexander the Great, for Calisthenes died in 327 B. C., i. e., four years before the death of Alexander.

Hammurabi, as Marquardt[1] and Lehmann[2] have done. If this date means anything, it must mean the beginning of Semitic rule in Babylon.[3] The date is further corroborated from another Greek source.

Chronology of Berossos

Berossos was a Babylonian priest, living in Greece in the time of Alexander the Great. He wrote a history of Babylonia, in three volumes, in which he outlined the history of that land from the beginning to the time of Alexander. Berossos' works have perished, and we have now only some quotations from them, collected from the writings of Syncellus and Eusebius, who, however, had access only to the quotations of Alexander Polyhistor.

Schwarz[4] has collected these references, and according to him, Berossos gave the following data:

	10 kings before the Flood	432,000 years
Dyn. I.	86 kings after the Flood	34,090 years
Dyn. II.	8 Median usurpers	224 years
Dyn. III.	11 kings	248 years
Dyn. IV.	49 Chaldean kings	458 years
Dyn. V.	9 Arabian kings	245 years
Dyn. VI.	45 kings	526 years
	From *Nabonassar* to C*yrus*	209 years
	From C*yrus* to death of *Alexander*	215 years
		1901 years

[1] *Chronologische Untersuchungen*, pp. 14 ff.

[2] *Zwei Hauptprobleme*, pp. 112 ff.

[3] Rost, *Untersuchungen*, *MVG.*, 1897, 2, p. 111, accepts this date, but assumes that Babylon fell in 330, and that this year was the same as the year 1903, given by Calisthenes. Rost therefore places the rise of *Dynasty A* in 2232 B. C. This is, however, impossible. Babylon fell in 331 B. C.

[4] Pauly-Wissowa, *Real Encyclopedie*, II, p. 314.

If we now add thereto 323,[1] we obtain the year 2224, representing the beginning of some dynasty of Babylonia, which had eleven kings, and as Berossos does not designate this dynasty by a special name, he might mean the dynasty of Babylon, i. e., the *Hammurabi Dynasty* which began in 2223 B. C. This is ten years later than the date given by Simplicius, and this difference may very well depend upon the imperfect condition in which the text of Berossos has been handed down to us; perhaps also on leaving out the fractions of years, which *King-List A* and undoubtedly also Simplicius counted. The essential fact remains that the data of Berossos confirm in the strongest manner the date given by Simplicius, and also, as we shall see presently, the date of *Hammurabi*, given by *Nabonidus* as well as the date of *Amraphel*, given in Gen., chap. 14.

But von Gutschmid[2] and Peiser[3] have called attention to the fact, that the Babylonians reckoned the time in cycles of *sars*, each *sar* comprising 3,600 years. Berossos says that the ten kings before the Flood had reigned 120 cycles or *sars*, i. e., 432,000 years. Then follows the period "after the Flood" to the fall of the Babylonian Empire and the accession of the Persians. This period comprises the following dates, as quoted by Syncellus and Eusebius:

86 kings after the Flood	34,080 years
8 Median usurpers	224 years
11 kings	248 years
49 Chaldean kings	458 years

[1] Alexander died in the year 323 B. C.
[2] *Kleine Schriften*, Vol. II, pp. 101 f.
[3] *ZA.*, Vol. VI, pp. 264 ff.

9 Arabian kings	245 years
45 kings	526 years
8 Assyrian kings	122 years
6 Chaldean kings	87 years
Total,	35,990 years

This total lacks an even 10 years in 10 *sars* or cycles of 36,000 years. Von Gutschmid has therefore altered the third date, 248 years, of the 11 kings of *Dynasty A* of Babylon to 258 years, which would give a full cycle from the Flood to the fall of the Babylonian Empire, and I believe that this emendation is correct. In this case the Berossos list agrees well with the date given by Simplicius, adding 1686 years to 538 B. C., the accession year of *Cyrus*, which gives us the year 2234-3 B. C.

If we then take the date of Simplicius, 2233 B. C., for the beginning of *Dynasty A* of Babylon, and apply thereto the data furnished by *King-List B*, we obtain the following—

Chronology of Dynasty A

Name of King	Length of Reign	Date
1. *Sumu-abi*	15 years	2233–2218 B. C.
2. *Sumu-la-ilu*	35 years	2218–2184 B. C.
3. *Zabu*	14 years	2184–2169 B. C.
4. *Apil-Sin*	18 years	2169–2151 B. C.
5. *Sin-muballit*	30 years	2151–2121 B. C.
6. *Khammurabi*	55 years	**2121–2066** B. C.
7. *Samsu-iluna*	35 years	2066–2031 B. C.
8. *Abeshu*	25 years	2031–2006 B. C.
9. *Ammi-ditana*	25 years	2006–1981 B. C.
10. *Ammi-sadugga*	21 years	1981–1960 B. C.
11. *Samsu-ditana*	31 years	1960–1929 B. C.

Hammurabi died in 2066 B. C., and *Burna-Buriash* in 1380 B. C. *Nabonidus* states that there were 700 years between *Hammurabi* and *Burna-Buriash*.

In regard to thè differences between the *King-Lists* and the *Date-Lists* in the *Hammurabi Dynasty*, the following solution is offered:

1. *Sin-muballit* reigned, according the the *Date-Lists*, twenty years, according to the *King-List*, thirty years. This would indicate that he was overpowered by *Eri-Aku* in 2131 B. C., but continued to live for ten years more, and died in 2121 B. C.

2. *Hammurabi* reigned forty-three years according to the *Date-Lists*, and fifty-five years according to the *King-List*. This would mean that *Eri-Aku* continued as suzerain for the first twelve years of *Hammurabi*, and that, in 2109, *Hammurabi* subdued *Eri-Aku*, and became king of Northern arid Middle Babylonia. *Hammurabi's* victory over Elam in his thirtieth year would be in 2080 B. C., and his victory over *Eri-Aku* in his thirty-first year would be in 2079 B. C.

For the five following reigns I would suggest that the *King-List* gives the reigns from accession to accession, while the *Date-Lists* give the reigns from death-year to death-year. According to this supposition we would get the following scheme:

	King-List	*Date-Lists*	Total Length of Reign
5. *Sin-muballit*	30 y. 2151–2121	20 y. 2151–2131	30 y. 2151–2121
Eri-Aku		22 y. 2131–2109	
6. *Hammurabi*	43 y. 2121–2066	55 y. 2109–2066	55 y. 2121–2066
7. *Samsu-iluma*	35 y. 2066–2031	38 y. 2066–2028	38 y. 2066–2028
8. *Abeshu*	25 y. 2031–2006	28 y. 2028–2000	31 y. 2031–2000
9. *Ammi-ditana*	25 y. 2006–1981	37 y. 2000–1963	43 y. 2006–1963
10. *Ammi-zadugga* ...	21 y. 1981–1960	17 y. 1963–1946	35 y. 1981–1946
11. *Samsu-ditana*	31 y. 1960–1929	(17 y. 1946–1929)	31 y. 1960–1929

The theory of Sayce,[1] that in the *King-Lists* allowance is made for rival princes who were deemed illegitimate and hence not mentioned, while in the *Date-Lists* we have naturally only the names and the years of legitimate rulers, might be allowed in the cases of *Sin-muballit* and *Hammurabi*, but is contradicted by the dates of the following kings, which are longer in the *Date-Lists* than in the *King-Lists*.

Dynasty B, of Uru-kha

Dynasty A, of Babylon, fell in 1929 B. C. *Dynasty C*, "the *Kassite Dynasty*," came to power in 1782 B. C. This leaves a period of 147 years, which should then be assigned to *Dynasty B*, of Uru-kha. But *King-List A* accords 368 years to this dynasty. Can this discrepancy be explained in a satisfactory way? It is this lengthy period of 368 years, that accounts for scholars having placed *Dynasty A* so early. If *Dynasty B* preceded the *Kassite Dynasty*, its kings must have reigned from 2150 to 1782 B. C., and *Dynasty A* must then be pushed 304 years back, i. e., to 2454–2150 B. C.

But the *Dynasty of Uru-kha* is identical with *Dynasty B*, of the Sea-Land, or Southern Babylonia, which did not come under Semitic rulers before the thirty-first year of *Hammurabi*, in 2079 B. C.[2] And it is from this time, therefore, that we must count its eleven kings and

[1] *PSBA.*, Vol. XXI, p. 18.

[2] In *Date List A* the thirty-first year of *Hammurabi* (2079 B. C.) is called: "*The year in which the land of Ê-Mutpal [was conquered]*." On the legal documents the same year is referred to as, "*The year of Hammurabi the king in which with the help of Anu and Bêl he established his good fortune and his hand cast to the earth the land of Ê-Mutpalum and Eri-Aku the king*." This event happened in 2079 B. C. *Eri-Aku* was king of the *Sea-Land*, which stood under the tutelage of god *Ae* of Eridu. Up to this time *Hammurabi* is protected only by *Anu* of Sippara and *Bêl* of Nippur, as *Ae* of Eridu was

368 years. The first kings of this dynasty were then vassal-kings under the overlord of Babylon. Taking the year 2079 B. C. as its first year, and applying thereto the dates on *King-List A*, we obtain the following

Chronology of Dynasty B of Uru-kha

Name of King	Length of Reign	Date
1. *Ilu-ma-ilu*	60 years	2079–2019 B. C.
2. *Ki-an-ni-bi*	56 years	2019–1963 B. C.
3. *Damqi-ilu-shu*	26 years	1963–1937 B. C.
4. *Qadushshi*	15 years	1937–1922 B. C.
5. *Mil-ki-pal*	24 years	1922–1898 B. C.
6. *Gul-ki-shar*	55 years	1898–1843 B. C.
7. *Kir-gal-dara-bar*	50 years	1843–1793 B. C.
8. *A-dara-kalama*	28 years	1793–1764 B. C.
9. *Êkur-ul-anna*	26 years	1764–1739 B. C.
10. *Me-lam-ma*	8 years	1739–1731 B. C.
11. *Ea-gâmil*	20 years	1731–1711 B. C.

That this reckoning is in no way hypothetical, but is correct, can be proved.

Dates of Nebuchadrezzar I and Bêl-nâdin-aplu

Hilprecht has published the inscription on a boundary-stone, dated in the fourth year of King *Bêl-nâdin-aplu*.[1] In this inscription it is stated that a certain *Gir-ki-shar*, king of the *Sea-Land*, had donated a piece of land to the goddess *Ninâ*, which had remained in her possession for 696 years down to *Nebuchadrezzar (I)*, but that a seculari-

Eri-Aku's protector. The overthrow of *Eri-Aku* leaves the *Sea-Land* without a king. In order to affiliate this land with Babylon and also for the purpose of securing a buffer-state against *Ê-Mutpal* and Elam, *Hammurabi* appointed a Semitic prince, *Ilu-ma-ilu*, son of *Nabshemea* of Erech, to be the first king of the *Dynasty of the Sea-Land* as a vassal under Babylon.

[1] *BE.*, Vol. I, pl. 30, text 83.

Obverse

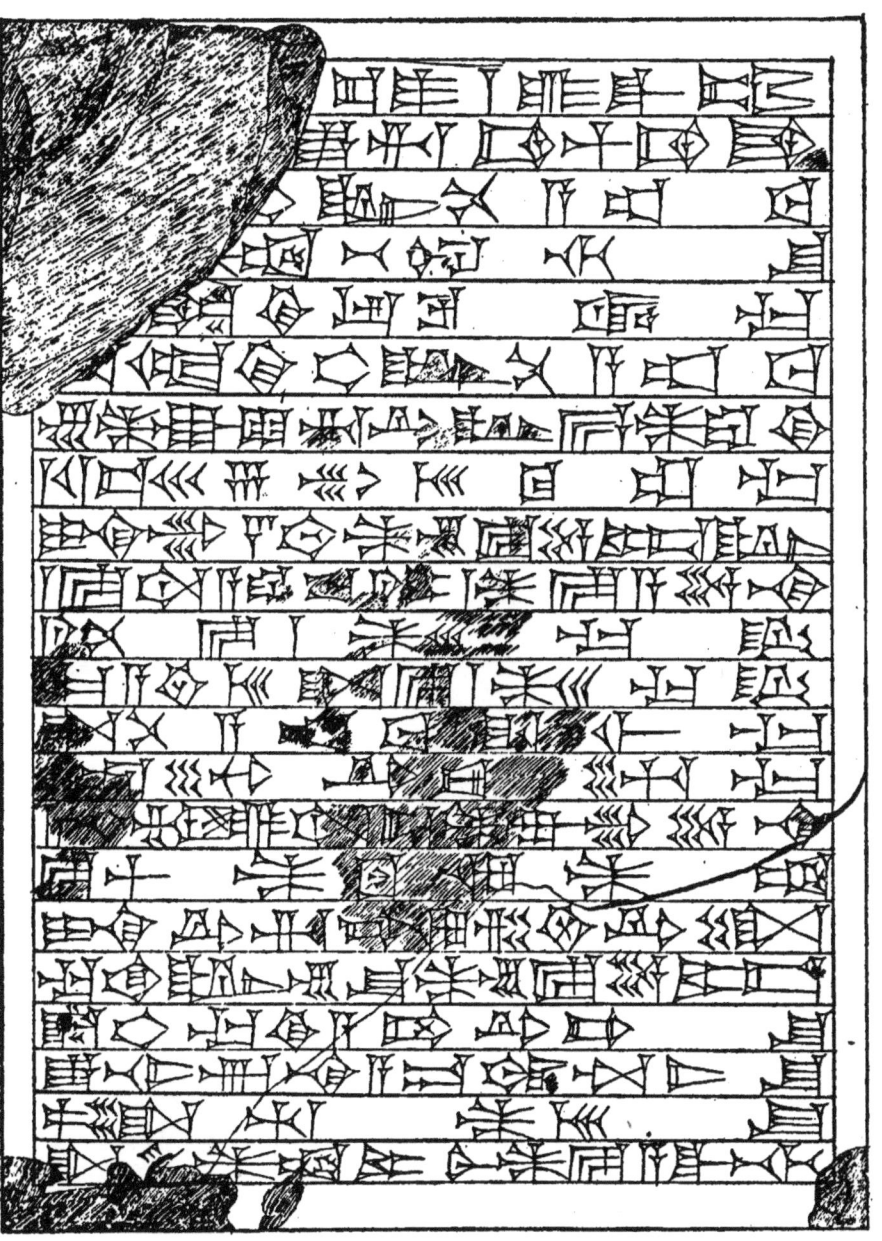

BOUNDARY STONE OF BÊL-NÂDIN-APLU
(From *BE.*, Vol I. pl. 30.)

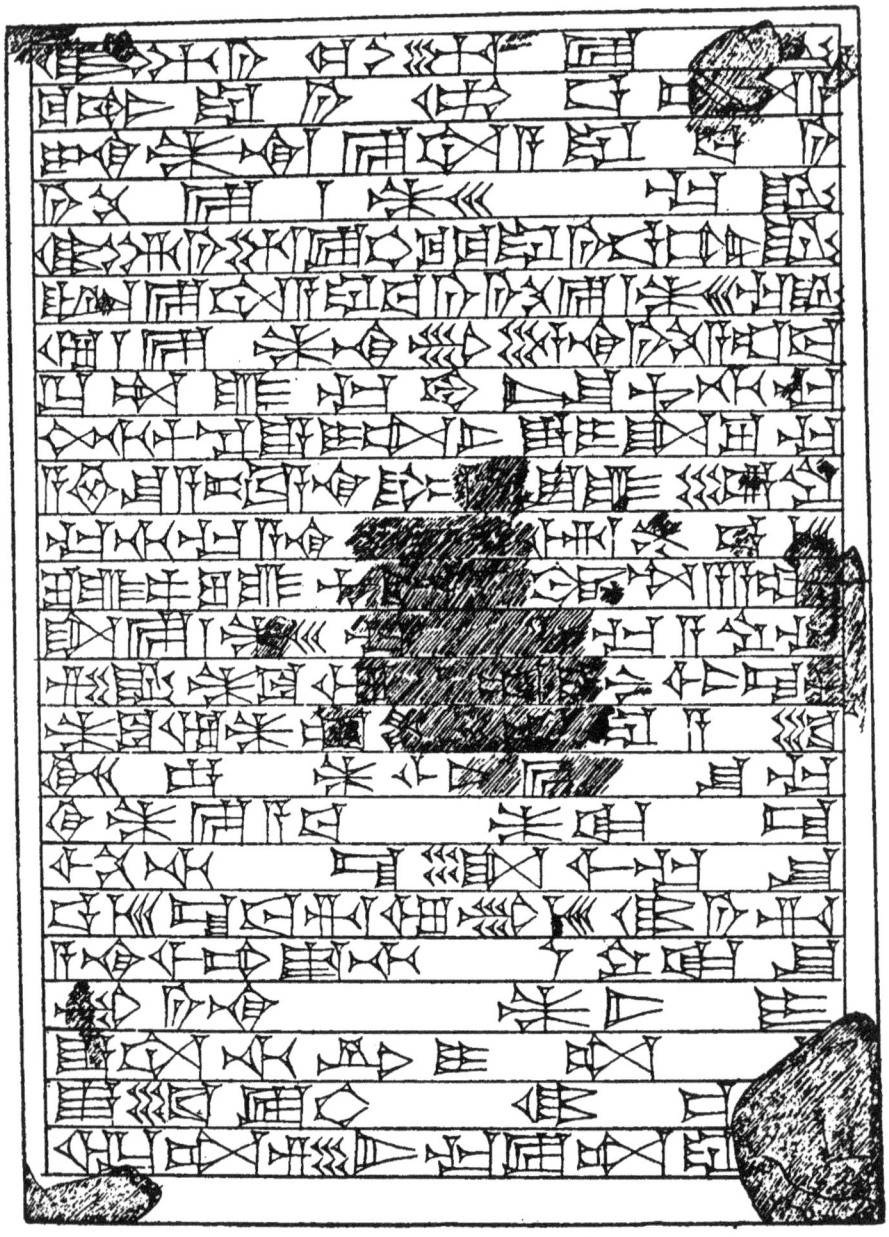

BOUNDARY STONE OF BÊL-NÂDIN-APLU
(From *BE.*, Vol. I, pl. 31.)

zation of it had taken place, and that King *Bêl-nâdin-aplu* in his fourth year corrected this.

Gir-ki-shar, king of the *Sea-Land*, has been taken as identical with *Gul-ki-shar*, the sixth king of *Dynasty B*, and notwithstanding the objections of Lehmann and Rost, many scholars are agreed that this is the fact. We do not know in what year *Gir-ki-shar* donated this land, but 696 years from his death-year, 1843 B. C., brings us to the year 1147 B. C. This date should indicate the accession year of *Nebuchadrezzar I*. From the *Synchronistic History* we know that *Nebuchadrezzar I* was a contemporary of *Ashur-rêsh-ishi* of Assyria, to whom we assigned the date 1160–1125 B. C. In *King-List A* there is a lacuna, for the first seven kings of *Dynasty D*, of Pashe, covering the period 1205–1116 B. C. We know that the name of the first king of this dynasty began with *Marduk - - - -*, and that he reigned for eighteen years, 1205–1187, and we cannot therefore place *Nebuchadrezzar I* at the beginning of this dynasty. Scholars are therefore generally agreed that *Nebuchadrezzar I* and *Bêl-nâdin-aplu* immediataly preceded *Marduk-nâdin-akhê*, who became king in 1116 B. C. The year 1147 B. C. agrees therefore excellently with the accession year of *Nebuchadrezzar I*, to whom we may assign the period 1147–*circa* 1130 B. C., and to his son *Bêl-nâdin-aplu* the period *circa* 1130–1116 B. C.

This date then is admirably suited for *Nebuchadrezzar I*, both as to his contemporaneity with *Ashur-rêsh-ishi* and his distance of 696 years from *Gir (Gul)-ki-shar*. It leaves forty years for the four remaining unknown kings of *Dynasty D*, of Pashe, 1187–1147, which is also reasonable.

The bearing of this date is of immense importance in

the history of this time. The first kings of *Dynasty B* were vassal-kings under the last kings of the *Hammurabi-Dynasty*, from 2079 B. C. to 1929 B. C. *Qadushshi* was the king of the *Sea-Land*, who finally became supreme ruler of Babylonia, although he and his successors continued to live in the southern capital, *Uru-kha*, or *Uru-Ninâ*, well known under the name of *Ninâ*, from the *Tel-lôh* inscriptions, as a mighty city in that province. The *Kassites* had entered Babylonia as early as the time of *Samsu-iluna*, but were then repulsed. In the beginning of the eighteenth century B. C., in 1782, during the weak rule of the kings of *Dynasty B*, they succeeded in making their leader, *Gandish* or *Gande*, king of Kâr-Duniash by which name they designated middle Babylonia. *Dynasty B of the Sea-Land*, continued in the meantime to rule Southern Babylonia or the *Sea-Land* to 1711 B. C., when *Adumetash* then king of Kâr-Duniash, became king of Middle and Southern Babylonia.[1]

The fall of *Dynasty B of the Sea-Land* is referred to in *Chronicle K2*.[2] According to this document, *Ea-gâmil*,

[1] According to chronicles *K1* and *K2* we learn the following facts:

(1) *Eri-Aku* survived into the reign of *Samsu-iluna*, and renewed his attack on Babylon in the hope of regaining his lost prestige in, and crown of, that land.

(2) These chronicles state definitely that *Ilu-ma-ilu*, the first king of *Dynasty B*, of the Sea-Land, was living in the time of *Samsu-iluna*, and that after *Eri-Aku's* war, this king, *Ilu-ma-ilu*, rebelled against *Samsu-iluna* of Babylon, in order to secure his independence. Two battles, disastrous for *Samsu-iluna*, were fought on the shore of the Persian Gulf. It was in this war, probably, that *Samsu-iluna* died, for *Ilu-ma-ilu* continued the war with *Abeshu*, son of *Samsu-iluna*. This important fact corroborates my chronology as presented above, because, according to that, *Ilu-ma-ilu*, who reigned for 60 years, died in the 12th year of *Abeshu*.

(3) My contention, that the *Dynasty of Uru-kha* was identical with the *Dynasty of the Sea-Land*, is here shown to be correct.

[2] Cf. above, p. 53.

DATES OF NEBUCHADREZZAR I AND BÊL-NÂDIN-APLU 87

the last king of this dynasty, invaded Elam. It is probable that he lost the ensuing battle, and fled back again to his own country. In any event, this chronicle continues by mentioning a counter-invasion of the Sea-Land by *Ulam-Buriash*, a Kassite king of Elam, and states that *Ulam-Buriash* overpowered *Ea-gâmil* and conquered the Sea-Land. According to my calculation, this conquest took place in 1711 B. C.

King[1] assumes that this *Ulam-Buriash* is identical with *Ula-Burariash*, son of a King *Burna-Burariash*, mentioned in an inscription on a stone knob:[2]

"*Knob of diorite, the property of Ula-Burariash, the son of king Burna-Burariash, the king of the Sea-Land. Whosoever shall destroy this name and shall write his own (in place thereof), may Anu, Bêl, Ea, Marduk, and Ninmakh destroy his name!*"

I am inclined, however, to question King's identification. Not only is the spelling of the two names different, but the chronicle referred to above states definitely that *Ulam-Buriash* was a brother of *Bitiliashu I*.

The same chronicle mentions in its last section that *Agum*, the son of *Bitiliash* also conquered the Sea-Land. This *Agum* can hardly be identical with *Agum-shi*, the predecessor and probably also the father of *Bitiliashu I*. I would therefore identify him with *Adumetash*, the reading of which name is very uncertain. He may have been a younger brother of *Dushiashu*, and have succeeded him.

The situation may then be explained somewhat after this manner. The *Kassites* had taken possession of the mountains of Anzan in northern Elam, and had established

---
[1] *Chronicles Concerning Early Babylonian Kings*, Vol. I, p. 152.
[2] Cf. Weissbach, *Babylonische Miscellen*, p. 7, Tab. I, no. 3.

there a kingdom of their own. About 2058 B. C. they attempted the conquest of Babylonia, but were repulsed by *Samsu-iluna*. Chronicle *K2* mentions an invasion of Babylonia by the *Hittites* in the time of *Samsu-ditana*, and this invasion may have weakened the kingdom to such an extent that *Qadushshi*, fifth king of the Sea-Land, was able to conquer Babylon and drive away *Samsu-ditana*. The kings of the Sea-Land then ruled all Babylonia until the year 1782 B. C., when the *Kassites* again invaded Babylonia, laid siege to the city of Babylon, and, under their leader *Gandish* (*Gande*, or *Gaddash*) succeeded in capturing the city. This capture of Babylon is mentioned in a neo-Babylonian copy of an inscription by this *Gaddash*[1], in which he terms himself "*king of the Four Regions, king of Shumir and Akkad, king of Babylon,*" and in which he also asserts that he had restored the temple of *Bêl* (*Marduk*) of Babylon, which was destroyed "in the conquest of Babylon" (*ina ka-šad Ba-ba-lam*). From this time on it is to be expected that there would be constant disturbances of the peace between the Kassite kings and those of the Sea-Land. The *Kassites* in Babylonia, in the meantime, continued to govern their old possession, the *Kashshu* region of Elam. *Agum-shi* may therefore have appointed his older son *Bitiliash I* to reign over Babylonia, and his younger son *Ulam-Buriash* to rule the *Kashshu* district of Elam. It is conceivable that *Ea-gâmil*, king of the Sea-Land, tried to weaken the Kassite power by an attack on the *Kassites* in Elam, but that he lost the battle, was driven back, and was then attacked by *Ulam-Buriash*, who conquered the Sea-Land and became its king. Having achieved this success, *Ulam-Buriash* assumed total sov-

[1] Cf. Winckler, *Untersuchungen*, p. 156, no. 6.

ereignty over the Sea-Land, disregarding his nephew, *Agum*, who had become king of Babylonia two years before (1714 B. C.). This gave *Agum* an opportunity of sending an army into the Sea-Land in order to force recognition of himself upon its king, his uncle, and make him his vassal. To this dynasty of Kassite kings in the Sea-Land *Burna-Burariash* and *Ula-Burariash* would have belonged. The latter's inscription quoted above lacks any trace of worship of Kassite divinities, and his mention of only the well-known old gods of Babylonia together with the Sumerian *Ninmakh* shows that this inscription was made quite late, when the *Kassites* has already become thoroughly Semitized.

The intervention of the *Kassites* in the affairs of Babylonia is the signal for the independence of Assyria, which could not be ruled from the *Sea-Land*, when another power controlled Middle Babylonia. The great empire that *Hammurabi* had created had now become disrupted. Assyria became independent, and instead of "judges" (*pateses*) we find henceforth kings, who soon begin to contest stubbornly the power of the *Kassite* kings of Kâr-Duniash, a contest that is carried on for several hundred years, as attested by the *Synchronistic History* and *Chronicle P.* Palestine and Syria, Mesopotamia, and the provinces north of Elam and east of the Tigris become now also independent of Babylonia. The map of the world is changing, and we shall have occasion to come back to this period of transition more than once in the following researches.

The dates given in the historical inscriptions are thus in no way "round numbers, of doubtful weight and doubtful application,"[1] as has been claimed so often by scholars.

[1] Rogers, *History of Babylonia*, Vol. I, pp. 316 f.

The Conquest of Babylonia

When *Dynasty A* of Babylon succeeded in establishing itself in Babylonia, it was not as supreme kings of the whole land, but as lords over a small district. None of the early rulers of this dynasty is called king in the legal documents of that period, until the time of *Sin-muballit* and *Hammurabi*.[1] This fact is significant, and demands an explanation. Who were the overlords of Babylonia at that time? Our thoughts, of course, turn to Elam, whose army *Hammurabi* overthrew in 2080 B. C. But the *Elamites* were only usurpers, who held sway over some parts of Babylonia at short intervals. Furthermore, *Hammurabi* is called king before his thirtieth year, which shows that he was recognized by that title before the overthrow of the E*lamites*. *Sin-muballit* is also once styled a king. The title of king must therefore have been acquired by *Sin-muballit*, some time near the end of his reign. A date in the reign of *Sin-muballit* might give us a clue. His seventeenth year is called "*the year in which he took the city of Isin.*"[2] This capture therefore took place in 2135 B. C. This city had been up to this time the capital of the *Dynasty of Isin*, and its kings were the possessors of the proud title, "*Kings of Isin, Kings of Shumir and Akkad.*" By the conquest of that city the lord of Babylon became *de facto* king of Babylonia.

Before we enter more fully into this question, let us glance at the expansion of the power of the First Dynasty of Babylon. A study of the royal *Date-Lists* of that

---

[1] *Sumu-abi* is once called "King;" cf. Ranke, *BE.*, Ser. D, Vol. III, p. 166; *Sumu-la-ilu* is also once called King, *ibid.*; *Zabum* is never called king; *Apil-Sin* is twice called king, *ibid.*, p. 60. Cf. also *BE.*, Ser. A, Vol. VI, p. 55, where *Sumu-la-ilu* is once called king.

[2] Or, "*the year in which the city of Isin was taken.*"

THE CONQUEST OF BABYLONIA

dynasty will place before us an almost perfect picture of its growth, and I add, therefore, the more important data of these *Date-Lists*.

King	Year of Reign	Date B. C.	
Sumu-abi	9	2225	Wall of city of Dilbat built.
"	10	2224	Crown of god Ni of *K*ish made.
"	13	2221	City of Kazallu laid waste.
Sumu-la-ilu	3	2217	Khalamba slain.
"	5	2215	Wall of city of Babylon built.
"	13	2207	City of *K*ish destroyed.
"	18	2202	Jakhar-zêr-ili flees from Kazallu.
"	19	2201	Fortress of *K*ish destroyed.
"	20	2200	Wall of city of Kazallu destroyed.
"	25	2195	Jakhar-zêr-ili of Kazallu slain.
"	28	2192	City of Barzi (=Borsippa?) taken.
"	29	2191	Wall of Sippara built.
Zabum	12	2172	Wall of Kazallu destroyed.
Apil-Sin	1	2169	Wall of Ba*t*zi (=Borsippa?) built.
"	2	2168	Wall of Babylon built.
Sin-muballit	1	2151	Wall of Rubatum built.
"	7	2145	Wall of Zakardada built.
"	11	2141	Wall of Muru built.
"	12	2140	Wall of Marad built.
"	14	2138	People of Ur slain.
"	15	2137	Wall of Eresh built.
"	17	2135	City of Isin taken.
(*Usurper*	22	2131–09	Eri-Aku *K*ing of Babylonia.)
Hammurabi	4	2106	Wall of Malga destroyed.
"	7	2103	[City] of Isin [taken].
"	21	2089	Wall of Bazu [built].
"	25	2085	Wall of Sippara built.
"	30	2080	Army of Elam slain.
"	31	2079	Land of Ê-Mutpal captured.
"	38	2072	City of Umliash destroyed.
Samsu-iluna	9	2058	Army of the *K*assites defeated.
"	10	2057	Walls of Ur and Erech built.
"	16	2051	Wall of Dadi built.
"	24	2043	Wall of *K*ish [built].

The often-recurring mention of building or restoration of the "walls" of cities indicates that these walls had been razed, and this could of course have happened only after a city had been besieged and captured. I assume, therefore, that the enemies were in most cases the rulers of the First Dynasty of Babylon, and that when the city was finally brought into submission, the Babylonian ruler set about to rebuild the walls and protect the city. That this is the correct explanation can be inferred from the treatment of *Borsippa* and *Ur*.

It is surprising to find how small this Babylonian kingdom was at the rise of this dynasty. The walls of Babylon were rebuilt in 2215. This city had thus been captured some short while before, probably in the first years of *Sumu-la-ilu*, about 2219 B. C. His predecesor, *Sumu-abi*, had captured *Dilbat*, *Kish*, and *Kazallu*, and their walls were rebuilt. *Nippur* was the only city the wall of which was not rebuilt, and the probability is that it was their first possession in Babylonia, and that it had come into their hands either through mutiny and rebellion, or by some sudden attack. The temple library of *Nippur* bears traces of great confusion and destruction in the time of *Bur-Sin II*,[1] but precisely at this time *Sumu-abi* and the First Dynasty came to power. *Bêl* of *Nippur* was the chief protector of its early kings, and when *Sippara* was captured, the god *Anu* of that city, and *Bêl*, became the patrons of these kings, until about 2109 B. C., when *Hammurabi* made Babylon his capital, an event which he describes in the prologue to his *code* as an act of *Anu* and *Bêl*, who transferred the suzerainty over Babylonia to *Marduk*, chief protector of the city of Babylon:

[1] Cf. Hilprecht, *BE.*, Series A, Vol. XX, p. 54.

THE CONQUEST OF BABYLONIA

"*When the lofty Anu, king of the Annunaki, and Bêl, lord of heaven and earth, he who determines the destiny of*

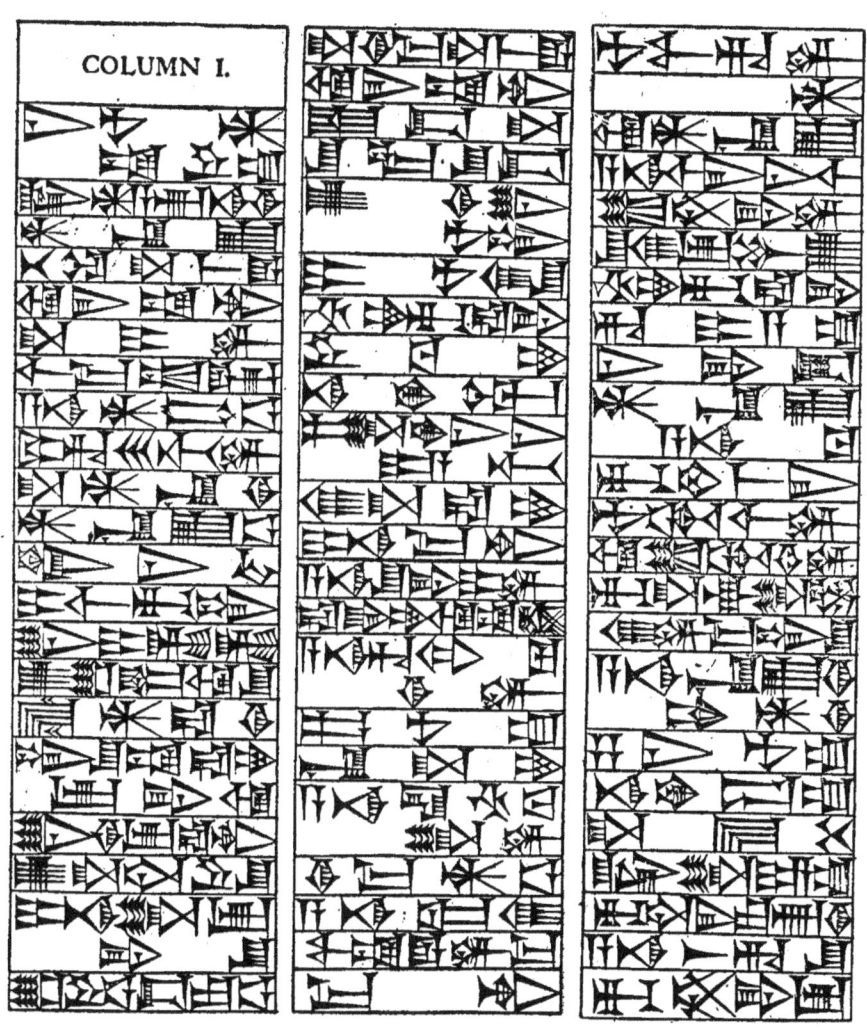

CODE OF HAMMURABI
Col. I.
(From R. F. Harper's *Code of Hammurabi*.)

the land, committed the rule of all mankind to Marduk, the chief son of Ae; when they made him great among the

Igigi; when they pronounced the lofty name of *Babylon;* when they made it famous among the *Regions*[1] and in its midst established an everlasting kingdom whose foundations were firm as heaven and earth—at that time, Anu and Bêl called me, Hammurabi, the exalted prince, the worshiper of the gods, to cause justice to prevail in the land, to destroy the wicked and the evil, to prevent the strong from oppressing the weak, to go forth like the sun over the Black-Head Race, to enlighten the land and to further the welfare of the people. Hammurabi, the governor named by Bêl, am I."[2]

The facts are clear. *Hammurabi* became king in 2109 B. C. His second year is named: "*The year in which righteousness* [*was established*],"[3] or, on the contracts of that year: "*The year in which Hammurabi* (*established*) *the heart of the land in righteousness.*"[4]

This event must have taken place in the year following his accession. "The establishment of righteousness" refers evidently to his overthrow of *Eri-Aku*. He was "named governor by *Bêl*," which indicates that his right to the throne came from the god of *Nippur*, the chief protector of the early kings of this dynasty. It seems as if *Hammurabi* in his revolt against *Eri-Aku* first of all captured Babylon. When he succeeded in freeing Northern and Middle Babylonia, which he probably accomplished the next year, he chose Babylon as his capital, the gods of *Nippur* and *Sippara* consenting thereto. *Marduk* became then chief protector of this dy-

[1] The *Four Regions* of Babylonia, the kingdom of which therefore came into *Hammurabi's* hand at this time. See below p. 117.

[2] *Code of Hammurabi*, Col. I, ll. 1-55.

[3] *Date-List A*, second year of *Hammurabi*.

[4] Meissner, *Altbabylonisches Privatrecht*, No. 49.

nasty, and in fact received the title of *Bêl* or "lord," which belonged originally to *Bêl* of *Nippur*, or in other words, Babylon superseded *Nippur* as capital of the First Dynasty in the first year of *Hammurabi*, 2109 B. C. That Babylon was not the capital of this dynasty from the time that *Sumu-abi* became king is evident from the fact that *Sumu-la-ilu* rebuilt its wall in 2215 B. C., which suggests that he must have conquered the city and razed its wall some time before that. Again we find that *Apil-Sin* rebuilt its wall in 2168 B. C., which presupposes a revolt in and a recapture of this city. It could, therefore, not have been the capital of these kings, at least not while it was in revolt against them.

Kish, north of *Nippur*, had been captured by *Sumu-abi*, but revolted and was recaptured by *Sumu-la-ilu*, and its wall rebuilt in 2201 B. C.

Kazallu, another city north of *Nippur*, had also been captured by *Sumu-abi*, but it rebelled in 2202, 2195, and 2172 B. C.

Borsippa was captured in 2192, and its wall rebuilt in 2169 B. C.

Sippara was captured by *Sumu-la-ilu*, probably shortly before 2191, when its wall was rebuilt. We know that *Immerum* was king of *Sippara* in the time of *Sumu-la-ilu*, and its capture means the overthrow of that king and the end of the old dynasty of *Sippara* or *Agade*. *Anu*, the protecting deity of Northern Babylonia and chief god of *Sippara*, now becomes also the patron god of the Babylonian kings.

After the conquest and fortification of *Borsippa* in 2169 B. C., the conquest was gradually pushed southward along the western bank of the Euphrates. This land was known as *Mar-tu* or *Amurru*, "the westland." Its cities were captured and then the walls were rebuilt: in *Rubatum*, 2151; *Zakardada*, 2145; *Muru*, 2141; and *Marad* 2140 B. C.

In 2138 B. C., *Sin-muballit* extended his conquests on the western bank of the Euphrates to the city of *Ur*, which was then taken, and the year was named: "*The year in which the people of Ur were slain with the sword.*" It has been thought that this battle referred to *Kudur-Mabug's* capture of *Ur*, but this is impossible, for the simple reason that it is unthinkable that the Babylonian king would name a year after the success of his worst enemy. The *Date-Lists* point, without exception, everywhere, to Babylonian achievements and victories. The victory over *Ur* was therefore a victory won by *Sin-muballit*, who had now succeeded in extending his power that far south on the west side of the Euphrates. We know that *Eri-Aku* was king of *Larsa*, and his capture of that city would indeed be important enough to name a year after it, had that been in line with the principle underlying these *Date-Lists*, but this capture of *Larsa* is never referred to. On the other hand, it would be natural that *Eri-Aku*, as king of Southern Babylonia, should name one of his years after that event.

While the power of the First Dynasty had thus extended considerably on the west side of the Euphrates, *Nippur* was still its most southern city east of that river. But three years later, 2135 B. C., *Isin* falls, the great *Dynasty of Isin* is overthrown by *Sin-muballit*, and his conquest is pushed that far south in Middle Babylonia.

An unexpected change then takes place. *Sin-muballit*, who had for twenty years victoriously expanded his

THE CONQUEST OF BABYLONIA

kingdom and by the fall of *Isin* had become king of Babylonia, suddenly meets a heavy reverse at the hands of *Kudur-Mabug*, a prince of *Ê-Mutpal*, and his son *Eri-Aku*. It is probable that the land east of the *Shatt-el-Hai* river had for a long time belonged to *Kudur-Mabug*. Shortly before 2131 B. C., he had succeeded in capturing *Larsa*, over which he placed *Eri-Aku* as king.

In 2131 B. C., *Kudur-Mabug* and his son *Eri-Aku* succeeded in overthrowing all of Babylonia, which was placed under *Eri-Aku*, whose vassal *Sin-muballit* became until his death in 2121 B. C. This historically important fact is recorded in two inscriptions of *Kudur-Mabug*:

"*Kudur-Mabug, lord of Ê-Mutpal, son of Simti-Shilkhak, and Eri-Aku (Ri-im-Sin), his son, the exalted shepherd of Nippur, the rebuilder of Ur, king of Shumir and Akkadî.*"[1]

"*To Nannar, his king, has Kudur-Mabug, lord of Martu, son of Simti-Shilkhak, built Nannar's temple, Ê-nun-Makh, because he has heard his prayers, for his own life, and for the life of his son, Eri-Aku, king of Larsa.*"[2]

The last inscription is evidently the older. Here is *Eri-Aku* king only of *Larsa*, while *Kudur-Mabug* is lord of *Mar-tu*, i. e., the land west of the Euphrates, in which *Ur* was located.

In the first inscription *Eri-Aku* is "Shepherd of *Nippur*," which indicates that he rules the capital of *Sin-muballit* and is king of Middle Babylonia. Several legal documents have been discovered, in which the oath-formula reads: "*By Anu, Bêl, and Eri-Aku*," which goes

---

[1] Kanephore in the Louvre.

[2] IR., 3, No. III. It was a votive-inscription, placed by *Kudur-Mabug* in the temple of the Moon-god in Ur. See cut on next page.

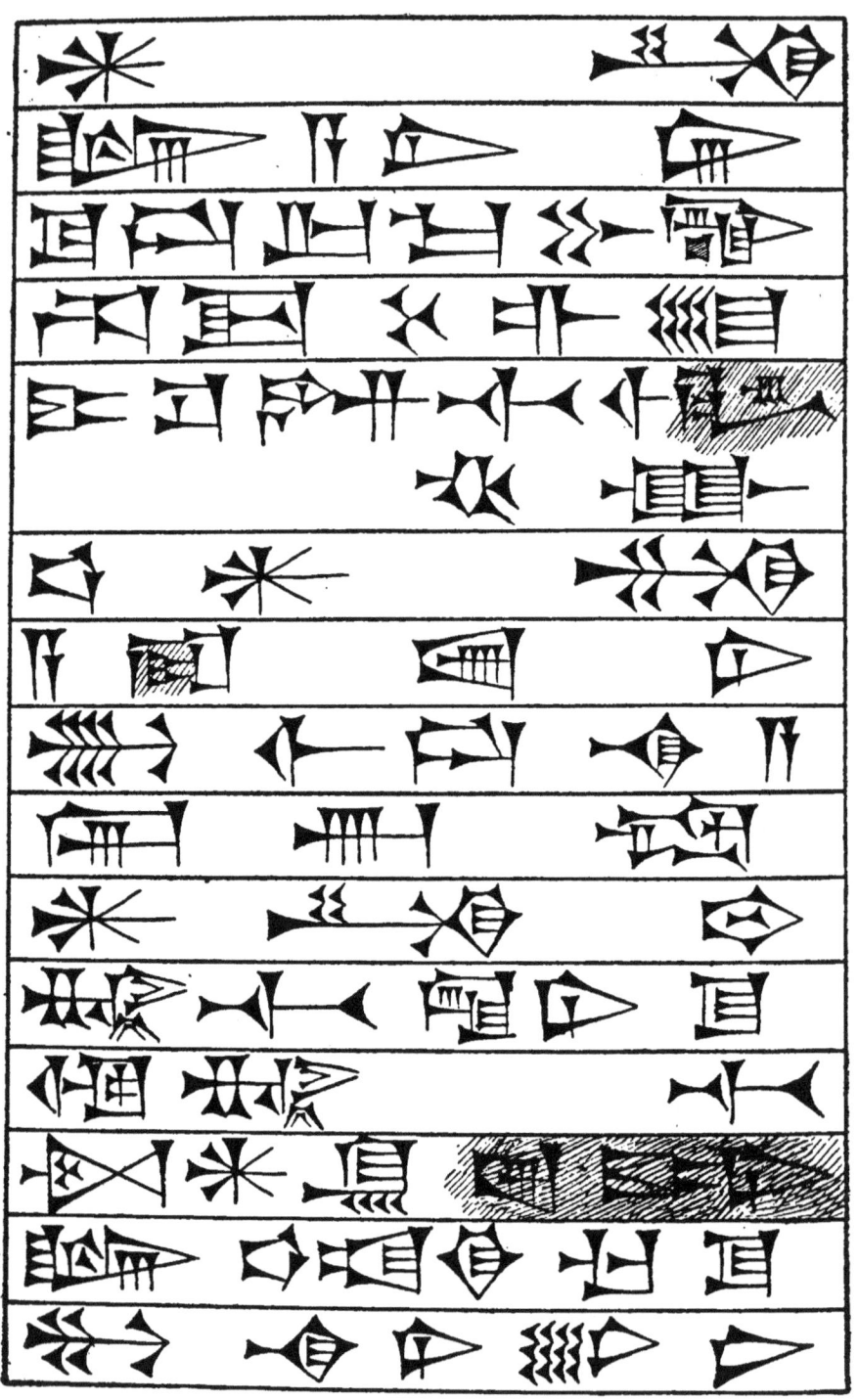

INSCRIPTION OF K*UDUR*-MABUG
(From *IR.*, 3, No. III)

to show that *Eri-Aku* ruled both *Sippara* and *Nippur*, i. e., Northern and Middle Babylonia.

But *Eri-Aku* is also styled "*king of Shumir and Akkad*," a title carried by the kings of *Isin*, and this indicates that *Eri-Aku* possessed the southern cities of Babylonia as well. This means then a conquest of *Isin* by *Eri-Aku*. This capture was so important that *Eri-Aku* named a number of years as "such and such a year after the capture of *Isin*." This dating has commonly been placed in connection with *Sin-muballit's* seventeenth year, when *Isin* also was taken, but that is impossible, for that was a conquest by *Sin-muballit*, and *Eri-Aku* had to reconquer it before he could date his years from its fall. *Isin* was in the hands of *Eri-Aku* until the seventh year of *Hammurabi*, when this latter king reconquered it, i. e., it was in the possession of *Eri-Aku* from 2132/1 to 2103/2 B. C., or twenty-nine years, and this is also the highest year after the capture of *Isin*, which is recorded for *Eri-Aku's* reign.[1]

Sin-muballit died in 2121 B. C., and was succeeded by his son *Hammurabi*, who continued as a vassal under *Eri-Aku* for twelve years, until 2109 B. C. Unfortunately we do not know the exact course of events in that year, but my assumption is that *Hammurabi* led a rebellion against *Eri-Aku*, took Babylon and then Nippur, whereby he became king of Middle Babylonia. *Malga* was captured in 2106, and *Isin* fell into the hands of *Hammurabi* in 2103/2 B. C.

The conquest of *Mar-tu*, the land to the west of the Euphrates, was then taken up; *Bazu* was captured, and its walls rebuilt in 2089 B. C.

[1] The highest date reads, "*thirtieth year of the capture of Isin*," which may comprise 29 years and a few days.

Sippara was captured and its walls rebuilt in 2085 B. C. As this fact is mentioned in the prologue to the *code*, that *code* must have been promulgated subsequent to that year.

Hammurabi finally dealt the deathblow to the army of *Elam* in 2080 B.C., and the following year, 2079 B.C., *Eri-Aku* was overthrown and *Ê-Mutpal* captured. *Hammurabi* was now king of *Babylon*, king of *Kish*, king of the *Four Regions*, and king of *Shumir* and *Akkadî*, i. e., all Babylonia had come under his hand, and his and his successors' subsequent achievements were directed chiefly in strengthening their possessions and developing the resources of the empire.

We have thus seen that the rulers of the First Dynasty did not become kings of *Isin* before 2135 B. C., and it was not until this time, that they had a legal right to be called "kings."

Original Home of the Babylonians

The people that conquered Babylonia and established *Dynasty A of Babylon* was Semitic, but belonged neither to the same group of Semites who founded the Dynasties of *Agade* or *Kish*, nor to the neo-Babylonians or Assyrians. Their language, which we shall designate as Old Babylonian, differed in many respects from the other Babylonian and the Assyrian dialects. This people pronounced *Shamshu* as *Samsu*, *Shumu* as *Sumu*, etc., and their vocabulary differed considerably from that of the other Babylonians. Their manner of forming proper names shows marked deviations from the usual Babylonian nomenclature, and several new forms and usages are discernible.

These phenomena are so numerous and so plain that

scholars, ever since the civilization of this dynasty became known, have considered it to be of a hetereogeneous descent, for they have been quite unable to explain how this civilization could arise from Babylonian soil. The people of *Dynasty A of Babylon* has therefore been regarded as a race foreign to Babylonia, a race which invaded that land some time before 2233 B. C., conquered a part of it, and established their government and their line of rulers over it. The main problem before scholars, therefore, is to ascertain the original home of this race.

It was at first assumed that this dynasty was of *Kassite* descent. The only plausible support for this theory was the reading of the name *Hammurabi* as *Khammuragas*. This is a possible reading, but no additional relationship between the two races could be found to support the theory, and when it was discovered that the name must be read *Khammurabi* the hypothesis was given up.

Pognon, followed by *H*ommel and a host of other scholars, then proposed to assign this dynasty to an Arabic origin. They based their theory on the fact that a number of proper names in the Old Babylonian show an unmistakable affinity with Old Arabic dialects, and especially with the language of *Ma'in*, the so-called Minean dialect; e. g., the Babylonian *Shamshu* is pronounced *Samsu*, both in Old Babylonian and in Minean. In the name *Samsu-ilu-na*, "the sun-god is our god," the ending *-na*, "our," is Arabic, corresponding to *H*ebrew *-nu* and Assyro-Babylonian *-ni*. In *Ammi-zadugga*, "god Ammi is righteous," the root "*zadugga*" is not found in the Assyro-Babylonian dialects, but is common in the South Semitic languages—Arabic, Ethiopic, and Sabaean—as well as in the *H*ebrew, Canaanitic, and Aramaic dialects. In a number of Old Babylonian proper names like *Yadakhu-Nabû, Yabnik-ilu, Yakhzar-ilu, Yakub-ilu*, etc., the first part is a verbal form in the imperfect third person singular. The preformative sign *ya*, "he," is not Assyro-Babylonian, which uses *i-*, Hebrew *yi-*, but corresponds with the Arabic *ya-*. In view of these, and a number of similar phenomena, it was concluded that the people of the *Hammurabi Dynasty* had come from Arabia. This supposition developed finally the curious theory that a number of great migrations, each at an interval of 1,000 years, had emerged from Arabia,[1] the second of which was the great Amoritic migration, and that the *Hammurabi Dynasty* resulted from this. The chief difficulty with this theory is that it cannot be shown that an Arabic people lived in Arabia at this time. On the contrary, evidence points to the conclusion that the first Arabic settlements began in Arabia at a much later date. On the other hand, the proper names of this dynasty show a number of affinities with West-Semitic—Canaanitic, and Hebrew—forms, and this led scholars to modify their views to the extent of regarding the *Hammurabi Dynasty* as of Canaanitic origin. This term has lately been changed to West-Semitic, and a double theory is proposed, one assuming that the *Hammurabi Dynasty* came from Canaan, the other suggesting that the Old Babylonians and the Canaanites came from the same, at present unknown, locality.

Ranke,[2] however, has led the inquiry in a new direction by his interesting comparison of a number of Old Babylonian names with the so-called Cappadocian names. To this he added last year his own view in regard to the

[1] Paton, *Early History of Syria*, pp. 3 ff.
[2] *BE*, Series D, Vol. III, pp. 39 f.

original home of these Babylonians.[1] He remarks that in the time of *Zabum* these new settlers in Babylonia were called *Mârê-Amurrum*, "sons of the West-land," or better, "Amorites," and that such West-Semitic names are more numerous during the first part of the *Hammurabi Dynasty* than later. He therefore regards these Babylonians as nomads who had come from the Arabian and Syrian plateaus and settled in Babylonia, where, after a long interval, they succeeded in establishing one of their descendants as king of Babylon.

This view seems to me well taken, but instead of postulating a gradual settlement of shepherds from the Arabian and Syrian deserts, extending over a long period, it occurs to me that this settlement was the result of a well-organized migration from northern Syria and Mesopotamia. To regard this district as the original home of this people would be to explain the many peculiarities found in the proper names of the *Hammurabi Dynasty*, and it is perhaps possible to assign a plausible cause of this invasion.

The divine name *Sumu*, found, e. g., in *Sumu-abi* and in *Sumu-la-ilu*, was that of the chief god of the city of *H*amath in northern Syria, where he was worshiped under the name of *Ashima*,[2] compounded from the Samaritan definite article *a-* and *shima*, "name." He undoubtedly represents *Shem*, the deified ancestor of the Semitic race. His worship is not found to have occurred outside of northern Syria and the *Hammurabi Dynasty*, and the occurrence of this divine name in their proper names suggests strongly that these early Babylonians originally came from northern Syria.

[1] *BE.*, Series A, Vol. VI, pp. 16 ff.
[2] II Kings 17:30.

The names of two kings of this dynasty, *Apil-Sin* and *Sin-muballit*, are compounded with *Sin*, the name of the Moon-god. This god was worshiped in Ur of Chaldea and in Haran of Mesopotamia. But as Ur belonged at this time to the kings of Isin, the Babylonians could not worship him in his own temple, and it seems improbable that kings would be named after a god with whom they had no relation. It must therefore have been *Sin* of Haran after whom these kings were named, and as they were devout worshipers of this *Sin*, erecting temples and shrines to him in several north-Babylonian cities almost as soon as these cities were captured, I assume that this people must have come from a region where *Sin* of Haran was worshiped, i. e., from northwestern Mesopotamia. In this region, northern Syria and northwestern Mesopotamia, the matriarchal institution persisted down to the time of *Eleazar* and *Jacob*, but the worship of *Ammi*, "the (divine) uncle," and *Akhi*, "the (divine) brother" is a characteristic of the matriarchate. Now *Ammi*, *Akhi*, and *Abi*, "the (divine) father," appear very frequently in the composition of proper names of the *Hammurabi Dynasty*.

This region around the upper Euphrates, between the Mediterranean and the river Balikh, which I assume to have been the original home of the people of the *Hammurabi Dynasty*, is the identical district occupied by the Mitani people.

This Mitani conquest must in all probability be assigned to the twenty-third century B. C. It stands in connection with three other migrations. About 2500–2400 B. C. the *Elamites*, belonging to the Anzan-Susun(ka) race, conquered Elam and established the dynasty to which -*Kudur*

ORIGINAL HOME OF THE BABYLONIANS   105

Nankhundi (2280 B. C.) and *Chedor-laomer* belonged. Coming from the east, probably from the regions of the Caspian Sea, this people occupied Elam and drove out the old inhabitants of western Elam. This gave rise to the *Armenian* migration from Elam, Anzan, and Ê-Mutpal along the Tigris into the region of Kurdistan, and especially the tract of land lying between the lakes of Urmia and Van, where they established the kingdoms of Muzazir, Man, and Van. This last kingdom superseded the old kingdom of Ararat or Urartu, with its capital Turushpâ or Tushpâ, on the southeastern shore of lake Thospitis (or Van). This occupation displaced the old inhabitants of Urartu, who moved westward and settled the regions of Kurkhi and Shubari (later Shubria). This people is known by its worship of god *Teshup* and his daughter *Sha-Ush-kas*, and through these divine names we are enabled to trace the migrations and expansion of this race. The old city Tushpâ or Turushpâ, on the cliffs overhanging Lake Van, was named after this god *Teshup*, as was also Lake Thosp(itis) or Thosp(is). The city of Pituru in Kirkhu seems to have been their capital.

From this land the Teshup-people pushed southward and westward. In their southward advance they conquered mount Masius. This highland is undoubtedly identical with the inscriptional *Ki-Mash*, "highland of Mash," and also with the biblical *Mash*[1] or *Mesha*.[2] But this mountain was the old home of the *Joqtanide* Arabs, who are said to have dwelt "*from Mesha as thou goest unto Sephar, a mountain of Qedem.*" Qedem, or the *H*auran region, was still in the time of *Ashurbanipal* the abode of

[1] Gen. 10:23.
[2] Gen. 10:30. Mesha is the Aramaic emphatic form of *Mash*.

Arabic tribes, and the land east of the river *H*abor was known as Arbaja, or the Arabic land. This identification explains the frequent recurrence of Arabic verbs, pronouns and nouns in proper names of the *Hammurabi Dynasty*. As the two peoples had lived almost as neighbors, we should naturally expect to find a mutual interchange of ideas and language.

Between the rivers Balikh and *H*abor was the land of Êbir-nâri,[1] "the land across the river (Habor)," the biblical Eber-hannahar,[2] which was the original abode of the *H*ebrew race, and relationship between *H*ebrew and Old Babylonian is thus natural and to be expected.

When the Teshup-people moved southward, occupying mount Masius, the Arabs of that land were pushed farther south, and, retreating along the river *H*abor and crossing the Euphrates, they settled in Qedem, "the east-land," and in the *H*auran mountains.

Simultaneously with this movement southward, the Teshup-people seems also to have expanded westward, and crossing the upper Tigris they settled around the upper Euphrates, where they established in Comagene the kingdom of Khani-rabbat, also known by the name of Mitani. Here the Teshup-people came upon the people of the *Hammurabi Dynasty* and drove them from their old abode.

Following the Euphrates, or perhaps after a futile attempt to locate in the region around the city of Ashur,[3] along the Tigris, this latter people entered Babylonia and began its conquest.

The location of their original home in northwestern Mesopotamia and northern Syria, south of Cappadocia,

---

[1] *ABL.*, no. 706, rv. 3. [2] Josh. 24:2, 14, 15. [3] See below, p. 148.

PLATE III

Reverse

CHRONOLOGICAL TABLET OF THE DYNASTIES
OF UR AND ISIN

(From *BE*, Ser. A, Vol XX, Pl XV.)

explains, finally, the occurrence of Cappadocian and Mitanic names in the *Hammurabi Dynasty*.

Dynasty of Isin[1]

When *Sin-muballit* conquered the city of *Isin* in his sixteenth year, 2135 B. C., a great dynasty was overthrown. We know of this dynasty from a number of monuments, and have perceived that it must have consisted of a mighty line of kings who ruled a large kingdom. The succession of its kings, and its relation to that of *Ur*, have, however, not been exactly clear up to the present. Last winter Hilprecht published[2] a very important tablet, giving a list of the kings of *Isin* and *Ur* and also the length of their reigns. We are from this enabled to trace Babylonian chronology correctly 342 years back of *Sin-muballit's* capture of *Isin* in 2135 B. C.

Dynasty of Isin

Name of King		Length of Reign	Date
1. *Ishbi-Ura*		32 years,	2360–2328 B. C.
2. *Gimil-Ilishu*,	{ son of preceding }	10 years,	2328–2318 B. C.
3. *Idin-Dagan*,	"	21 years,	2318–2297 B. C.
4. *Ishme-Dagan*,	"	20 years,	2297–2277 B. C.
5. *Libit-Ishtar*,		11 years,	2277–2266 B. C.
6. *Ur-Ninib*		28 years,	2266–2238 B. C.
7. *Bur-Sin (II)*,	"	21 years,	2238–2217 B. C.
8. *Itêr-KA-sha*,	{ brother of preceding }	5 years,	2217–2212 B. C.

[1] After I had written this chapter, Hilprecht's volume, containing the remarkable tablet given below, appeared. I then embodied this inscription, omitting my discussion of this period, in which I endeavored to weigh the evidence as carefully as possible. I had reached the conclusion that we could not date *Ur-Gur* (or *Ur-Engur*) earlier than 2475 B. C. It was therefore a pleasure to me to find that I was only two years away from the exact date. My discussion of the Sargonic period, which was based on the conclusion I had reached in regard to the date of *Ur-Engur*, remains unchanged.

[2] *BE.*, Vol. XX, text 46, and discussion of it, pp. 39–56b.

9. ? - - - -.	7 years,	2212–2205 B.
10. Sin (?) - - - - - - - - 6 months		2205–2204 B.
11. Bêl-bâni	24 years,	2204–2180 B.
12. Za-me(?) - -e (?)	3 years,	2180–2177 B.
13. ? - - - - -	5 years,	2177–2172 B.
14. Ea - - -	4 years,	2172–2168 B.
15. Sin-mâgir	11 years,	2168–2157 B.
16. Dâmiq-ilishu	23 years,	2157–2135 B.
16 kings	225 years, 6 months	2360–2135 B. C.

Dynasty of Ur

Name of King	Length of Reign	Date
1. Ur-Engur	18 years,	2477–2459 B. C.
2. Dungi, son of preceding	58 years,	2459–2401 B. C.
3. Bur-Sin (I) "	9 years,	2401–2392 B. C.
4. Gimil-Sin "	7 years,	2392–2385 B. C.
5. Ibi-Sin	25 years,	2385–2360 B. C.
5 kings	117 years,	2477–2360 B. C.

Dynasty of Agade

The *Dynasty of Ur* succeeded that of *Agade*. Three kings of this latter dynasty, *Shargani-sharali* (Sargon), *Narâm-Sin*, and *Bingani-sharali*, are known. *Narâm-Sin* is referred to by *Nabonidus*, in a building inscription at *Sippara*, as follows:

"*The foundation-stone of Narâm-Sin, which no king before me had found for 3,200 years, Shamash, the great lord of Ebarra, showed to me.*"

This carries the date of *Narâm-Sin* back to about 3750 B. C. *Narâm-Sin* was the son of the great *Sargon I*, king of *Agade*. This *Sargon* is well known from a number of his inscriptions, from his *Omen-tablets*, and also from the legend about his birth. He became king of *Agade*, then of Babylonia, and finally of *Martu*.

The date mentioned above has been the source of a good deal of speculation. Niebuhr[1] even doubted the existence of this *Sargon*, and when the excavations at

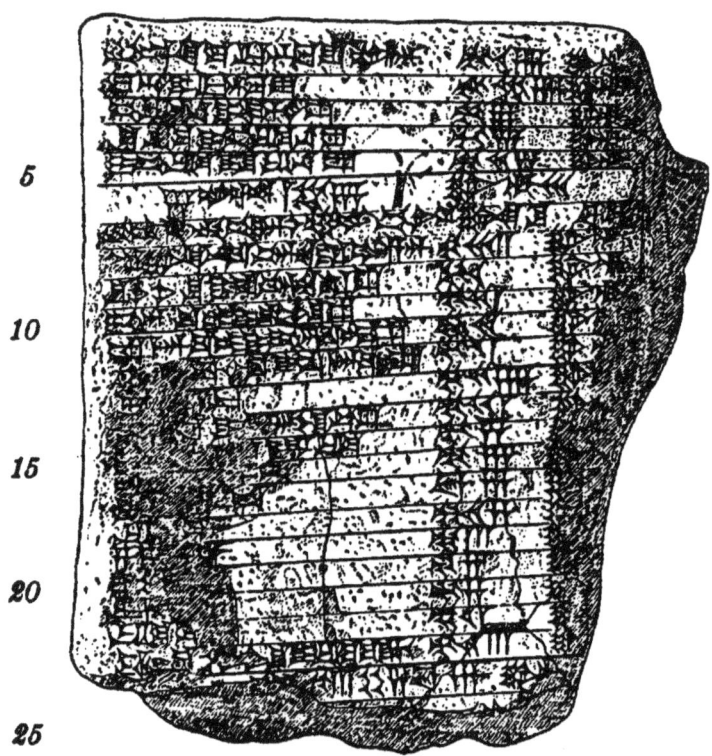

CHRONOLOGICAL TABLET OF THE DYNASTIES OF
UR AND ISIN
(From *BE.*, Ser. A, Vol. XX, Pl. 30.)

Nippur brought to light a number of bricks, stamped with the name of *Sargon* and *Narâm-Sin*, indeed even when the stamp was found, with which these bricks were impressed, scholars like Niebuhr[2] regarded both the brick-inscriptions and stamp as falsifications by the priests

[1] *Chronologie*, p. 75. [2] *Ibid.*

of *Bêl*. Later discoveries have revealed the fact that legal documents were dated in certain years of the reign of

BUILDING INSCRIPTION OF NABONIDUS, MENTIONING
NARÂM-SIN AND SARGON
(From *VR.*, 62, *b*, ll. 46–65.)

Sargon and *Narâm-Sin*, and no one today doubts the existence of these kings.

PLATE IV

Obverse

CHRONOLOGICAL TABLET OF OLD BABY-
LONIAN KINGS

(From *BE*, Ser. A, Vol. XX, Pl. XV)

The date, however, is still an unsettled question. Several scholars take it at its face value. Lehmann,[1] on the contrary, doubts its accuracy. He argues that we should read 2200 for 3200, and many scholars have lately accepted his theory. Now it is true that archaeology supports his emendation, so far as available data are concerned.

The form of cuneiform signs, used in the inscriptions of *Sargon* and *Narâm-Sin*, belongs unquestionably to a later date than that of the early *Telloh* inscriptions, and are much nearer to that of the *Hammurabi* period. To this should be added, that in the temple-platform at *Nippur* bricks stamped with the name of *Dungi* appear immediately above those stamped with the names of *Sargon* and *Narâm-Sin*. The conclusion is inevitable that *Sargon* must have lived shortly before *Dungi*, because in the later strata of *Bêl's* temple at *Nippur*, there is a large space of debris between *Dungi* and *Kuri-Galzu*. Now, there were about 1100 years between *Kuri-Galzu* and *Dungi*, but if *Sargon* lived about 3800 B. C., there would be about 1400 years between him and *Dungi*, and it would be expected that there would be at least as large a space of debris between the temple-platforms of *Sargon* and *Dungi*, as between those of *Dungi* and *Kuri-Galzu*. Still there is no space whatever between the two first-named platforms. The latter king built his platform immediately upon that of *Sargon* and *Narâm-Sin*. It seems, therefore, impossible to reconcile the archaeological data with the date, 3200, of *Nabonidus*. Still it seems as if Lehmann's solution—the subtraction of 1,000 years—involving, as it does, an error of the scribe, is highly improbable. It has therefore occurred to me that the date might be based on astro-

[1] *Zwei Hauptprobleme*, pp. 172 ff.

nomical calculations, rather than on actual chronological data, and that thus a solution may be found by which the date of *Nabonidus* can be brought into harmony with the data of archaeology.

I mentioned above (p. 2) that there was a calendar reform in the time of *Nabonassar*, about 747 B. C. That calendar reform was called forth by the fact that at that time the sun came to rise in the sign of *Aries* at the vernal equinox, and an "*Aries-era*" was then begun. Before that time the sun rose in the sign of *Taurus* at the vernal equinox. That time we may designate as the "*Taurus-era*," within which the *Hammurabi* period falls. But Winckler[1] has shown that several myths and religious customs of the old Sumerian period were based on the fact, that in that period the sun rose at the vernal equinox in the sign of *Gemini*, and that therefore that period belongs to the "*Gemini-era.*"

The *Omen-tablets* of *Sargon*, with their numerous astronomical data, indicate that a new era, the "*Taurus-era*," began with *Sargon* and lasted down to *Nabonassar*. From *Nabonassar* to *Nabonidus* there was an even period of 200 years, and the interval between *Sargon* (or *Naràm-Sin*) and *Nabonidus* was therefore an era + 200 years.

In the time of *Nabonidus* such an era may have been counted as an even 3,000 years,[2] and an "era" + 200 years would therefore be 3,000 + 200 years in the time of *Nabonidus*, and would account for *Nabonidus'* "3,200 years."

But Berossos also tells us that *Nabonassar* in his cal-

[1] *KAT*3., p. 332.

[2] The Hindus had such eras of 1,000 years, called *Avatarae*, or periods comprising a third of a Sign of the Zodiac.

endar reform had destroyed all previous records. This may mean that they reckoned its past history by "eras", and that each era was made to be an even 3,000 years.

Such an era, indicated by the earth entering from one zodiacal sign into another at the vernal equinox, does not take 3,000 years, but only about 2,146 years. The Babylonians were acute astronomical observers, and could not fail to observe when the earth passed into a new zodiacal sign. If this happened some time before *Sargon*, he would be expected to readjust their calendar and astronomical calculations according to this new order, and his *Omen-tablets* were a result thereof.

So far as we know, the calendar reform necessitated by this new era was not introduced until the time of *Sargon*, and it was therefore regarded as a "*Sargon-era.*" *Nabonidus*' 3,200 years would then be explained as "*the Sargon-era*" + 200 years. Now it is possible that *Nabonidus* made this inscription in the year 547 B. C., and there would then be exactly 200 years from *Nabonassar* to his own date. The time before *Nabonassar* he regarded as a whole era (designated by him as "3,000 years").

These "3,000 years," or even 2,146 years, do not help us therefore to assign the date of *Sargon*. It is contrary to all archaeological evidence to assign his date to 3800 B. C. Even 2900 B. C., or 2750 B. C., as Lehmann has suggested, is too early. There were only three kings of this dynasty, *Sargon*, *Narâm-Sin*, and *Bingani*, and all that we can reasonably assign to them is seventy years. The dates of the succeeding dynasties cannot be brought higher up than about 2477 B. C. The *Dynasty of Agade* can therefore not be assigned to a higher date than 2550–2477 B. C.

That this calculation is approximately correct can be

shown. *Telloh* became a dependency under *Sargon*. The *patesi* of *Telloh*, in the time of *Sargon*, was *Lugal-ushum-gal*. Now we know his successors in the *patesi*-office of *Telloh*, namely *Ur-Ê*, *Ur-Bau*, *Nammakhni*, *Gudea*, and *Ur-nin-Girsu*. The last named was a vassal of *Dungi*, of the *Dynasty of Ur*. This gives us about one hundred and fifty years from the accession of *Sargon* to the death of *Dungi*, or about twenty-five years to each *patesi* of *Telloh*. To assign the date of 3800 B. C., as Radau and his followers have done, is to assume that each of these *pateses* of *Telloh* ruled about two hundred and fifty years. Even Lehmann's, Thureau-Dangin's, and Eduard Meyer's date, 2750 B. C., is too high, because it means that each *patesi* of *Telloh* in this period ruled about sixty years. The date of *Sargon* (*I*) can hardly be earlier than 2550 B. C., but may be a few years later.

The shifting of the "spheres of influence" in Babylonia in this comparatively short period of four hundred and fifty years, from *Agade* to *Ur*, then to *Isin*, and finally to *Babylon*, presents not only some interesting historical data but calls for some explanation of what I am tempted to call "sudden" changes. It is evident that there must have been some undercurrents that are not now visible, but which contributed to transform and shape the events of those days. Whether those undercurrents consisted in great migrations of nations or not may perhaps not be possible to decide. There are, however, some traces of great events that have become known to us, and although we are not able now to determine with certainty on these phenomena, we may be able to offer some suggestions that will help us to appreciate the history of that time.

The legend about *Sargon* has undoubtedly a historical

kernel. He is said to have come down on the Euphrates, floating in a reed chest, and having been saved by a water-carrier of *Agade*, to have been reared there and become finally king of that place. May not this indicate a Semitic migration from the north, along the Euphrates, down to *Agade*? Now the Bible mentions a certain *Serug*,[1] a descendant of *Shem*. If I am right, the names of these patriarchs may stand for ancient Semitic dynasties. Several scholars think that *Serug* represents *Sargon of Agade*, and in my opinion, it stands for the *Sargon Dynasty of Agade*. We know that both *Sargon* and his son *Narâm-Sin* were regarded as gods, and the "god-" determinative was appended to their names. *Sargon*, Bab. *Shargani*, may have arisen from *Serug-an, an* being the god-determinative which the biblical author omitted.

There was an ancient locality in Northern Mesopotamia between the Euphrates and the Balikh rivers, that was called *Sarug*, and it is possible that the *Sargon Dynasty* and the Semites of *Agade* came from this place.

Sargon conquered, not only *Agade*, but a large part of Babylonia, *Martu*,[2] the kingdom of *Gutium* in *Kurdistan*, and also made war expeditions into *Elam*. While *Sargon* (*I*) only mentions as his title the first one that he

[1] Gen. 11:20–23.

[2] *Sargon's* conquest of M$artu^{ki}$ has generally been regarded as a conquest of Syria and Palestine. This is now disproved by the new *Chronicle K1*. In this document M$artu^{ki}$ is referred to as a land bordering on "the Sea of the East," or the Persian Gulf. *Sargon* is here said to have crossed this sea when he began his campaign against the "West-land," and his spoil was brought from the "West-land" over the Persian Gulf to his dominion in the Sea-Land and Babylonia. This fact is entirely unexplainable if the "West-land" be Syria and Palestine, but becomes quite clear, if the "West-land" be the region on the western bank of the lower Euphrates. *Sargon* never came further north or west than northern Mesopotamia (*Subartu*) and did not enter Syria or Palestine. The conquest of that land was carried out by his son, *Narâm-Sin*.

acquired when he became king of *Agade*, namely *Sharali*, "city-king," his son *Narâm-Sin* assumed the proud title "*king of the Four Regions.*" What this title precisely means is still a debated question. Several scholars have assumed that it denotes the four world-regions, including Syria in the west and the highlands of Media to the east. I am not prepared to accept this explanation.

When the *Dynasty of Ur* came to power, *Ur-Engur* is at first only "*king of Ur.*" Later on he assumes the title, "*King of Shumir and Akkad.*" The meaning of this title is also an unsettled question. *Dungi*, the successor of *Ur-Engur*, begins his reign with only the title "*King of Shumir and Akkad,*" but after a time he assumes another, "*king of the Four Regions.*" This title is carried by all his successors of the *Dynasty of Ur*.

When the *Dynasty of Isin* comes to power, its kings are not entitled "*kings of the Four Regions,*" but only "*kings of Shumir and Akkadî.*"

Ur-Ninib founded a new line of rulers in *Isin*, succeeded by *Bur-Sin II* and his brother. But it is in the reign of *Bur-Sin II*, 2238–2217 B. C., that the *Hammurabi Dynasty* is established, 2233 B. C. We have seen above that this dynasty possessed nothing of Babylonia, south of *Nippur*, until the latter part of the reign of *Sin-muballit*. But it occupied *Nippur*, which was the capital of *Ki-en-gi*.

As *Sin-mâgir* and *Dâmiq-ilishu* are both known as "*kings of Shumir and Akkad,*" it is evident that the kings of *Isin* could be called "*kings of Shumir and Akkad,*" without possessing *Nippur*, the old capital of *Ki-en-gi*.

Kingdom of Shumir and Akkad

Many scholars, and notably Winckler, have argued that the kingdom of *Shumir and Akkad* was located somewhere in southern Babylonia, although a definite region has not yet been proposed. The references to it generally indicate a location to the south. There was a city on the *Shatt el-Hai* river, known in the inscriptions as *Gir-Su*^{ki}. It is possible that this name was read *Su-Gir*^{i}, and if so, it can be identified with *Shumir*, for *g* in *Sugir* may have been a nasal-palatal, and the name was then pronounced *Sumgir* or *Sungir*, from which we get the Babylonian *Sumir* (later, *Shumir*) and Hebrew *Shinᶜar*. *Shumir* was the name that superseded *Ki-en-gi*, the old name of Middle Babylonia, and this change took place when the seat of government of that land was removed from *Nippur* to *Gir-Su*^{ki}.

A sister city of *Gir-Su*^{ki} was $^{an}Ninâ^{ki}$. We do not know the correct reading of this name, but it was dedicated to a goddess, whose name was written with the same sign as the one denoting Nineveh. Nor do we know the Sumerian name of Ishtar of Nineveh. We are aware, however, that she was known in *Mitani* as $^{an}\tilde{S}a$-$uš$-kas. Although I am not able to prove it definitely, it is possible that she is identical with the goddess *Akkadi*, and if that be the case, then we may have, in this city of $^{an}Ninâ^{ki}$, the origin of the name of *Akkadî*^{ki}, which would then denote the "*Land of the goddess Akkadî*." The title *Shumir and Akkad* would then denote "Middle and Southern Babylonia," the land on both sides of the *Shatt el-Hai* river, between the rivers Euphrates and Tigris.[1]

Kingdom of the Four Regions

We must also inquire what the title "*king of the Four Regions*" means. It is almost certain that it must origi-

[1] The goddess *Akkadi* may originally have been associated with Ishtar of Erech, and the land of *Akkadû* would then have been located near the city of

nally have denoted the four cardinal points, and, as the name goes very far back, it must have applied to Babylonian localities. The view-point must have been a centrally located important city of Babylonia, and as such there is only one choice, the ancient city of *Nippur.* The *"Four Regions"* would then represent four localities east, south, west, and north of *Nippur.* Of such places there is of course a large number from which to choose. But as a suggestion I would call attention to the biblical statement that *"the beginning of Nimrod's kingdom was Babel, and* Erech *and* Akkad *and* Calneh *in the land of* Shinar.[1] Nippur was the old capital of *Ki-en-gi* or *Shinar.* Babel was to the north-west. Erech was an ancient city and the most important one in the southwestern part of *Ki-en-gi.* Akkad was an important city in the south-east. With *Kalneh* I would compare the ancient city of Mount (*Kharsag-*) *Kalama.* A change of *m* to *n* is not unusual (compare Shu*m*ir and Shi*n*ar). The city, "the mount of the world," lay to the east of *Nippur.* The "east wind" was regarded as the wind from the mountain, and this "mountain" may once have been the great mountain of *Kharsag-kalama,* close by *Dûr-ili.*

The title *"king of the Four Regions"* would then carry with it suzerainty over Middle Babylonia. That *Dungi* of *Ur* and his successors ruled over this region is certain.[*] So did also *Narâm-Sin.* The First Dynasty, of

Erech. At any rate, it is certain, that *Nabû-ushabshi* of Erech (*K.* 528; Harper *ABL.,* No. 269, rev. 9) calls his land the land of *Akkadû* Similarly we find in the Rassam-cylinders, that what *Ashurbanipal* once calls the land of the city Erech, he calls at another time the land of *Akkadû.* This land, therefore, cannot be identical with *Agade* in Northern Babylonia, but the latter may have been a settlement from it. See further, on these names, my treatise, *Researches in Assyrian Geography.*

[1] Gen. 10:10.

Babylon, however, did not come into possession of all of this region until the time of *Sin-muballit*, and this is the reason why the first rulers of this dynasty up to that time were not styled *"kings of the Four Regions."* This king conquered both *Isin* and *Ur*, and was accordingly entitled to be known as *"king of Shumir and Akkad,"* as well as *"king of the Four Regions."* It was only for a few years, however, that he was permitted to enjoy this honor, and the first king that assumed these proud titles was *Hammurabi*.

The above investigations give, then, the following results:

The Dynasty of *Agade*	arose ca. 2550 B. C.
The Dynasty of *Ur*	arose in 2477 B. C.
The Dynasty of *Isin*	arose in 2360 B. C.
The Dynasty of *Babylon*	arose in 2233 B. C.
The Dynasty of the *Sea-Land*	arose in 2079 B. C.

This table of dynasties gives the outline of the shifting of power from one city to another. This transference of the supremacy from city to city does not necessarily indicate that dynastic rule altogether ceased in the subdued city. On the contrary, it is not only possible, but it can be shown that kings—probably vassals—continued to rule in those cities after their supremacy had passed away.

In the time of *Sumu-la-ilu* we thus find a certain *Immerum* king in Babylonia. The evidence seems to indicate that he was king of Northern Babylonia, and probably resided in *Sippara*. *Buntakhtun-ila* is another king of this period, and presumably also king of *Sippara*. These kings must then be regarded as members of a dynasty succeeding that of *Sargon of Agade*.

Over *Ur* we likewise find a king, *Gungunu*, in the time of *Ishme-Dagan*, suzerain of Babylonia, of the *Dynasty of Isin*. This must indicate that after the fall of the *Dynasty of Ur*, vassal kings continued to rule that city.

Kings of Larsa

Larsa never attained to the dignity of being the capital of Babylonia. Yet the monuments acquaint us with a number of its kings, but as their succession is not certain, I shall only mention their names:

Nûr-Adad
Sin-iddinam, his son
- - - - -
Eri-Aku (or, *Rim-Sin*).

Dynasty of Erech

Erech preceded *Agade* as the capital of Babylonia. Its kings belonged to a powerful dynasty that ruled, not only Babylonia, but all Western Asia as well. Only three of its kings are known.

Lugal-zaggisi seems to be the founder of this dynasty. He calls himself "*king of Erech*," "*king of Kalama (Calneh)*," which seems to imply that he ruled only over that city. His successors were *Lugal-kigubnidudu* and *Lugal-kisalsi*, who bear the title "*kings of Erech, kings of Ur*," indicating that they had extended their power over the city of *Ur* also. Their inscriptions are written in the Sumerian language, but several Semitisms occur in them, and it seems, therefore, safe to conclude that this dynasty was of Semitic origin.

The rise of this *Dynasty of Erech* can hardly be placed earlier than 125 years before the *Dynasty of Agade*, i. e., about 2675 B. C. As its first king, *Lugal-zaggisi*, calls himself "*king of Erech, king of Kalama,*" and as *Kalama* is probably identical with *Kharsag-Kalama*, the biblical *Calneh*, we may perhaps see an indication that this dynasty came into Babylonia from the east, i. e., from the Aramaean countries east of the Tigris, to which *Kharsag-Kalama* belonged.

After the fall of the *Dynasty of Agade*, before the *Dynasty of Ur* had subdued Babylonia, we meet with two kings, *Sin-gâshid* and *Sin-gâmil*, who style themselves "*kings of Erech.*" It seems probable that when the *Dynasty of Agade* fell, the larger cities of Babylonia asserted their independence, and that these kings ruled *Erech*, not only in the time of *Ur-Engur*, but until *Dungi* was able to subdue *Erech*. It is almost certain that *Sin-gâshid* was a contemporary of *Dungi*, probably in the first part of his reign. *Sin-gâmil* also seems to have been an independent king. It is probable that he was a predecessor of *Nabshemea*.

From this time on we hear nothing of the kings of *Erech*. But in the *Hammurabi* period there is a nobleman of *Erech*, called *Nabshemea*, whose son *Ilu-ma-ilu* is called king. This *Ilu-ma-ilu* can hardly be any other than the king of the same name, who founded *Dynasty B of the Sea-Land*.

Gishkhu

At this time there existed a land east of the Tigris, called *Gishkhu* or *Gish-ban (Gish-ukh)*, whose rulers were *pateses* either under the kings of *Kish* or those of *Telloh*. The first known of them was *Ush*. Another was *Gunam-mide*, contemporary of *Ê-an-na-dum* of *Telloh*. *En-à-kal-li* and his son *Ur-lum-ma* were *pateses* under *Kish*, and also kings of *TE*. *Ili* is also a *patesi* from this time.

U-kush, another *patesi* of this land, is better known through his son *Lugal-zag-gi-si*, the founder of the Dynasty of Erech. *Ê-zu-ab* is entitled king, and belongs to the period immediately preceding that of *Sargon* of *Agade*. From the time of *Dungi* and *Bur-Sin I*, two *pateses* of *Gishkhu*, *Ur-ne-sù* and *Galu-utu* are known.

Subsequent to this time this land is not mentioned, and the probability is that it became incorporated into the land of *Anzan* or Elam.

Dynasty of Telloh

Prior to the *Dynasty of Gishkhu* is that of *Telloh*. Through the excavations at that city, a long line of rulers—kings and *pateses*—is known to us. Among the first of these seems to have been a king, *Uru-ka-gi-na*. One of his successors, *En-khe-gal*, was also king.

Uru-ka-gi-na may have become king about 2950 B. C., but hardly earlier. His dynasty was evidently overthrown by the kings of *Gishkhu*, for the next rulers of *Telloh*, *Lugal-shug-gur* and *Gur-sar*, were only *pateses*, and so was *Gu-ni-du*, son of *Gur-sar*.

But *Ur-Nina*, a son of *Gu-ni-du*, becomes king, showing that he had been able to throw off the yoke of *Gishkhu*. His successors, *A-kur-gal* and *E-an-na-dum*, are styled both kings and *pateses*, indicating the changing fortunes in the wars between these rulers and those of *Gishkhu*.

From the time of *En-an-na-dum I*, brother of *Ê-an-na-dum*, all the rulers of *Telloh* are only *pateses*. A number of these are known, in direct succession from *En-an-na-dum I*: *En-teme-na*, *En-an-na-dum II*, and *Lum-ma-dur*. Here the succession is broken off, but some time after we find a certain *Lugal-an-da* as *patesi* of *Telloh*.

Here again is a gap in the succession, until we reach the time of *Sargon* and *Narâm-Sin* of *Agade*, when *Lugal-ushum-gal* and *Ur-Ê* were successive *pateses* of *Telloh*.

The next known rulers of *Telloh* were *Ur-Ba'u* and his nephew, *Nam-makh-ni*. Then comes the great *Gudea*, and his son *Ur-nin-Gir-su*, who was *patesi* of *Telloh* and vassal of *Dungi* of *Ur*. It is not certain whether *Ur-Ba'u* was the immediate successor of *Ur-Ê*, or whether *Gudea* followed *Nam-makh-ni*, but in view of the fact that we possess a large number of monuments from this period, and only these rulers are known, it seems probable that we have the full list of rulers for this time. If this be so, it is impossible to place *Sargon of Agade* earlier than we have done, for otherwise we must allot too long reigns to these *pateses* of *Telloh*, none of whom, except *Gudea*, seems to have ruled for any considerable period.

Of later *pateses* of *Telloh* the monuments mention *Ur-nin-sun*, *Galu-ka-ni*, *Kha-la-lama*, *Al-la-mu*(?), and *Ur-kal*.

Dynasty of Kish

The *Dynasty of Kish*, a city of Babylonia, was partly contemporary with that of *Telloh*. Several of its kings are known—*Ma-an-ish-tu-su*, *Me-silim*, *Lugal-da-ak*, *Al-zu-zu-a*, *En-ne-ugun*, *Ur-sag-ud-da*, *Lugal-tar-si*, *Uru-mu-ush*; and it may have lasted for about two hundred and fifty or two hundred and seventy-five years, i. e., about 2950–2675 B. C.

In the inscriptions of this dynasty occur several Semitisms, and we have to assume, either that it was of Semitic origin, or else that *Kish* had been a Semitic settlement before the kings of this dynasty occupied this region.

From this dynasty we must trace the royal title, "king

of hosts," *Shar Kish*, Ass. *Shar kishate*, especially coveted by the Assyrian kings.

Dynasty of Ki-en-gi

The earliest ruler in Babylonia, so far as is now known from the monuments, was *En-shag-kush-an-na*. His capital was undoubtedly *Nippur*, and his title was "*Lord of Ki-en-gi.*" His date may provisionally be assigned to about 3100 B. C.

The Sumerians

We have often referred to the land of *Shumir*, and we have suggested above that this name originated in the city of *Gir-Su*^{ki} or *Su(m)-Gir*^{ki}, and finally was applied to and superseded *Ki-en-gi*, the old name of Babylonia. The people that gave the name of *Shumir* to Babylonia must therefore have been a foreign race which invaded the Euphrates valley, and that people is now generally known as the Sumerians. They are supposed to have carried with them and to have introduced the art of writing, now known as "*cuneiform* script." Their language has been studied by Assyriologists, of whom the greater number declare it to have been a non-Aryan, non-Semitic tongue, probably related to that of the Turanian—Turkish or Finnish—group of languages. A few Assyriologists have contended, however, that this "*Sumerian*" language is only an artificial script, adopted by the Semitic priests of Babylonia. This latter view is, however, untenable. Alike untenable, it seems to me, is the "Turanian" theory of its origin.

Ed. Meyer has lately taken up this question in an admirable study on the Sumerians and Semites in Babylonia,[1] and he reaches the following conclusions: (1) that

[1] *Sumerier und Semiten in Babylonien.* Berlin, 1906.

as far as the monuments show, there were from early times two physically and linguistically different races living side by side in Babylonia, the Semites and Sumerians, the latter dating from the end of the fourth millennium B. C., and centering around *Telloh;* (2) that there is no cogent reason for assuming that there ever existed a pure Sumerian period in Babylonia, when Semites were unknown in that land; (3) that Northern Babylonia had been peopled by Semites from earliest, perhaps pre-Sumerian, times, and that the two races became fused, both in language and religion, but that Sumerians never occupied Northern Babylonia, except that Sumerian kings might have ruled it for short intervals; (4) that the Sumerians entered Babylonia from the east, and were not related to the Semites.

No one, I presume, will question these conclusions, for the monuments, the physical characteristics of the people, their language, and religion, will hardly permit of a different interpretation. Still it seems to me, that with the help of the knowledge we possess at present in regard to early Babylonia, we can safely take at least one step further.

The Sumerians wrote from left to right. Still there must have been a time when the script read from right to left. As Thureau-Dangin[1] has shown, the vertical position of some signs at least must have preceded the horizontal. This shows that the signs then faced toward the right, and that writing was therefore from right to left. As this change was introduced by the Sumerians, the preceding stage of writing must belong to an older people, that was not Sumerian, nor could that people have been Semitic, for the Semites adopted the Sumerian system.

[1] *L'écriture cunéiforme,* pp. xi ff.

Several ideograms, like *E-A, ZU-AB, KI-EN-GI*, show that they were read originally from right to left. When the Sumerians changed the script so as to run from left to right, they still continued to write the signs of these ideograms in the old order, and the Semites did likewise. This phenomenon points to a pre-Sumerian as well as a pre-Semitic origin.

The cuneiform script was originally hieroglyphic or picture-writing. This phenomenon disappears gradually in the Sumerian inscriptions, not only in those on baked clay, but also in those on stone or metal. The Egyptian and *H*ittite inscriptions show that where the hieroglyphic writing was aboriginal with the people, it was kept up continuously. The wedge-system was then of Sumerian origin, and was applied by the Sumerians to the ancient Babylonian hieroglyphic writing.

The numerous values attached to the Babylonian signs indicate a very composite origin, i. e., they were accommodated to fit several languages, each adding to it the sounds that were peculiar in that language, to express the idea symbolized by the original sign. In several of those signs we find traces of Egyptian and Semitic, as well as of the pure Sumerian language.[1]

We must then inquire: What people was it, that introduced the original Babylonian picture-writing? At present we know only of one people which answers all the conditions embodied in this question, and that people was the Egyptian, or rather the ancestors of that people, that developed the Egyptian civilization in the Nile Valley.

Many circumstances and phenomena in the Egyptian

---

[1] To these might be added the proto-Aryan language, for several cuneiform values betray an unmistakably Aryan origin.

civilization indicate that its cradle was in the Euphrates Valley. The use of bricks in constructing the earliest temples, mastabas, and pyramids in Egypt point to a Babylonian, not an Egyptian, origin. The Egyptian pantheon, the rites and myths of the Egyptian religion, although largely fused with older African elements, show such a close affinity with the early Babylonian religion, that we must postulate a relationship between them.

Many of the Egyptian hieroglyphic values are identical with those of the Babylonian cuneiform signs, e. g., Bab. *Ê*, "temple," "house"=Hebrew *Hê(-kal)* =Eg. *H(et)*. More important is the similarity in signs. Cf., e. g., the sign for Bab. *A*, "water;" if it be written horizontally it is evidently the same as Eg. *Mw*, "water;" Bab. *KI*, "city," with its surrounding country, and Eg. *N(t)*, "city," both exhibiting the idea of an encircled and inclosed area, divided in four quarters or regions, and probably designating the original Babylonian idea of the "*Four Regions.*" Bab. *SAD*, Sum. *KUR*, "highland," and Eg. *St,* "highland;" Bab. *MU*, "year," and Eg. *rnp(t)*, "year," were symbolized in both cases by a blossoming reed. Such instances can be multiplied many times over, and the similarities cannot in so large a number of signs be purely accidental.

Many Egyptian local names, especially those of the old kingdom, betray affinity with Babylonia. So, e. g., seems Eg. *Abyd(os)*, the home of *Osir(is)*, identical with Babylonian *Ab-zu*^{ki}, which was the original home of the god *A-sir (sur); In* or *On* (=*H*eliopolis) is identical with *Unu* or (*Ud-*) *Unu*, (Larsa,) the sun city of Babylonia, not to mention such Egyptian names as *Turra*, Troja, (*Din-Tir*) and *Babil*.

Still more evident is this relationship in the language; and the Erman school even assumes that the Egyptian is a sister language of the Semitic. This applies to a number of Egyptian words, large enough to make up a primitive vocabulary, where it is impossible to assume that we deal with words borrowed from the Semitic; and still their Semitic origin cannot be denied. But this applies especially to the grammatical structure of the Egyptian language, where the Semitic kinship is evident almost everywhere.

All these phenomena seem to suggest that an Egyptian people, probably the ancestors of the historical Egyptians, had lived in Babylonia in ancient times, probably in Middle, and later on in Southern Babylonia, and simultaneously with the Semites of Northern Babylonia. To differentiate them from the prehistoric Egyptians, I shall call them "Hamites." This people adopted a hieroglyphic writing, which later was developed by the Sumerians into the cuneiform writing, while their own descendants developed it into the Egyptian hieroglyphic system.

The Hamites in Southern Babylonia were overpowered by the Semites some time in the latter part of the fourth millennium B. C., and a part of them migrated into Egypt. This migration might have taken place about 3350 B. C. The Hamites of Middle Babylonia became largely Semitized under Semitic rule and the influence of Semitic religious ideas. From the name of the land, *Ki-en-gi*, where they lived, they became known as "Canaanites," a halfbreed race of Semites and Hamites. It is from this period and from this kingdom that we should probably date the term *"king of the Four Regions."*

About 3000 B. C., a new people came from the east and

settled in Southern Babylonia near *Telloh*. They came from a mountainous region somewhere between the Caspian Sea and Elam, adopted and changed the system of writing then found in Babylonia into the "wedge"-system, assimilated several Semitic religious forms and beliefs with their own, and succeeded in establishing a flourishing civilization, of which *Telloh* became the center. This people we now know by the name of Sumerians.

About 2750 B. C. these Sumerians succeeded in subduing *Nippur* and the land of *Ki-en-gi*. This gave rise to the Canaanite migration from *Ki-en-gi* to the west. *Bêl* of *Nippur* becomes *Baal* of Canaan; *Ki-en-gi(n)* becomes *Ki-na-akh-na* or *Ki-na-akh-khi*. The temple of Tyre was founded 2300 years before *H*erodotus, i. e., about 2740 B. C., and 2800 B. C. is about the date that we must assign to *Ur-Ninâ's* kingship in *Telloh*. For the older *Bêl* of *Nippur*, *En-kid* or *En-lil*, "lord of the land," was introduced, and *Ki-en-gi* became known as *Sumir*. The combination of the *Telloh* region with that of *Nippur* gave rise to the term *Shumir and Akkad*.[1]

The supremacy of *Telloh* was overthrown by the *Dynasty of Erech* about 2675 B. C. This dynasty was Semitic, but, having come from east of the Tigris, it was probably nearest allied to the Aramaic race, the cradle of which seems to have been in that region.

The subsequent development of Babylonia is chronologically certain. The Semitic *Dynasty of Agade* came to

---

[1] A branch of this migration from Middle Babylonia settled in Northern Egypt, around and in the city of Heliopolis. The Fifth Dynasty of Egypt, which came to power in 2729 B. C., was Heliopolitan, and from that time dates the royal title, *Sa-Re* "son of the sun-god." Cf. King and Hall, *History of Egypt*, pp. 102 ff.

power about 2550 B. C., the *Dynasty of Ur* succeeding it in 2477 B. C. The *Dynasty of Isin* succeeded that of *Ur* in 2360 B. C., and the *Hammurabi Dynasty* began to rule in 2233 B. C. *Kudur-Mabug's* and *Eri-Aku's Dynasty* in the *Sea-Land* dates from about 2135 B. C. and was superseded by *Dynasty B of the Sea-Land* in 2079 B. C. The *Kassites* established their kingdom of *Kâr-Duniash*, with *Babylon* as their first capital, in 1782 B. C. Then followed *Dynasty D of Pashe* in 1205 B. C., and *Dynasty E of the Sea-Land* in 1073 B. C.

C. ASSYRIAN CHRONOLOGY

For the chronology of Assyria prior to 893 B. C., when the *Limmu-Lists* begin, we must depend exclusively upon the information contained in the *Amarna Letters*,[1] the *Synchronistic History*,[2] *Chronicle P*,[3] the *Genealogies*,[4] and the chronological references given in the historical inscriptions.

Early Assyrian Kings

In dealing with dates of the dynasties of the *Kassites* and *Pashe*, we have several times had occasion to refer to contemporary kings of Assyria. These references enable us to conjecture, approximately at least, the chronology of Assyria in these periods.

Reviewing the results already gained, with the addition of the data given in the chronological material presented above, we are now enabled to present the following list of early Assyrian kings.

---

[1] See above, p. 32 f.
[2] *Ibid*, p. 33 ff.
[3] *Ibid.*, p. 40 ff.
[4] *Ibid.*, p. 57 ff.

ASHUR-NÂDIN-AKHÊ AND HIS SONS

Ashur-nirara III

The letter of *Adad-shum-nâzir* of Babylonia, referred to above,[1] was addressed to two Assyrian kings, *Ashur-nirara* and *Nabû-dâni*. We noticed then that their reigns must antedate that of *Ashur-bêl-nishêshu*, i. e., must be prior to 1450 B. C. The two Assyrian kings were evidently father and son, who were coregents in the city of Ashur, and the dates of their reigns may be conjecturally stated as *circa* 1500–1450 B. C.

Ashur-bêl-nishêshu

According to the *Synchronistic History*,[2] *Ashur-bêl-nishêshu*, king of Assyria, was a contemporary of *Kara-Indash*, king of Babylonia. His reign may be set provisionally at *circa* 1450–1430 B. C.

Ashur-nâdin-akhê and His Sons

In the *Amarna Letters*,[3] *Ashur-uballit*, king of Assyria, refers to his father, *Ashur-nâdin-akhê*, as having received gold from *Amenhotep III*, king of Egypt. *Ashur-uballit* addressed his letter to *Amenhotep IV*, and the wording of the letter indicates that *Amenhotep III* had died before the accession of *Ashur-uballit*. From the *Sychronistic History* and *Chronicle P*[4] we learn that *Ashur-uballit* was a contemporary of *Kara-Khardash* and *Kuri-Galzu II*, kings of Babylonia. We learn also that *Muballitat-Sherûa*,[5] a daughter of *Ashur-uballit*, was married to *Kara-Khardash*, and that their son, *Kadashman-Kharbe I*, was a coregent with his father. But *Kara-Khardash* and his son reigned hardly more than three years (*circa* 1380–1377 B.C.) preceded by the long reign of *Burna-Buriash*, 1405–

[1] P. 64.
[2] P. 34.
[3] No. 15, l. 19.
[4] See above, p. 40.
[5] *Ibid.*, p. 34.

1380 B. C. The accession of *Ashur-uballit* cannot have occurred before 1402 B. C., the death-year of *Amenhotep III*, and as he was grandfather of *Kadashman-Kharbe I*, who died in 1377 B. C., it follows that *Ashur-uballit* must have been a man of at least forty-five or fifty years of age when he became king.

Now the *Synchronistic History*[1] informs us that *Buzur-Ashur*, king of Assyria, was a contemporary of *Burna-Buriash*, king of Babylonia. But, as stated above, *Burna-Buriash* began to reign between 1407 and 1402 B. C.,[2] probably about 1405 B. C. *Buzur-Ashur* must therefore have reigned after 1405. This makes it necessary to assign *Ashur-nâdin-akhê*, father of *Ashur-uballit*, to a period preceding that of *Buzur-Ashur*, because *Ashur-nâdin-akhê* was a contemporary of *Amenhotep III*. As we have no reason to assume that *Buzur-Ashur* was a usurper, we must regard him as an older son of *Ashur-nâdin-akhê*, and brother of *Ashur-uballit*. I would therefore suggest the following dates for these three kings:

Ashur-nâdin-akhê   1430–1415 B. C.
Buzur-Ashur   1415–1400 B. C.
Ashur-uballit   1400–1370 B. C.

Bêl-nirari, Ârik-dîn-ilu, and Adad-nirari I

Ashur-uballit was succeeded by his son *Bêl-nirari*,[3] who was a contemporary of *Kuri-Galzu II*.[4] This latter king reigned from 1377–1353 B. C., and was succeeded by his son *Nazi-Maraddash*, 1353-1327 B. C. From the *Synchronistic History*[5] as well as from *Chronicle P*[6] we

---
[1] Above, p. 34.   [2] *Ibid.*, 65.
[3] Cf. the *Genealogies* above, p. 59.
[4] Cf. *Synchronistic History* above, p. 34.
[5] *Ibid.*, p. 36.   [6] P. 40.

know that *Adad-nirari I*, of Assyria was a contemporary of *Nazi-Maraddash*, of Babylonia. But the *Genealogies*[1] show that *Ârik-dîn-ilu* was a son of *Bêl-nirari* and father of *Adad-nirari I*, and his reign therefore falls between those of the two latter kings. This enables us to conjecture the following dates for these three kings:

Bêl-nirari	1370–1355 B. C.
Ârik-dîn-ilu	1355–1340 B. C.
Adad-nirari I	1340–1325 B. C.

Shalmaneser

The reign of *Tukulti-Ninib I* has been defined above.[2] It must antedate the year 1283 B. C., the death-year of *Shagarakti-Shuriash*, for this latter king was the object of *Tukulti-Ninib's* attack. The *Bavian Inscription*[3] assigned this war to the year 1289 B. C. From his *Annals*[4] it is evident that he had at that time been king for some years, as he had carried on several campaigns against the kings of Nairi before he attacked Babylon. We can therefore hardly assign his accession to a date later than 1295 B. C.

Shalmaneser I was the father and precedessor of *Tukulti-Ninib I*, and son and successor of *Adad-nirari I*.[5] His reign would therefore fall about 1325–1295 B. C.

Tukulti-Ninib I and His Successors

In *Chronicle P*[6] it is stated that the god *Marduk* dwelt in Assyria for $Y+6$ *years*, until the time of *Tukulti-Ashur*, king of Assyria, when *Marduk's* statue was brought back. The decimal of the number is broken away, but we may be able to conjecture it. We know that this statue was

---

[1] P. 59. [2] P. 73. [3] P. 60 ff.
[4] Cf. King, *Records of Tukulti-Ninib I*.
[5] Cf. the *Genealogies*, above, p. 59.   [6] See p. 44.

brought to Assyria in 1274 B. C. by *Tukulti-Ninib I*, who was succeeded in 1266 B. C. by his son *Ashur-nâzir-pal I*. From the *Synchronistic History* we know that *Bêl-kudur-uzur* of Assyria was slain by *Adad-shum-uzur* of Babylonia, probably in 1237 B. C., and was succeeded by *Ninib-apil-Êkur*. From this time on, the succession of Assyrian kings is known with certainty for more than one hundred and fifty years. The only place left for *Tukulti-Ashur* must therefore be between *Ashur-nâzir-pal I* and *Bêl-kudur-uzur*. These three kings reigned from 1266 B. C., to 1237 B. C. It is not unlikely that the siege of Ashur, when the statue of *Marduk* was recaptured and brought to Babylonia, cost *Ashur-nâzir-pal I* his life and made *Tukulti-Ashur* king. The reasonable date for this event would be 1248 B. C., which would give 20+6 years for *Marduk's* stay in Ashur. The reigns of these four kings would then be fixed approximately thus:

Tukulti-Ninib I,	circa 1295–1266 B. C.
Ashur-nâzir-pal I,	1266–1248 B. C.
Tukulti-Ashur,	1248–1243 B. C.
Bêl-kudur-uzur,	1243–1237 B. C.

Ashur-dân I

In the great cylinder-inscription of *Tiglath-pileser I* we read:

"*At that time the temple of Anu and Adad, the great gods, my lords, which in former times Shamshi-Adad (II), ruler of Ashur, son of Ishme-Dagan (II), ruler of Ashur, had built, after six hundred and forty-one years was falling down. Ashur-dân (I), king of Assyria, had torn down that temple but had not rebuilt it; for sixty years the foundations thereof had not been laid. In the beginning of my reign, Anu and*

PLATE V

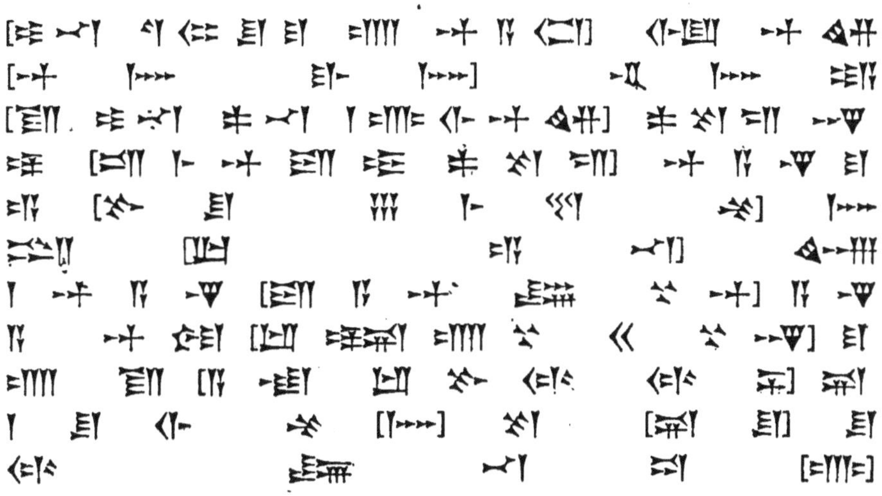

CYLINDER-INSCRIPTION OF TIGLATH-PILESER I

GIVING THE DATES OF ISHME-DAGAN, SHAMSHI-ADAD AND ASHUR-DÂN I

(From *AKA*., Vol. I, p. 95.)

ASHUR DÂN I

Adad, the great gods, my lords, who love my priesthood, gave command that I should rebuild their dwelling."[1]

From the same cylinder-inscription we learn that *Ashur-dân I* had been a mighty and successful ruler, who had reigned over Assyria for a very long time, "*and attained to gray hairs and a ripe old age.*"[2] The only adequate reason why *Ashur-dân I* did not rebuild the temple of *Anu* and *Adad* must be his death, and the *sixty years* must then refer to the period between the death of *Ashur-dân* and the accession of *Tiglath-pileser I*. This period includes the reigns of *Mutakkil-Nusku* and *Ashur-rêsh-ishi*, of whom the latter was by far the more powerful, and to whom the larger part of this period must be assigned.

The father of *Ashur-dân I* was *Ninib-apil-Êkur*, who became king not later than 1237 B. C. From the *Synchronistic History* we know that *Ashur-dân I* was a contemporary of *Zamama-shum-iddin*, king of Babylon 1208–1207 B. C.

From a comparison of the cylinder-inscription of *Tiglath-pileser I* with the boundary stone of *Marduk-nâdin-akhê*, it is evident that *Tiglath-pileser I* must have reigned at least six years before the sacking of *Ekallâte* in 1107 B. C.

From the *Synchronistic History*[3] we learn further that *Ashur-bêl-kala*, son of *Tiglath-pileser I*, was contemporaneous both with *Marduk-Shâpik-zêr-mâti*, 1093–1081 B.C., and *Adad-apil-iddina*, 1081–1073, and that he married a daughter of the latter. On the basis of these data, I would reconstruct the Assyrian chronology of this period in the following manner:

[1] *AKA.*, Vol. I, pp. 95, 96.
[2] *Tiglath-pileser I*, cylinder-inscription, Col. VII, l. 54.
[3] See above, p. 38.

Ninib-apil-Êkur,	1237– circa 1225 B. C.
Ashur-dân I,	circa 1225–1185 B. C.
Mutakkil-Nusku,	1185–1160 B. C.
Ashur-rêsh-ishi,[1]	1160–1125 B. C.
Tiglath-pileser I,	1125–1085 B. C.
Ashur-bêl-kala,	1085–1065 B. C.
Shamshi-Adad III,	1065–1050 B. C.

The Pateses of Assyria

The above data cover practically all that we know about the chronology of the early Assyrian kings down to 1050 B. C.

Besides this, we have a few inscriptions referring to more ancient rulers of Assyria, who are not, however, styled kings, but *pateses*, indicating that Assyria was a dependency of another power at the time.

Shamshi-Adad II

In the inscription of *Tiglath-pileser I*, quoted above,[2] it is stated that *Shamshi-Adad*, a *patesi* of Ashur, son of *Ishme-Dagan*, had built the temple of *Adad* and *Anu* 641 years before it was torn down by *Ashur-dân I*. This number points back to about 1826 B. C., which would fall within the reign of this *patesi*, preceded by that of *Ishme-Dagan II*. I would therefore fix their reigns approximately as follows:

Ishme-Dagan II	circa 1850–1830 B. C.
Shamshi-Adad II	circa 1830–1800 B. C.

Shamshi-Adad I

I have denoted the *Shamshi-Adad*, to whom *Tiglath-pileser I* referred in his inscription, as the second of that

---

[1] For the discussion of his date, see above p. 85.

[2] P. 137 and cf. Addenda.

name. I have done this for the reason that some inscriptions refer to another *Shamshi-Adad*, whose reign must fall considerably earlier than 1825 B. C., and I shall provisionally designate him as *Shamshi-Adad I*.

There is a contract dated in the fourth year of *Hammurabi*, in which we find the oath formula "*by Marduk, Hammurabi, and Shamshi-Adad.*" As the last name is not Babylonian, Ranke[1] and King[2] interpret it as the name of the *patesi* of *Ashur* in the time of *Hammurabi*. We know from the *Letters* and the *Code of Hammurabi*, that Ashur was at this time a dependency of Babylon, as was also Nineveh. *Shamshi-Adad* was, therefore, a *patesi Ashur* in the time of *Hammurabi*.

As this contract was dated in the fourth year of *Hammurabi*, *Shamshi-Adad* must have ruled as early as 2106 B. C., and his accession may be set down as *circa* 2110 B. C.

There is an inscription of a *patesi* of *Ashur* named *Samsi-Adad*, son of *Igur-kabkabu*,[3] which King[4] suggests may be the *Samsi-Adad* of the time of *Hammurabi*.

This inscription reads: "*Samsi-Adad, patesi of Ashur, the son of Igur-kabkabu, builder of the temple of Ashur.*"[5]

Igur-kabkabu

Igur-kabkabu was thus the father and predecessor of this *Shamshi-Adad*, and as *Ishme-Dagan* was the father of *Shamshi-Adad II*, this *Shamshi-Adad* must be another *patesi* of that name. The probability is that he is identical with the one mentioned on the contract from the fourth year of *Hammurabi*. The spelling of the name *Samsi-Adad*

[1] *EB.*, Ser. D, Vol. III, p. x.
[2] *Tukulti-Ninib I*, pp. 55 f.
[3] *AKA.*, Vol. I, p. 2.
[4] *Ibid.*
[5] *IR.*, 6, No. 1.

instead of *Shamshi-Adad* points to the Babylonian influence of the *Hammurabi* dynasty. (Cf. *Samsu-iluna* and *Samsu-ditana*.)

This seems corroborated by an inscription of *Adad-nirari III* (812–783 B. C.) in which he says:

"(I, *Adad-nirari*, am) *a descendant of Bêl-kapkapu, an ancient king, who lived in the remote time of the dynasty of Sulili, whom Ashur duly called (to be king) in days of old.*"[1]

Igur-kabkabu and *Bêl-kabkabu* may very well be identical, for *Igur* represents *Ê-kur*, the temple of Bêl at Nippur, and *Ê-kur* is thus often used for Bêl. Compare the name *Ninib-apil-Ê-kur*, "*Ninib* the son of *Ê-kur*," but Ninib was the son of Bêl. *Ê-kur* is here used for *Bêl*, as *Ê-sharra* is used for *Ashur*, lord of the temple of *Ê-sharra*. (Compare the name *Tukulti-apil-Ê-sharra* = "*Tiglath-pileser*.")

Sulili I take to be a corruption of *Sumu-la-ilu*, second king of *Dynasty A of Babylon*. We know that *Sumu* was pronounced as *Suwu*, and often shortened to *Su*. Thus we find that *Sumu-abi* is often written *Su-abu* in the contracts, and the same phenomenon occurs again in the last line of *Chronicle K 1*.[2] *Su-lili* may therefore very well represent *Su-la-ilu*, for *Sumu-lu-ilu*. *Adad-nirari III* therefore assigns *Bêl-kabkabu* to the "remote" time of the dynasty or kingdom of *Sumu-la-ilu*. Now it is well known that the later kings of *Dynasty A* referred to *Sumu-la-ilu* as the founder of their dynasty, indicating that the first king, *Sumu-abi*, did not belong to that family.

This seems to indicate that *Bêl-kabkabu* lived in the time of *Dynasty A*, and may therefore be identical with *Igur-kabkabu*, father of *Samsi-Adad* and this latter *patesi*,

[1] *AKA.*, Vol. I, p. xviii, n. i.   [2] See above, p. 51. .

be identical with *Shamshi-Adad I*, contemporary of *Hammurabi*.

This leads us to still another comparison. The Berlin Museum possesses a prism inscribed by *Esarhaddon*, in which he gives an outline of the history of *Ashur's* temple in the city of Ashur. In this inscription *Esarhaddon* states that the temple of Ashur had been built by a certain *Ushpia*, was later rebuilt by a certain *Irishu*, the son of *Ilu-shûma*, and was once more restored, after the lapse of 126 years, by *Shamshi-Adad*, the son of *Bêl-kabi*, and finally, 434 years after this restoration, it was burned down.

King[1] suggests that this *Bêl-kabi* is identical with *Bêl-kabkabu* and *Igur-kabkabu*, and this identification seems to me not only possible but very probable. The *Shamshi-Adad* of *Esarhaddon's* inscription is therefore identical with *Shamshi-Adad I*, contemporary of *Hammurabi*, whose accession I assigned above to 2110 B. C. According to this reckoning, *Bêl-kabi* would have ruled about 2130–2110 B. C.

Bêl-tâbi

Ranke has lately carried this one generation earlier, for he has found a tablet, dated in the time of "*Sin-muballit, Bêl-tâbi* and his wife,"[2] and he argues that *Bêl-tâbi* is an Assyrian name and probably represents a still earlier *patesi* of *Ashur*.

The date of *Bêl-tâbi* would then be about 2150–2130 B.C.

Erishu and Ilu-shûma

In the prism of *Esarhaddon* mentioned above, a certain *Irishu*, the son of *Ilu-shûma*, is said to have rebuilt the

---

[1] *Chronicles Concerning Early Babylonian Kings*, Vol. I, pp. 127 f.
[2] *EB.*, Vol. VI, Part I, p. 9.

temple of Ashur some 126 years before it was again restored by *Shamshi-Adad I*. A brick inscription of this *Irishu*[1] has been discovered, reading:

"*Irishum, patesi of Ashur, the son of Ilu-shûma,*[2] *patesi of Ashur, unto Ashur his lord for his own life and for the life of his son* [.... *has dedicated*]."

The names, both of *Irishum* and his father *Ilu-shûma*, have lately[3] been found in an inscription of *Irishum*.

The fact that *Irishu* restored the temple of Ashur, originally built by *Ushpia*, makes it certain that this *Irishu* is identical with the *patesi Erishu*, mentioned on a fragment published by Scheil,[4] where *Erishu* is said to have restored a temple built by *Aushpia(i)*.

The British Museum possesses a fragment of a late Assyrian copy of a votive inscription[5] on which mention is made of the temple Ê-kurgigal, built by the *patesi Ikunum*, son of *Erishum*. There is no doubt that this *Erishum* is identical with *Erishu*, mentioned above, and also with *Irishu*, the restorer of the temple of Ashur. The identification of these names, as well as *Erishum's* restoration of that temple, has been verified by four identical building inscriptions of *Shalmaneser I*,[6] part of which reads:

"*When Ê-kharsag-kurkura, the temple of Ashur, my lord, which Ushpia (variant = Aushpia) the priest of Ashur,*

[1] *BM.*, No. 91,130; published in *IR.*, 6, No. 2; Winckler, *ZA.*, Vol. II, pl. III, No. 10; *AKA.*, Vol. I. pp. xv and 1.

[2] This name was formerly misread as *Khallu*.

[3] It was made known in December, 1903. Cf. *MDOG.*, no. 20, p. 28.

[4] *RT.*, Vol. XXII, p. 156.

[5] K., 8805+K., 10,238+K., 10,880, and cf. *AKA.*, Vol. I, p. xvii, n. 3.

[6] Berlin Museum, nos. 859, 860, 783, and 890. Cf. *MDOG.*, no. 21, pp. 30, 34, 38, and 48.

my forefather, had built aforetime, and it fell into decay, and Erishu, my forefather, the priest of Ashur, rebuilt it; 159 years passed by after the reign of Erishu, and that temple fell into decay, and Shamshi-Adad, the priest of Ashur, rebuilt it; (during) 580 years that temple which Shamshi-Adad, the priest of Ashur, had built, grew hoary and old—(when) fire broke out in the midst thereof . . . . . , at that time I drenched that temple in its circuit."

This inscription is of special interest to us for several reasons: (1) Having been written by *Shalmaneser I*, it dates back to the fourteenth century B. C.; (2) It furnishes us with several names of early Assyrian *pateses;* (3) It helps us to locate, chronologically, several of these early *pateses.*

The *patesi Shamshi-Adad*, mentioned in these building inscriptions, cannot be the one mentioned by *Tiglath-pileser I*, for his reign falls about 100 years earlier. He must therefore be the *Shamshi-Adad* who was contemporary with *Hammurabi*. Now we found above that *Shamshi-Adad I* began to rule about 2110 B. C., and the restoration of the temple of *A*shur must therefore be later than that time. *Hammurabi* mentions in the prologue to his code[1] that he had restored the protecting deity to the city of *A*shur, which event should undoubtedly be placed in connection with the restoration of *A*shur's temple.

The date of *Erishu* can be defined quite precisely. He was the son of *Ilu-shûma*, but this *Ilu-shûma* is undoubtedly identical with *Ilu-shûma* of *Chronicle K1*. This *patesi* had some transaction with *Su-abu*, who is none other than *Sumu-abi*, the first king of *Dynasty A of Babylon*. This latter king reigned from 2233–2218 B. C.,

[1] Col. iv, l. 58.

and *Ilu-shûma's patesiat* must fall near that time. *Erishu*, therefore, was a contemporary of *Sumu-la-ilu*, but his reign may possibly have extended into that of *Sumu-abu;* more than this, it is probable that the catch-line at the end of *Chronicle K1* refers to a war between *Ilu-shûma* and *Sumu-abi*.

The date of *Erishu* on the prism inscription of *Esarhaddon* avers that only 126 years had elapsed from *Irishu* to *Shamshi-Adad I*, while the building inscriptions of *Shalmaneser I* claim 159 years for the same period. There seems to be a contradiction between these two numbers, but it is possible that *Esarhaddon*'s date refers to the death-year of *Irishu*, while the *Shalmaneser* inscription refers to his accession year, or the year of his restoration of *Ashur*'s temple. *Erishu* would then have reigned at least 33 years.

If we assume that *Shamshi-Adad I* rebuilt the temple of *Ashur* in the year 2085 B. C., which would give that *patesi* a reign of at least 25 years (2110–2085 B. C.), *Erishu* would have reigned from 2244 to 2211 B. C.

Ikunum was the son and successor of *Erishu*, and his reign would then fall after 2211 B. C.

Ilu-shûma, father and predecessor of *Erishu*, also reigned before 2239 B. C. But he was a contemporary of *Sumu-abi*, who began to reign in 2233 B. C. Can this be reconciled? It may be urged that I have placed *Shamshi-Adad's* restoration of the temple too early, and if that date be lowered, say ten years, the reign of *Ilu-shûma* would be partly contemporary with *Sumu-abi's*. This might seem at first the best way of overcoming the difficulty. There are, however, some other facts to be considered, before making a choice in either direction.

A small cylinder was found at Kalat-Sherqât (Ashur) in the autumn of 1904.[1] This inscription records the history of the building of the city wall of Ashur. It was inscribed by a *patesi* of Ashur, *Ashir-rîm-nishêshu*, son of *Ashir-nirari* and grandson of *Ashir-rabi*, and he says: "*The city-wall which Kikia, Ikunum, Shar-kenkâte-Ashir and Ashir-nirari, the son of Ishme-Dagan, my forefathers, had built, was fallen, and for the preservation of my life . . . . I rebuilt it.*"

This *Ishme-Dagan* can hardly be identical with the *patesi* of the same name who was the father of *Shamshi-Adad II*, for, in order to admit of a reasonable time between the successive restorations of this city wall, his reign must have preceded that of *Shamshi-Adad II*. I would therefore designate him as *Ishme-Dagan I*, and his son as *Ashir-nirari I*, and assign their reigns to about 1900 B. C.

Ashir-rabi, Ashir-nirari II, and *Ashir-rîm-nishêshu*, should perhaps be assigned to 1750–1700 B. C.

Ikunum is known, for he was the son and successor of *Erishu*. *Kikia* must therefore have preceded *Ilu-shûma*, perhaps by 200 years.

There remains then only *Shar-kenkâte-Ashir*, who followed *Ikunum*, and to whom we must assign a date. But there is a gap between the reigns of *Ikunum* and *Bêl-tâbi*, contemporary of *Sin-muballit*, and I assume therefore that we should assign the reign of *Shar-kenkâte-Ashir* to this period, i. e., about 2200–2150 B. C. This would, however, indicate that two successive, or at least almost successive *pateses*, *Ikunum* and *Shar-kenkâte-Ashir*, restored the same city wall, which would presuppose that it had been razed in the meantime.

[1] Cf. *MDOG.*, no. 25, pp. 66 f.

Founding of the Assyrian Kingdom

In the monolith inscription found at Zenjirli, *Esarhaddon* emphasizes the antiquity of his dynasty by saying: "[I, Esarhaddon, am a descendant] of the ancient royal seed of Bêl-ibni, son of Adasi, the founder of the kingdom of Assyria."[1]

This statement is corroborated by the last section of *Chronicle K1*[2] and the first section of *Chronicle K2*,[3] in which mention is made of a certain gardener, *Bêl-ib-ni*, who was elevated to the throne by a king, *Ura-imitti*. With *King*[4] I believe that this *Bêl-ib-ni* is the same as the one to whom *Esarhaddon* refers, and I also believe that *King* has rightly identified him with the *Beletaras* of Agathias.[5] This *Beletaras* is described by Agathias as having been a gardener before he became king and founded the kingdom of Assyria. But the predecessor of *Beletaras* was *Beleous*, a name which Eusebius and Syncellus render as *Belochus*, who after an interval followed *Ninus* and *Semiramis*, and he should then be the *Ura-imitti* of the *Babylonian Chronicles*. This equation is possible, for the reading of the signs in the name *Ura-imitti* is only provisional.

Otherwise we know of no *Assyrian* king by the name of *Bêl-ibni*. In the *Dynasty of Isin*, however, the eleventh king is called *Bêl-bâni*, and it is possible that this name should be read *Bêl-ib-ni*. The name of his predecessor is mutilated, but it appears to have begun with the sign *Uru* - - -, and thus he may be identical with *Ura-imitti* of the

---

[1] *AKA.*, Vol. I, p. xvii, n. 23.
[2] See above, p. 51.   [3] *Ibid.*
[4] *Chronicles Concerning Early Babylonian Kings.* Vol. I, pp. 62 ff.
[5] *Hist.*, Lib. II, 25.

Chronicles. He reigned only six months, and to all appearances there was a change in the dynasty with the accession of *Bêl-bâni.* This latter king came to the throne in the year 2205 B. C. As it is certain that there was a king, *Bêl-ibni*, in Isin, and as it is equally certain that the kings of Isin ruled upper Asia and the regions around the Zâb rivers, it seems to me that it is the *Bêl-bâni* of Isin with whom we should identify the *Bêl-ibni* of the *Esarhaddon* inscription. That *Bêl-bâni* of Isin is identical with *Bêl-ibni* of the *Chronicles*, there can hardly be any doubt.

But if it can be shown that the reign of *Bêl-ibni*, whom *Esarhaddon* calls the founder of the Assyrian kingdom, is contemporary with the reign of *Bêl-bâni* of Isin, then we could hardly help admitting that the two kings are identical.

Barbarus and Castor place the revolt of Media from Assyria in the sixty-seventh year before the first Olympiad, i. e., in 843 B. C. This is corroborated by Ktesias, who avers, according to Diodorus,[1] that the eight Median kings reigned 283 years before the accession of Cyrus, who became king of Media in 559 B. C. If we add 283 years to that date, we arrive at the year 842 B. C. as the year of the Median independence. Now Ktesias held that the Assyrian empire fell in the preceding year, 843 B. C. This date seems to be corroborated by Herodotus, who affirms that, "*while the Assyrians were governing upper Asia for 520 years, the Medes were the first who began to secede from them.*"[2]

520 years added to the year 843 brings us to the year

[1] II, 33 ff.
[2] I, 95, 'Ἀσσυρίων ἀρχόντων τῆς ἄνω Ἀσίης ἐπ' ἔτεα εἴκοσι καὶ πεντακόσια, πρῶτοι ἀπ' αὐτῶν Μῆδοι ἤρξαντο ἀπίστασθαι.

1364 B. C., i. e., to the reign of *Bêl-nirari*. But *Adad nirari I* avers that he was "*the grandson of Bêl-nirari, the priest of Ashur, who destroyed the hosts of the Kashshi, and whose hand has conquered all his enemies, who enlarged boundary and frontier.*"[1] If *Bêl-nirari's* conquest extended to the *Kashshi*, Media (*A*tropatene) was certainly included in it.

On the other hand the year 843 B. C. falls in the middle of the reign of *Shalmaneser II*, and it is at this time that we find serious uprisings recorded in the regions of the Kurdistan.

According to Diodorus,[2] the *A*ssyrian kingdom was ruled by 30 kings, who reigned for 1,360 years, but Agathias[3] assigns to it only 1,306 years, to which we should add 55 years of the reign of *Belus*. The two last numbers added to 843 give us the year 2204 B. C., which should be the accession year of *Belus*, and the founding of the Assyrian kingdom. This is the year of the accession of *Bêl-bâni* as king of Isin.

The Greeks rendered the *A*ssyrian name *Ninib* by *Ninus*, and according to one set of traditions the reign of *Ninus* preceded that of *Belus* by 62 years. But *Ur-Ninib* became king of Isin exactly 62 years before the accession of *Bêl-bâni*. Now the chronological table of the *Dynasty of Isin* shows plainly that there was a break in that dynasty at the accession of *Ur-Ninib*. He and his four successors, therefore, belonged to a separate family. The names of the kings, nos. 6–10, show that it was not *S*emitic. Beginning with *Bêl-bâni*, a *S*emitic family ruled Isin, for all the kings succeeding him bear *S*emitic names.

[1] Tablet of Adad-Nirari (*BM*., no. 90, 978), obv. 23–27; cf. *AKA*., Vol. I, pp. 6 f.
[2] II, 21, 25. [3] Diodorus, II, 25.

Ur-Ninib, who may indeed be identical with *Ninus*, ruled also over all upper Asia, and may have been the king who first conquered the city of Ashur.

Bêl-bâni, or *Bêl-ibni*, is then the *Belus* of the classical authors, and corresponds to *Beletaras* of Agathias.

Ktesias avers also that the *Beletarus Dynasty* of Assyria lasted for 526 years. This date brings us to the year 1678 B. C., which is a reasonable date for the overthrow of the *patesiat* and the establishment of the independent Assyrian kingdom.

When *Esarhaddon* referred to *Bêl-ibni* as a king and founder of the Assyrian kingdom, he could not mean that *Bêl-ibni* lived in Ashur, for we know that the earliest rulers of Assyria were not kings, but *pateses*. What he really affirms is that *Bêl-ibni* was the first Semite recognized by the city of Ashur and its *pateses* as their king and lord. And it was from this royal line of Isin that *Esarhaddon* and the whole *Sargon Dynasty* of Assyria reckoned their descent.

If, therefore, I rightly understand the development of events as they shaped themselves in the history of Assyria, they were somewhat as follows: About 2500 B. C. (the period of the *Sargon Dynasty* of Agade) *Kikia*, and later on, *Aushpia*, were *pateses* and high-priests ruling in the city of Ashur, the latter founding the temple of Ashur, the former building the wall of that city.

About 2267 B. C., *Ur-Ninib*, king of Isin, conquered the city of Ashur, and, by the name of *Ninus*, he came to be regarded as its founder. He then proceeded to appoint his viceroys, or *pateses*, among whom we should count *Ilu-shûma*, *Erishum*, and *Ikunum*. In the reign of *Ilu-shûma* the Semites living around *Haran* were driven away, and under their leader, *Sumu-abi*, may have marched eastward and attempted the conquest of the city of Ashur. *Ilu-shûma* succeeded, however, in defending himself, and the Semites under *Sumu-abi* turned southward, invaded Babylonia, and succeeded in capturing the city of Nippur, where they established a kingdom of their own; *Dynasty A of Babylon*, with *Sumu-abi* as their first king. After 15 years *Sumu-abi* was overthrown by *Sumu-la-ilu*, the founder of the *Hammurabi* family.

Ilu-shûma may then have reigned from about 2267 to 2244, *Erishum* from 2244 to 2211, and *Ikunum* from 2211 to 2204 B. C

In the latter year *Bêl-bâni*, the gardener, and son of *Adasi*, became king of Isin, laid siege to Ashur, razed its walls, drove away or slew *Ikunum*, and placed *Shar-ken-kâte-Ashir* as *patesi* over Ashur, who undertook to rebuild the walls of the city which had been built by his predecessor, but were destroyed in the siege of the city. When *Sin-muballit* captured Isin in 2135 B. C., Ashur became a dependency, and *Bêl-tâbi*, *patesi* of Ashur, his vassal. *Bêl-tâbi* was succeeded by *Bêl-kabi*, who ruled Ashur in the time of *Eri-Aku's* usurpation. With the accession of *Hammurabi*, *Shamshi-Adad I* became *patesi* of Ashur. He may have rebuilt the temple of Ashur in the year 2085 B. C., which is 159 years after the accession of *Erishu*, and 126 years after his death.

According to *Esarhaddon*, there elapsed 434 years, according to *Shalmaneser I*, 580 years, from the restoration of the temple of Ashur by *Shamshi-Adad I* to that by *Shalmaneser I*. Both numbers seem hopelessly corrupt. Instead of *Shalmaneser's* date, 9 sossi + 40 = 580, we should expect 12 sossi + 40 = 760 years, which would bring us into the reign of *Shalmaneser I*.

CHAPTER III
EGYPTIAN CHRONOLOGY
A. THE CHRONOLOGICAL MATERIAL

Our knowledge of Egyptian chronology[1] at present is far from satisfactory. This is due, however, not to the scarcity of material, but rather to its abundance. This material, coming to us from several sources—(1) the Bible; (2) Assyrian and Babylonian monuments; (3) classical authors; (4) above all, from the monuments of the Egyptians themselves—exhibits so many contradictions, that Egyptologists and historians differ radically in their theories on Egyptian chronology.

Formerly Egyptian chronographers depended almost entirely on the *Epitomes* from Manetho, and it was then believed that we possessed a fairly trustworthy chronology of Egypt. In the last century the Egyptian monuments became the object of persistent study by a number of eminent scholars, and finally yielded an intelligible meaning. Chronological data occur frequently on these monuments, but they often differ from the data furnished by classical authors. This fact has lately led a number of Egyptologists to discard entirely the chronological references of the Greek and Roman authors, in order to build

---

[1] I have consulted the following modern works on Egyptian chronology: Lepsius, *Das Königsbuch*, 1858; Eduard Meyer, *Aegyptische Chronologie*, 1904; Breasted, "Chronology of Egypt," in *Ancient Records of Egypt*, Vol. I, pp. 25-47, 1906; Petrie, *History of Egypt*, Vols. I-III, 1899; Sethe, *Untersuchungen zur Geschichte und Altertumskunde Aegyptens*, 1896-1905; Lehmann, *Zwei Hauptprobleme*, 1898; Rost, *Untersuchungen*, 1898; Marquart, *Chronologische Untersuchungen*, 1899; Brugsch-Bey, *Egypt under the Pharaohs*.

up an Egyptian chronology, based solely on the monuments.

But here again we are met by a new obstacle. These monuments do not always agree with each other, nor do they cover the entire field of Egyptian chronology, and the result is, that those scholars, who depend only on the monuments, are often compelled to resort to assumptions in order to fill up *lacunae* in the texts, and even great periods, seemingly not covered by the monuments. The two schools of Egyptian chronographers consequently differ about 2,000 years in their calculations of dates in Egyptian history.

It seems, therefore, evident, that a serious mistake must exist somewhere in this material. Indeed, it is possible that the error may be divided, and counted against both these procedures of establishing the Egyptian chronology.

It seems impossible that classical authors, who lived when the Egyptian language was still spoken, and who had many opportunities of conversing with literary men of Egypt, should have failed so utterly to grasp this subject, and should have erred so gravely in recording Egyptian dates. Nor is it possible to argue that these errors must be attributed to careless copyists. Although it must be admitted that some errors have arisen through misunderstanding and miscopying, it is absurd to claim that almost every Egyptian date in Greek authors is wrong. Those authors had as keen a sense of truth and exactness as any modern scholar, and difficulties in Egyptian chronology are not and will not be settled by flat statements that "Manetho is wrong whenever we are able to check him," and the like.

On the other hand, we have no right to impeach the

testimony of genuine monuments. It is the task of the modern Egyptian chronographer to steer his course between this Scylla and Charybdis, if he hopes to reconstruct an Egyptian chronology which will command the confidence of modern science.

Our first task will therefore be to present all the material bearing at any point on Egyptian chronology. On this basis, with all the differences placed before us, we shall then inquire for the principles underlying Egyptian chronology, and if it then be found that these differences, in a large part, must be ascribed to a system which included co-regencies and contemporary dynasties, we shall then proceed to find some incontrovertible dates, and on these dates we shall reconstruct its historical dates from all the data furnished, applying them according to these principles of Egyptian chronology.

Cuneiform Data

From the Assyrian and Babylonian inscriptions some light is shed upon Egyptian chronology, but it must be remembered that they refer primarily to the *Sargonic* period of Assyria, the Neo-Babylonian period, and Persian supremacy, i. e., to a time subsequent to 750 B. C., and therefore are not treated in this volume. An exception to this, however, appears in the *Amarna Letters*, discussed above,[1] and belonging to the reign of *Amenhotep III* and *Ikhnaton* of the Eighteenth Dynasty.

Biblical References

The Bible frequently refers to this period of Egyptian history. *Abram* sojourned for a time in Egypt during a severe famine. Another famine is recorded in the time

[1] See p. 32.

of *Isaac*, although that patriarch did not go down to Egypt. *Jacob* and *Joseph* settled in Egypt, and *Joseph* even became vizier of the *Pharaoh*. *Moses* and *Joshua* were born in Egypt, and the exodus of the Children of Israel took place from that land. Most of these dates are chronologically certain from the standpoint of the Bible, which, however, as it does not mention by name any contemporary king of Egypt, somewhat restricts us in employing its chronology for ascertaining Egyptian dates, until we have established a trustworthy chronology of the latter. Then, indeed, the biblical dates may and do become of immense value to us in settling a number of difficulties that beset both biblical and Egyptian historical questions.

Classical Authors

Greek and Roman writers often refer to the history of Egypt. Foremost among the former is *H*erodotus. But he nowhere purports to give anything like exact data, at least for the period under discussion in this volume. Nor is Egyptian chronology treated at length by any other classical authors, excepting only Manetho and Eratosthenes, concerning whose works brief references follow.

Manetho

*A*mong other works Manetho wrote in Greek a history of Egypt, containing three volumes. The first volume covered Dynasties I–XI, the second Dynasties XII–XIX, and the third, Dynasties XX–XXX.[1] This important work is lost, but we possess fragments of it, consisting partly of verbal quotations by Josephus, partly of extracts rendered by Josephus in his own words.

[1] The Thirty-first Dynasty was afterward added in some of the *Epitomes*.

Some unknown authors had also compiled *Epitomes* of the reigns of the Egyptian kings, which have been quoted by several classical authors.

Josephus

Josephus in his book, *Contra Apionem*, quotes largely from Manetho in order to show that the Children of Israel had once lived in Egypt. From the statements of Josephus it is evident that several texts of Manetho existed in his time, and also that Manetho in his history had made use both of the monumental records of Egypt and of Egyptian folklore. It is also evident that Josephus quoted from works of Manetho not belonging to his history of Egypt.

Josephus' quotations from Manetho are therefore of uneven value, although, so far as we now know, they are substantially accurate. As these quotations are of the utmost value for Egyptian chronology, I shall here give a translation of Josephus' text in full, divided into the following sections:

I. *History of the Hyksos.*—This is a verbal quotation from Manetho and reads as follows:[1]

Settlement of Hyksos

"*There was a king of ours, whose name was Timaeus.*[2] *Under him it came to pass, I know not how, that God was averse to us, and there came after a surprising manner men of ignoble birth out of the eastern parts, and had boldness*

---

[1] Josephus, *Contra Apionem*, I, 14, translated by W. Whiston. For a full commentary on this history, see my *Sidelights on Biblical Chronology*.

[2] Ἐγένετο βασιλεὺς ἡμῖν Τίμαιος. Bunsen, Fruin, and Lepsius (*Königsbuch*, p. 23) suppose that ἡμῖν is a corruption of Ammon, and that we therefore should read Ἀμυντίμαιος, and in him recognize King *Amenemhet IV* of the Twelfth Dynasty. This assumption, I believe, is quite correct, but we should probably identify him with *Amenemhet III*.

enough to make an expedition into our country, and with ease subdued it by force, yet without our hazarding a battle with them. So when they had gotten those that governed us under their power, they afterward burned down our cities, and demolished the temples of the gods, and used all the inhabitants after a most barbarous manner; nay, some they slew, and led their children and their wives into slavery."

Salatis

"At length they made one of themselves king, whose name was Salatis; he also lived at Memphis, and made both the upper and lower regions pay tribute, and left garrisons in places that were the most proper for them. He chiefly aimed to secure the eastern parts, as foreseeing that the Assyrians, who had then the greatest power, would be desirous of that kingdom, and invade them; and as he found in the Saite Nomos (Sethroite) a city very proper for his purpose, and which lay upon the Bubastic channel, but with regard to a certain theologic notion was called Avaris: this he rebuilt, and made very strong by the walls he built about it, and by a most numerous garrison of two hundred and forty thousand armed men which he put into it to keep it. Thither Salatis came in summer time, partly to gather his corn and pay his soldiers their wages, and partly to exercise his armed men, and thereby to terrify foreigners."

The Successors of Salatis

"When this man had reigned nineteen[1] years, after him reigned another, whose name was Beon, for forty-four years; after him reigned another, called Apachnas, thirty-six years and seven months; after him Apophis reigned sixty-one

---

[1] Whiston reads incorrectly "thirteen."

years, and then Janias fifty years and one month; after all these reigned Assis forty-nine years and two months. And these six were the first rulers among them, who were all along making war with the Egyptians, and were very desirous gradually to destroy them to the very root."

Meaning of the Hyksos' Name

This whole nation was styled HYCSOS, that is, shepherd-kings; for the first syllable HYC, according to the sacred dialect, denotes a king, as is SOS a shepherd; but this according to the ordinary dialect; and of these is compounded HYCSOS; but some say that these people were Arabians. Now, in another copy it is said, that this word does not denote kings, but on the contrary denotes captive shepherds, and this on account of the particle HYC; for that HYC, with the aspiration, in the Egyptian tongue, again denotes shepherds, and that expressly also: and this to me seems the more probable opinion, and more agreeable to ancient history."

Expulsion of the Hyksos

"These people, whom we have before named kings, and called shepherds also, and their descendants [as he says] kept possession of Egypt five hundred and eleven[1] years. The kings of Thebais and of the other parts of Egypt made an insurrection against the shepherds and there a terrible and long war was made between them. . . . . Under a king, whose name was Alisphragmuthosis, the shepherds were subdued by him, and were indeed driven out of other parts of Egypt, but were shut up in a place that contained

---

[1] This date should perhaps be corrected to 518, as given below (p. 160). This carries the Hebrew settlement in Egypt back to 2084 or 2077 B. C., i. e., **to the** time of Abraham. See Gen., chap. 12, and cf. below pp. 224, 229, 236.

ten thousand acres: this place was named Avaris. The shepherds built a wall round all this place, which was a large and strong wall, and this in order to keep all their possessions and their prey within a place of strength, but Thummosis, the son of Alisphragmuthosis, made an attempt to take them by force and by siege, with four hundred and eighty thousand men to lie round about them, but, upon his despair of taking the place by that siege, they came to a composition with them, that they should leave Egypt and go, without any harm to be done to them, whithersoever they would; and after this composition was made, they went away with their whole families and effects, not fewer in number than two hundred and forty thousand, and took their journey from Egypt through the wilderness for Syria; but, as they were in fear of the Assyrians, who had then the dominion over Asia, they built a city in that country which is now called Judaea, and that large enough to contain this great number of men, and called it Jerusalem."

II. *Josephus' Epitome of Manetho.*—Josephus then adds some excerpts from Manetho in regard to the reigns of the Egyptian kings of the Eighteenth and Nineteenth Dynasties. There can be no doubt that these excerpts were made directly from Manetho, and that Josephus made the blunder of transposing *Amenophis* (*Amenhotep I*) and *Khebron* (=*Thutmose II*). This *Epitome* reads:[1]

"*When this people or shepherds were gone out of Egypt to Jerusalem, Tethmosis, the king of Egypt who drove them out, reigned afterward twenty-five years and four months, and then died; after him his son Chebron took his kingdom for thirteen years; after whom came Amenophis, for twenty*

[1] Josephus, *Contra Apionem*, I, 15 a.

years and seven months; then came his sister Amesses, for twenty-one years and nine months; after her came Mephres, for twelve years and nine months; after her was Mephramuthosis, for twenty-five years and ten months; after him was Thmosis, for nine years and eight months; after him came Amenophis, for thirty years and ten months; after him came Orus, for thirty-six years and five months; then came his daughter Achencheres for twelve years and one month; then was her brother Rathotis, for nine years; then was Achencheres, for twelve years and five months; then came another Achencheres, for twelve years and three months; after him Armais, for four years and one month; after him was Ramesses, for one year and four months; after him came Armesses Miammoun, for sixty[1] years and two months; after him Amenophis, for nineteen years and six months."

III. *Manetho's history of the rise of the Nineteenth Dynasty.*—After this *Epitome* Josephus quotes again from Manetho's account of the rise of the Nineteenth Dynasty. In Josephus this section appears to be an immediate continuation of the history subsequent to *Amenophis* (=*Merneptah*), while in reality it was taken from a section following the history of *Amenhotep IV* (or *Achencheres*). Manetho's history of the rise of the Nineteenth Dynasty is as follows:[2]

"*After him came Sethosis and Ramesses, who had an army of horse, and a naval force. This king appointed his brother Armais to be his deputy over Egypt. (In another copy it stood thus—After him came Sethosis and Ramesses, two brethren, the former of which had a naval force, and in a hostile manner destroyed those that met him upon*

---
[1] For sixty-six.   [2] Josephus, *Contra Apionem*, I, 15 b.

the sea; but as he slew Ramesses in no long time afterward, so he appointed another of his brethren to be his deputy over Egypt.) He alse gave him all the other authority of a king, but with these only injunctions, that he should not wear the diadem, nor be injurious to the queen, the mother of his children; and that he should not meddle with the other concubines of the king, while he made an expedition against Cyprus and Phoenicia, and besides against the Assyrians and the Medes. He then subdued them all, some by his arms, some without fighting, and some by the terror of his great army; and being puffed up by the great successes he had had, he went still on the more boldly, and overthrew the cities and countries that lay in the eastern parts. But after some considerable time, Armais, who was left in Egypt, did all those very things, by way of opposition, which his brother had forbid him to do, without fear; for he used violence to the queen, and continued to make use of the rest of the concubines, without sparing any of them: nay, at the persuasion of his friends, he put on the diadem, and set up to oppose his brother. But then he who was set over the priests of Egypt wrote letters to Sethosis and informed him of all that had happened, and how his brother had set up to oppose him; he, therefore, returned back to Pelusium immediately, and recovered his kingdom again. The country also was called from his name Egypt, for Sethosis was himself called Egyptus, as was his brother Armais called Danaus."

IV. *Josephus' chronology of the Hyksos period.*—Josephus now goes on to use this material from Manetho to show not only the antiquity of his race, but also to fix the date of the expulsion of the *Hyksos*. In doing so, he evidently used other material of Manetho's than the document quoted by him, but as this has also a great value for Egyptian chronology, I shall here give a translation of the passage:[1]

"*This is Manetho's account. And evident it is, from the number of years by him set down belonging to this interval, if they be summed up together, that these shepherds, as they are here called, who were no other than our forefathers, were delivered out of Egypt, and came thence, and inhabited this country, three hundred and ninety-three years[2] before Danaus came to Argos; although the Argives look upon him as their most ancient king. Manetho, therefore, bears this testimony to two points of the greatest consequence to our purpose, and those from the Egyptian records themselves. In the first place, that we came out of another country into Egypt, and that withal our deliverance out of it was so ancient in time as to have preceded the siege of Troy almost a thousand years,[3] but then, as to those things which Manetho adds, not from the Egyptian records, but, as he confesses himself, from some stories of an uncertain original, I will disprove them hereafter particularly, and shall demonstrate that they are no better than incredible fables.*"

V. *Josephus' account of the Osarsiph story.*—Later on Josephus takes up, in the same book, a treatment of the *Osarsiph* story as given by Manetho. This he prefaces with a discourse of his own, referring again to the story about the rise of the Nineteenth Dynasty.[4]

---

[1] Josephus, *Contra Apionem* I, 16.

[2] The sum of all the numbers in the preceding section amounts to 327 years, but as *Ramses II* is there quoted with 60 instead of 66 years, we may add 6 years, and read 333 years, to which this number should be corrected. It is true that *Sethos* or *Seti I* is credited with 59 years, and that would almost fill up this gap, but it is evident, both from Josephus and other documents, that *Seti I* was a contemporary king with some other regent, and that Manetho therefore rightly passed him by in his chronological table.

[3] This number cannot refer to the Exodus, nor even to the expulsion of the *Hyksos*, but must be connected with the beginning of this sentence, i. e., it must refer to the first Hebrew settlement in Egypt which took place about 900 years before the fall of Troy. See *Sidelights on Biblical Chronology*.

[4] Josephus, *Contra Apionem*, I, 26 a.

"*And now I will turn my discourse to one of their principal writers, whom I have a little before made use of as a witness to our antiquity; I mean Manetho. He promised to interpret the Egyptian history out of their sacred writings, and premised this—that 'our people had come into Egypt many ten thousands in number, and subdued its inhabitants;' and, when he had farther confessed, that 'we went out of that country afterward, and settled in that country which we now called Judaea, and there built Jerusalem and its temple.' Now thus far he followed his ancient records; but after this he permits himself, in order to appear to have written what rumors and reports passed abroad about the Jews, and introduces incredible narrations, as if he would have the Egyptian multitude that had the leprosy and other distempers to have been mixed with us, as he says they were; and that they were condemned to fly out of Egypt together; for he mentions Amenophis,[1] a fictitious king's name, though on that account he durst not set down the number of years of his reign, which yet he had accurately done as to the other kings he mentions: he then ascribes certain fabulous stories to this king, as having in a manner forgotten how he had already related that the departure of the shepherds for Jerusalem had been five hundred and eighteen[2] years before; for Thmosis was king when they went away. Now, from his days, the reigns of the intermediate kings, according to Manetho, amounted to three hundred and ninety-three years, as he says himself, till the two brothers, Sethos and Hermeus; the one of which, Sethos, was called by that other name of Egyptus, and the other, Hermeus, by that of Danaus. He also says, that Sethos cast the other out of Egypt, and reigned fifty-nine years, as did his eldest son, Rhampses, reign after him sixty-six years. When Manetho, therefore, had acknowledged that our forefathers were gone out of Egypt so many years ago, he introduces his fictitious king, Amenophis.*"

[1] *Amenmeses.*

[2] Here again Josephus is confused. If the period from the expulsion of the *Hyksos* to *Amenophis=Amenmeses* was 333 (for Josephus' 393) years, it could not have been 518 years. This date should then be compared with that of 511 above (see p. 155), and be taken as the period from the *Canaanite* settlement in Egypt to the expulsion of the *Hyksos*, 2084-1566 B. C. If the date is to be applied as it stands, it would carry us to 1048 B. C., i. e., to about the fall of the *Ramessid* (Twentieth) *Dynasty.*

VI. *Manetho's account of Osarsiph.*—Now follows a quotation by Josephus from Manetho concerning *Osarsiph*. Manetho made no claim to base this part of his history on the Egyptian monuments, but we have nevertheless no reason to doubt its correctness, although Manetho mistakenly identified the "lepers" with the Jews instead of with the Philistines, and Josephus, who was ignorant of this historical fact (the Philistine occupation of Egypt about 1230 B. C.) denounces the whole story as a vile lie, fabricated by the enemies of the Jews in order to disgrace them.

The *Osarsiph* story rests, however, on a solid historical basis, and as that story is very important for the history of the time, I shall here give a translation of Josephus' quotation from Manetho, who said:[1]

"*This king[2] was desirous to become a spectator of the gods, as had Orus, one of his predecessors in that kingdom, desired the same before him; he also communicated his desire to his namesake Amenophis, who was the son of Papis, and one that seemed to partake of a divine nature, both as to wisdom and the knowledge of futurities. This namesake of his told him that he might see the gods if he would clear the whole country of the lepers and of the other impure people: the king was pleased with this injunction, and brought together all that had any defects in their bodies out of Egypt, and that their number was eighty thousand; whom he sent to those quarries which are on the east side of the Nile, that they might work in them, and might be separated from the rest of the Egyptians. There were some of the learned priests that were polluted with the leprosy;*

---

[1] Josephus, *Contra Apionem*, I, 26 b.
[2] *Amenophis=Amenmeses.*

but that still this Amenophis, the wise man and the prophet, was afraid that the gods would be angry at him and at the king, if there should appear to have been violence offered them; who also added this farther (out of his sagacity about futurities,) that certain people would come to the assistance of these polluted wretches, and would conquer Egypt, and keep it in their possession thirteen years: that, however, he durst not tell the king of these things; but that he left a writing behind him about all those matters, and then slew himself, which made the king disconsolate. After those that were sent to work in the quarries had continued in that miserable state for a long while, the king was desired that he should set apart the city of Avaris, which was then left desolate of the shepherds, for their habitation and protection, which desire he granted them. Now this city, according to the ancient theology, was Typho's city. But when these men were gotten into it, and found the place fit for a revolt, they appointed themselves a ruler out of the priests of Heliopolis, whose name was Osarsiph, and they took their oaths that they would be obedient to him in all things. He then, in the first place, made this law to them, that they should neither worship the Egyptian gods, nor should abstain from any one of those sacred animals which they have in the highest esteem, but kill and destroy them all: that they should join themselves to nobody but to those who were of this confederacy. When he had made such laws as these, and many more such as were mainly opposite to the customs of the Egyptians, he gave order that they should use the multitude of the hands they had in building walls about their city, and make themselves ready for a war with king Amenophis, while he did himself take into his friendship the other priests, and those that were polluted with them, and send ambassadors to those shepherds who had been driven out of the land by Tethmosis to the city called Jerusalem; whereby he informed them of his own affairs, and of the state of those others that had been treated after such an ignominious manner, and desired that they would come with one consent to his assistance in this war against Egypt. He also promised that he would, in the first place, bring them back to their ancient city and country, Avaris, and provide a plentiful maintenance for their multitude; that he would protect them and fight for them as occasion should require, and would easily reduce the country under their dominion. These shepherds were all very glad of this message, and came away with alacrity all together, being in number two hundred thousand men; and in a little time they came to Avaris. And now Amenophis, the king of Egypt, upon his being informed of their invasion, was in great confusion, as calling to mind what Amenophis, the son of Papis, had foretold him; and, in the first place, he assembled the multitudes of the Egyptians, and took counsel with their leaders, and sent for their sacred animals to him, for those that were principally worshiped in their temples, and gave a particular charge to the priests distinctly, that they should hide images of their gods with the utmost care. He also sent his son Sethos, who was also named Aramessis, from his father, Rhampses, being but five years old, to a friend of his. He then passed on with the rest of the Egyptians, being three hundred thousand of the most warlike of them, against the enemy, who met them.

Yet he did not join battle with them; but thinking that would be to fight against the gods, he returned back, and came to Memphis, where he took Apis and other sacred animals, which he had sent for to him, and presently marched into Ethiopia, together with his whole army, and multitude of Egyptians; for the king of Ethiopia was under an obligation to him; on which account he received him, and took care of all the multitude that was with him, while the country supplied all that was necessary for the food of the men. He also allotted cities and villages for this exile, that was to be from its beginning during those fatally determined thirteen years. Moreover, he pitched a camp for his Ethiopian army as a guard to king Amenophis upon the borders of Egypt, and this was the state of things in Ethiopia. But for the people of Jerusalem, when they came down together, with the polluted Egyptians, they treated the men in such a barbarous manner, that those who saw how they subdued the afore-mentioned country, and the horrid wickedness they were guilty of, thought it a most dreadful thing; for they did not only set the cities and villages on fire, but were not satisfied till they had been guilty of sacrilege, and destroyed the images of the gods, and used them in roasting of those sacred animals that used to be worshiped, and forced the priests and prophets to be the executioners and murderers of those animals, and then ejected them naked out of the country. It was also reported that the priest who ordained their polity and their laws was by birth of Heliopolis, and his name Osarsiph, from Osyris, who was the god of Heliopolis; but that, when he had gone over to these people, his name was changed, and he was called Moses. . . . . After this Amenophis returned back from Ethiopia with a great army, as did his son, Rhampses with another army also; and both of them joined battle with the shepherds and the polluted people, and beat them, and slew a great many of them, and pursued them to the bounds of Syria."

The Epitomes of Manetho

Beside these direct quotations from Manetho, there were also in existence at an early time a number of excerpts (*epitomes*) or lists, some giving all the kings of the more important dynasties, with the length of their reigns, others only the length of each dynasty (7-11, 13, 14, 16, 17, 20), also the number of years covered in each volume of Manetho's history, and here and there a short biographical notice, appended to the more prominent names. Three such *Epitomes* are now extant.

Africanus

The *Epitome* by Africanus (220 A. D.) is the most complete. A later recension of this occurs in the so-called *Excerpta Barbari*.

Eusebius

Another *Epitome* is recorded by Eusebius in his *Præp. Evang.* and the *Chronicon*, which has been preserved in an Armenian translation, and also has been quoted by Syncellus.

Syncellus

A third *Epitome* is given by Syncellus, differing considerably at several points from Africanus, Eusebius, and Josephus.

The Sothis-Book

Syncellus also compiled a so-called *Sothis-Book*, based on Manetho, as he expressly affirms, but several of these data were evidently taken from some other work on Egyptian history. As both names and dates in the *Sothis-Book* differ widely from all other lists, I add them here together with those of Syncellus:

EGYPTIAN CHRONOLOGY

Sothis-Book		Syncellus
Dyn. XIX—15 Kings		**Dyn. XV**—17 Kings
1. Mestraim (or *Menes*),	35 years	1. Mestraim (or *Menes*),
2. Kourodes,	63 years	2. Kourodes,
3. Aristarkhos,	34 years	3. Aristarkhos,
4. Spanios,	36 years	4. Spanios,
		5 and 6. Unknown,
5. The Serapis,	23 years	7. The Serapis,
6. Sesonkhosis,	49 years	8. Sesonkhosis,
7. Amenemes,	29 years	9. Amenemes,
8. Amasis,	2 years	10. Amasis,
9. Akesephthres,	13 years	11. Akesephthres,
10. Ankhoreus,	9 years	12. Ankhoreus,
11. Armiuses,	4 years	13. Armiuses,
12. Khamois,	12 years	14. Khamois,
13. Miamous,	14 years	15. Miamous,
14. Amesesis,	65 years	16. Amesesis,
15. Ouses,	50 years	17. Ouses,
	438 years	
Dyn. XX—8 Kings		**Dyn. XVI**—8 Kings
1. Rameses,	29 years	18. Rameses,
2. Ramessomenes,	15 years	19. Ramessomenes,
3. Ousimare,	31 years	20. Ousimare,
4. Ramessesios,	23 years	21. Ramessesios,
5. Ramessameno,	19 years	22. Ramessameno,
6. Ramesse Ioubasse,	39 years	23. Ramesse Ioubasse,
7. Ramesse Ouaphrou,	29 years	24. Ramesse Ouaphrou,
8. Konkharis,	4 years	25. Konkharis,
	189 years	
Dyn. XXI—6 Tanites		**Dyn. XVII**—6 Kings
1. Silites,	19 years	26. Silitis,
2. Baion,	44 years	27. Baion,
3. Apakhnas,	36 years	28. Apakhnas,
4. Aphophis,	61 years	29. Aphophis,
5. Sethos,	50 years	30. Sethos,
6. Kertos,	44 years	31. Kertos,
	254 years	
Dyn. XXII—14 Kings		**Dyn. XVIII**—14 Kings
1. Asseth,	16 years	32. Asseth,
2. Amosis,	26 years	33. Amosis or *Tethmosis*, son of *Asseth*,
3. Khebron,	13 years	34. Khebron,
4. Amemphis,	15 years	35. Amemphis,
5. Amenses,	11 years	36. Amenses,
6. Misphragmouthosis,	16 years	37. Misphragmouthosis o Amosis,
7. Misphres,	23 years	38. Misphres,
8. Touthmosis,	39 years	39. Touthmosis,
9. Amenophthis,	34 years	40. Amenophthis or *Mem*
10. Oros,	48 years	41. Oros,
11. Akhenkheres,	25 years	42. Akhenkheres,
12. Athoris,	29 years	43. Athoris,
13. Khenkheres,	26 years	44. Khenkheres,
14. Akherres,	8 years	45. Akherres,
	329 years	

THE THEBAN KINGS OF ERATOSTHENES

Dyn. XXIII—4 Kings	
1. *Armaios* or *Danaos*,	9 years
2. *Ramesses* or *Aigyptos*,	68 years
3. *Amenophis*,	8 years
4. *Thouoris*,	17 years
	102 years
Dyn. XXIV—6 Kings	
1. *Nekhepsos*,	19 years
2. *Psammouthis*,	13 years
3. *Kertos*,	16 years
4. *Rampsis*,	45 years
5. *Amenses* or *Ammenemes*,	26 years
6. *Okhuras*,	14 years
	133 years

Dyn. XIX—4 Kings	
46. *Armaios* or *Danaos*,	9 years
47. *Ramesses* or *Aigyptos*,	68 years
48. *Amenophis*,	8 years
49. *Thouoris*,	17 years
	102 years
Dyn. XX	
50. *Nekhepsos*,	19 years
51. *Psammouthis*,	13 years
52. ———	4 years
53. *Kertos*,	16 years
54. *Rampsis*,	45 years
55. *Amenses* or *Ammenemes*,	26 years
56 *Okhuras*,	14 years
	141 years

The Theban Kings of Eratosthenes

Eratosthenes wrote a chronography on the Theban kings, consisting of two lists, one containing 38, the other 53 kings, with short explanations of the meaning of the Egyptian names. This work is lost, but the list was quoted by Apollodorus, who again was quoted by *Panodorus*, from whom Syncellus rendered the first list of 38 names:

1.	*Menis*, Thinite,	62 years
2.	*Athothes*,	59 years
3.	*Athothes*,	32 years
4.	*Diabies*,	19 years
5.	*Pemphos*,	18 years
6.	*Toigaramakhos*, Memphite,	79 years
7.	*Stoikhos*,	6 years
8.	*Gosormies*,	30 years
9.	*Mares*,	26 years
10.	*Anouphis*,	20 years
11.	*Sirios*,	18 years
12.	*Khnoubis Gneuros*,	22 years
13.	*Rauosis*,	13 years
14.	*Biuris*,	10 years

15. *Saophis*,	29 years
16. *Saophis B.*,	27 years
17. *Moskheres*,	31 years
18. *Mosthes*,	33 years
19. *Pammes*,	35 years
20. *Apappous*,	100 years
21. *Ekheskosokaras*,	1 year
22. *Nitokris*,	6 years
23. *Myrtaias*,	22 years
24. *Thuosimares*,	12 years
25. *Sethinilos*,	8 years
26. *Semphronkrates*,	18 years
27. *Khouther*,	7 years
28. *Meures*,	12 years
29. *Khomaephtha*,	11 years
30. *Soikounios*,	60 years
31. *Peteathures*,	16 years
32. *[St]ammenemes*,	26 years
33. *Ammenemes*,	23 years
34. *Sistosikhermes*,	55 years
35. *Mares*,	43 years
36. *Siphthas*,	5 years
37. *Phrouoro*,	19 years
38. *Amonthartaios*,	63 years
38 kings reigned	1076 years

The Egyptian Inscriptions

The Egyptian monuments naturally offer us the best and most reliable material for Egyptian chronology. This material consists chiefly of the *King-Lists*, the *Palermo Stone*, the *Turin Papyrus*, the minimum dates, the *Sothis* festivals, and the New-Moon dates.

THE EGYPTIAN INSCRIPTIONS

The King-Lists

We possess at the present time three Egyptian *King-Lists*, the *Karnak-*, *Abydos-*, and *Sakkara-Lists*. They are in more or less fragmentary condition, and only furnish us with the order of kings, without any references to the length of their reigns. They disagree, not only with each other, but with the Manethonian, Eratosthenian, and Syncellan *Lists*, and the *Turin Papyrus*. On the other hand, it must be admitted that the scribes who compiled those lists could not have been so ignorant of the succession of Egyptian kings as to commit such apparent blunders, as is often claimed. It seems therefore as if these lists were meant to serve some other purpose than that of giving the succession of all the Egyptian kings, and the solution of these difficulties lies probably in the fact that these lists might give only the names of the kings that ruled over the city where these lists were made, or else that they give the genealogy of the king who was the author of his particular list.

The Karnak-List

This applies especially to the *Karnak-List*, erected by *Thutmose III* in Amon's temple at Karnak. It begins with (1) an illegible name; then follows (2) *Snofru;* (3) *Sahure;* (4) *Ini;* and (5) *Asosi;* Nos. 6 and 7 are illegible; (8) *Re-sekhem-Smen-tawi;* (9) *Mernere;* (10) *Pepi;* 11 is illegible; (12) *rp^{c}ti-Intef.* It is evident that *Thutmose III* intended to mention only those kings who had ruled over Thebes, and with whom he felt that he stood in blood-relationship.

The Abydos-List

Seti I placed in his temple in Abydos a list of kings, 76 in number, from *Menes* to *Seti I*. The value of this list

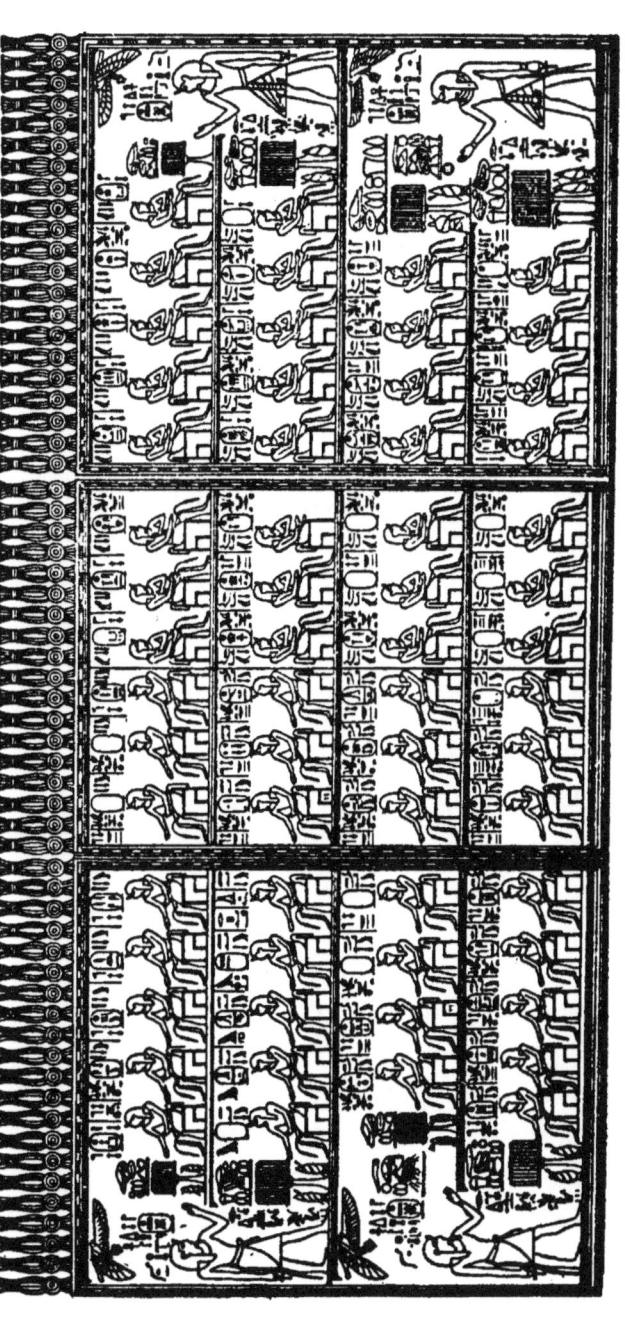

THE KARNAK LIST
(From Budge, *History of Egypt*.)

THE EGYPTIAN INSCRIPTIONS 171

cannot be overestimated. Still, it leaves out four kings at the end of the Second Dynasty, but furnishes in their stead another name, *Zazai*, of whom the other lists, except perhaps the *Turin Papyrus* (*Bebti*), know nothing. The inference is that these four kings did not reign in Abydos, where *Zazai* had made himself independent at that time. The same phenomenon occurs again after the numbers 16, 17, 18, 24, 25, 29. The Sixth Dynasty, Nos. 34–40, is given *in toto*. Then follow 16 names, of whom we otherwise know nothing, and after these the two last kings of the Eleventh Dynasty. This list was evidently meant to furnish the names of kings in Abydos, while the kings of the Eighth Dynasty ruled in Memphis, those of the Ninth and Tenth Dynasties ruled in Heracleopolis, and the first kings of the Eleventh Dynasty reigned in Thebes. Then follow all the kings of the Twelfth Dynasty, except *Sebeknefrure*, and immediately after, the kings of the Eighteenth Dynasty, beginning with *Ahmose*, but omitting *Hatshepsut*, *Amenhotep IV* and his successors, and ending with the kings of the Nineteenth Dynasty, *Haremhab*, *Ramses I*, and *Seti I*.

The Sakkara-List

Tunroi, a scribe of *Ramses II*, placed in his mortuary chamber at *Sakkara* a list of Egyptian kings, which, unfortunately, is only partially preserved. It contains 58 names, beginning with *Miebis*, who reigned in the middle of the First Dynasty, and then continues to the end of the Sixth Dynasty. It then takes up the two last kings of the Eleventh and all the kings of the Twelfth Dynasty, but gives these in reverse order. Thereafter it gives the same kings of the Eighteenth and Nineteenth Dynasties as are found in the *Abydos-List*, with the addition of *Ramses II*.

As *Ramses II* was a son of *Seti I*, the reason for the difference in the lists compiled in the reigns of these two kings can hardly have been a genealogical one, and we may therefore infer that *Tunroi* regarded his kings only as legitimate rulers over the Sakkara region.

The Palermo Stone

Of this remarkable document only a small part has been preserved. In its original form it gave the history of Egypt from predynastic time down toward the end of the Fifth Dynasty. On the obverse, the first line gave probably the names of the gods, who had ruled Egypt, then the kings of Upper Egypt, and finally the kings of Lower Egypt. Of these latter nine names are preserved: —*pu, Seka, Khayu, Tiu, Thesh, Neheb, Wazenez, Makh,* —*a.*

The rest of the stone gave the annals of the kings of United Egypt, beginning probably with *Menes*. For each year a rectangle is marked off on the stone, and within that rectangle are recorded the chief events of that year. This shows that in ancient Egypt the same custom of naming the year was followed as in ancient Babylonia, and the *Palermo Stone* corresponds, accordingly, with the Babylonian *Date-Lists*.

If the stone had been preserved intact, we would now be in possession of a correct chronology of the first four and a part of the Fifth Dynasty of Egypt. The extant fragment was broken somewhere from the middle of the stone, and this excludes even a close estimate of the length of the stone and the number of rectangles on each line.

Sethe and Ed. Meyer have attempted to restore the length of the stone, and upon their respective estimates they have based calculations for the number of years of the first three dynasties:

	Sethe	Meyer
Lines 2 and 3, First Dynasty........	253 years	210 years
Lines 4 and 5, Second Dynasty.....	302 years	224 years
Lines 6, Third Dynasty.............	100 (110) years	46 years
Total................	655 years	480 years

The Turin Papyrus

The Turin Museum possesses some fragments of a papyrus which once gave a complete chronology of Egypt, from the predynastic time down into the Eighteenth Dynasty. This papyrus has been broken into small fragments, now numbering about three hundred, but large parts of it are lost. Seyfarth, Sethe, Ed. Meyer, and others have attempted to reconstruct the order of these fragments, and the results which these scholars have achieved seem in the main acceptable and correct.

This papyrus gave not only the names and the order of the kings, but also the length of the reigns and of the dynasties, and here and there totals of years from *Menes* to the end of a certain king's reign, but these dates are often mutilated or entirely broken off, and there is constant uncertainty as to the proper arrangement of the fragments. It seems to me, therefore, that the exaggerated importance which some scholars have lately ascribed to this document should be somewhat minimized, especially if it be used for the purpose of showing that the Manethonian lists are almost wholly untrustworthy.

To this it should be added that the *Turin Papyrus* does not give the exact succession of kings of Egypt, but is confined to a certain city. For the dark periods, Dynasties VII–XI and XIII–XVII, it furnishes long lists of kings otherwise unknown. In those periods several contemporary dynasties ruled in their respective cities, and lists of those kings should therefore be accepted with caution. The *Turin Papyrus* stands in this respect on a par with the *Karnak-* and *Abydos-Lists*.

Nor should its dates of reigns always be accepted as final, viz., the Manethonian and Eratosthenian dates, for it is quite possible that a lower date in the *Turin Papyrus* may be accounted for by a coregency, of which the other lists have taken no account. We have already seen how common this phenomenon is in the Babylonian lists, and we should expect the same phenomena to occur again and again in Egypt.

In reconstructing the chronology of Egypt, the testimony of the *Turin Papyrus* can therefore not be allowed to exclude that of the other lists, but will enable us to check their data whenever we are absolutely certain of the relevancy of its testimony.

Minimum Dates

On the Egyptian monuments occur quite frequently references to certain years in a king's reign. Noting the highest year of each king, we are enabled to fix the lowest number of years that such a king could have reigned. We are, however, cautioned against the assumption that such dates should always indicate the full length of his reign. On the other hand, coregencies are seldom included in such statements.

PLATE VIII

Obverse

THE PALERMO STONE
(From Breasted, *History of Egypt.*)

This is mainly the material from which we must reconstruct the chronology of Egypt.

In order to apply this material, we must find some certain dates, where we can begin the reconstruction of this chronology. These desiderata are furnished by the *Sothic* and New-Moon dates.

B. ASTRONOMICAL DATES

The Sirius-Star

In Egypt the Calendar year consisted of 365 days, divided into 12 months of 30 days and five intercalary days. The Egyptians, however, discovered, quite early, that this year was one-fourth of a day too short. In four years this shortage amounted to a whole day; in 100 years the difference was 25 days; in 1,460 years it was a whole year; i. e., the Egyptians had counted 1,461 years, while only 1,460 Julian years had elapsed. They knew of this difference at the time, but did not pay serious attention to it, because in a lifetime it was hardly noticeable, amounting only to about 15 to 20 days. Their real New-Year's Day, the first of Thoth, fell on the twenty-first day of July. On that day Sirius or Sothis (=the Dog Star) was first seen, in the latitude of Memphis, to rise with and disappear in the glow of the rising sun, and this was called the *heliacal rising of Sothis.*

This happened, of course, once every year, and the space between each heliacal rising of Sirius was an even Gregorian year of 365 days, 5 hours, 48 minutes, and 48 seconds, but the Egyptians never discovered the real length of the Gregorian year, and were therefore satisfied to estimate their *Sothic* year as a Julian year of $365\frac{1}{4}$ days.

They did not, however, adjust the discrepancy between the Calendar year of 365 days and the *Sothic* year, by adding a leap-year day every fourth year. The discrepancy between the Calendar year and the *Sothic* year was permitted, as stated above, to accumulate indefinitely, and the outcome was, that only once in every 1,461 years did the New-Year's Day of the Calendar year coincide with the *S*othic New-Year, i. e., the heliacal rising of *S*irius occurred on the New-Year's Day of the Calendar only once in each 1,460 Julian years.

The Egyptians therefore celebrated annually not only the Calendar New-Year's Day, but also the annual feast of the heliacal rising of *S*irius.

Sothic Cycles

It is evident that if we could find a year when *S*irius rose on the Calendar New-Year's Day, we should be able to divide Egyptian chronology into *S*othic cycles of 1,460 years. If then the Egyptian inscriptions should offer us a certain year in the reign of some king, in which it was accurately stated how many days the Calendar New-Year's Day antedated the heliacal rising of *S*irius, we should be enabled to calculate that year with certainty, the mistake never being larger than three years, because *S*irius would continue to rise on the same day for three successive years. Both these desiderata are now at our disposal, and our first object will be to find the years when *S*irius rose on the Calendar New-Year's Day.

Censorinus

Censorinus, writing in 238 A. D., says that in that year the Calendar New-Year's Day was celebrated on the twenty-fifth of June, but that 99[1] years before, it was celebrated on the twenty-first of July, "on which day Sirius regularly rises in Egypt." As it takes four years for Sirius to fall one day behind the Calendar year, it would therefore have risen on the twenty-first day of July in the year 139 A. D. An even 99 years had elapsed between this Sothic date and the year 238 A. D., when Censorinus wrote. The difference in time between the Calendar New Year's Day and the rising of Sirius would in these 99 years amount to an even 25 days, and this is exactly the period from June 25 to July 21.

Censorinus' statement is thus proved to be correct, and the year 139 A. D. is an assured Sothic date, in which the New-Year's Day of the Calendar fell on the day of the heliacal rising of Sirius. As the Sothic Cycle consists of 1,460 years, the same phenomenon must have occurred every 1,460 Julian years before, i. e., in 1321 B. C., in 2781 B. C., and in 4241 B. C.

Era of Menophris

That these years were regarded as *termini* of *eras* can be shown in regard to the year 1321 B. C. Theon, a mathematician of Alexandria, has noted that 1,605 Egyptian years had elapsed from the beginning of the *Era of Menophris* to the beginning of the *Era of Diocletian*. This term of 1,605 Egyptian years corresponds to $1604^{1}/_{10}$ Julian years. The *Era of Augustus* ended, and the *Era of Diocletian* began, on June 13, 284 B. C. If we deduct

---

[1] Censorinus defined it as 100 years (*abhinc annos centum*) before 238 B. C., which, according to the Roman custom of including the last date in the number, carries us to the year 139 A. D. That this is the correct date is certain from the fact, that Censorinus also mentions the Roman consuls of that year, *imperatore Antonino Pio II et Brutio praesente consulibus*, who were consuls in 139 A. D.

1604$^1/_{10}$ years from this we are brought to the year 1321 B. C. This year, therefore, began an *Era*, here called the *Era of Menophris*. The only royal name of this time with which we can compare it is *Mn-ph(ti)-Re*, the throne-name of Ramses I. This king reigned, according to Josephus, 1 year, 4 months, and his reign began on or shortly before July 21, 1321 B. C., on which day *S*irius rose in that year.

This era is referred to by Manilius, according to *P*liny, who recorded that P. *L*icinius and Cn. Cornelius were consuls in the year 225 of this era.[1] *H*incks and Lepsius have emended this date to 1225, assuming that an *M* (*Mille* = 1,000) had fallen out of the *L*atin text. *P. Licinius* and *Cn. Cornelius* were consuls in the year 97 B. C., and these (emended) dates would carry us to 1321 B. C.[2]

Clement of Alexandria

The *Sothis* period is also mentioned by Chalcidius,[3] and Clement of *A*lexandria avers that the Exodus took place 345 years before the *Sothic* period, i. e., in 1665 B. C. Clement adds here the words, "*after Inachus*," which must indicate that the *Sothic* period began after the fall of Inachus, i. e., with the reign of *Danaus* in Argos. But *Danaus* is identical either with *Haremhab*, or with his successor, *Ramses I (Menophris)*, after whom this era was named.

---

[1] *Fuisse ejus conversionis annum P. Licinio, Cn. Cornelio Coss.* (M)CCXXV.

[2] According to the Roman custom of counting dates, the first year should be omitted, when adding or subtracting number of years.

[3] Comment. in Plat. Timaeum, *Canis* . . . . *hanc stellam Aegyptii Sothim vocant, cujus completus annus, qui Cynicus vocatur, annis mille quadringentis sexaginta.*

Era of 2781

The era of 2781 was also referred to in Manetho's *Sothis-Book*. Syncellus refers to it, but, readjusting it to his scheme of the duration of the world, he assigns its beginning to the year 2718 B. C. Manetho had stated that in the seven-hundredth year of that era (which was the fifth and last year of *Konkharis*) the *Hyksos* entered Egypt, and this would bring us to the year 2081 B. C.[1]

First Sothic Date

Within the *Sothic* cycle of 2781–1321 B. C. fall the Twelfth and Eighteenth Dynasties. It is very fortunate that three *Sothic* references have come down to us, one dated in the Twelfth, and two in the Eighteenth Dynasty, by which we are enabled to construct a reliable chronology of these two dynasties.

Among the papyri found at *Kahun* is a letter of a high-priest, addressed to his subordinates. In this letter it is stated that in the seventh year of *Sesostris III* the heliacal rising of Sirius would be celebrated on the sixteenth day of the eighth month, which means that in this year the Calendar New-Year's Day came seven months and fifteen days, or 225 days, earlier than the *Sirius*-festival. Multiplying this number 225 by 4, we get 900, which represents the number of years required for the Calendar New-Year's Day to come 225 days earlier than the heliacal rising of *Sirius*, since this *Sothic* cycle began in 2781 B. C. Subtracting 900 from 2,781, we obtain the year 1881 B. C. This papyrus was dated in the seventh year of *Sesostris III*, who accordingly became king in 1887 B. C.

---

[1] For this date of the *Hyksos*, see my *Sidelights on Biblical Chronology*.

The Second Sothic Date

On the *verso* of *P*apyrus Ebers occurs the following note:

Year 9, under the Majesty of the king of Upper and Lower Egypt Sezer-ka-Re, living forever:
New-Year's Festival, month 3, of the Shemu-season,[1] *day 9, the heliacal rising of the Sirius star.*

Sezer-ka-Re is the throne-name of *Amenhotep I*, and the *Shemu*-season is the third season of the year. This date refers, therefore, to the ninth day of the eleventh month, i. e., 10 months and 8 days or, 308 days, had elapsed from the Calendar New-Year's Day to the heliacal rising of Sirius. Multiplying this number by 4, we obtain 1,232, which represents the number of years that had elapsed from the beginning of this *Sothic* cycle in 2781 until the ninth year of *Amenhotep I*.

This note in *P*apyrus Ebers was therefore written in the leap-year period 1549–1546,[2] and *Amenhotep I* became king of Egypt some time between 1557–1554 B. C.

Third Sothic Date

Thutmose III celebrated a *S*irius-festival[3] on the twenty-eighth day of the eleventh month. This gives us 327 days, or 1,308 years, since the beginning of the *Sothic* cycle

---

[1] The Egyptians divided the year into three seasons, each consisting of four months, after which the five intercalary (*epagomene*) days were added:

Season	Months	Season	Months	Season	Months
1. *Akhet*	1. *Thoth* 2. *Paophi* 3. *Hathor* 4. *Khoiak*	2. *Pert*	1. *Tybi* 2. *Mechi*r 3. *Phamenoth* 4. *Pharmuthi*	3. *Shemu*	1. *Pachons* 2. *Pauni* 3. *Epiphi* 4. *Mesore*

5 intercalary (*epagomene*) days.

[2] I. e., this heliacal rising of Sirius might have taken place in any one of these years.

[3] On a calendar fragment from Elephantine. LD. III, 43 *e*.

in 2781. This Sirius festival would then have been celebrated about 1473 B.C. On the tablet on which this

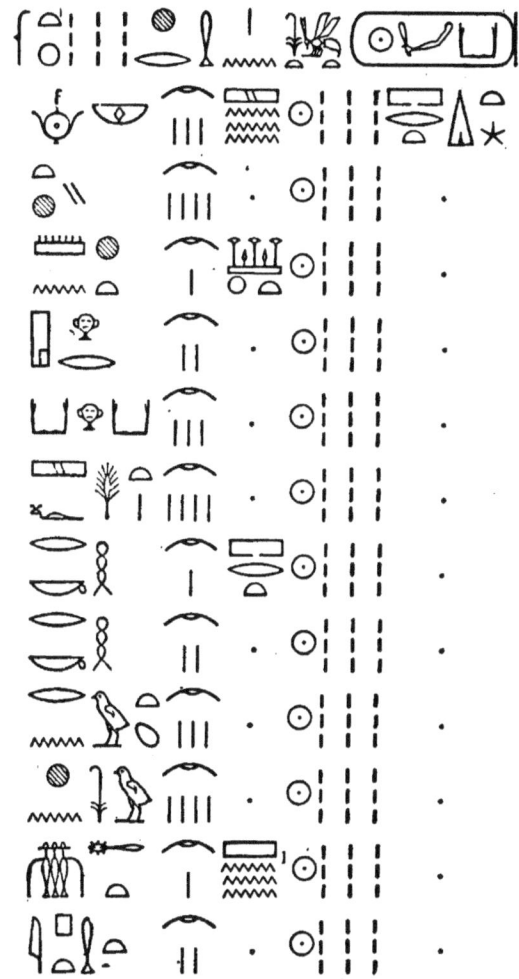

LIST OF MOVABLE FESTIVALS, ON REVERSE OF
PAPYRUS EBERS
(From Meyer, *Aegyptische Chronologie*.)

festival is recorded the year of *Thutmose's* reign has been broken away, and all that we can conclude from it is that this festival was celebrated during some year between

1473–1470 B. C., and that *Thutmose III* reigned at that time.

New-Moon Festivals

From the inscriptions of *Thutmose III* it is known that a New-Moon Festival was celebrated on the twenty-first day of *P*achon in the twenty-third year of his reign, and also that another New-Moon Festival was celebrated on the thirtieth day of Mechir in the twenty-fourth year of his reign.

Now it is certain that he began his reign on the fourth day of *P*achon. The twenty-first day of *P*achon of his twenty-third year is then the eighteenth day of that year of his reign. Of that year, then, there remained 365–18 or 347 days. From the twenty-first day of *P*achon to the thirtieth day of Mechir of this twenty-fourth year are 302 days, which should be added to the above number, giving a total of 649 days between the twenty-ninth day of *P*achon in his twenty-third year to the thirtieth day of Mechir in his twenty-fourth year.

It is certain that the twenty-third year of *Thutmose III* falls somewhere about 1480 B. C. There remains then to be found a year near 1480, in which there was a new moon on the twenty-first day of *P*achon and another, 649 days later, on the thirtieth day of Mechir.

By the help of *Oppolzer's* tables it would be possible to find these dates, if we could be sure which year—*S*irius or Calendar year—is here meant. Mahler assumed that these dates referred to the *S*irius-year. Eisenlohr has, however, shown that this is impossible, and that only the Calendar year could be meant. In this Eisenlohr is undoubtedly correct, and Mahler has later accepted his conclusion.

Both Mahler and Eisenlohr calculated on the basis of the New-Moon Festival having been celebrated on the day of the moon's conjunction. Lehmann has, however, doubted the accuracy of that method, and claims that the New-Moon Festival was celebrated on the day when the new moon became visible. And he then assumes that such a day comes about two days later than the astronomical New-Moon Day, and that therefore these dates of *Thutmose III* should be sought for in years when the astronomical new moon fell on the nineteenth of *P*achon and the twenty-eighth of Mechir. This view has been accepted by Ed. Meyer and Breasted.

This latter hypothesis cannot be admitted. The new moon may at one time be visible one day after the conjunction, and at another time not before the third or fourth, and these dates therefore would leave us in entire uncertainty. On the other hand, we know that the Babylonians were able to calculate correctly the conjunctions of the moon, and celebrated their New-Moon Festivals on the day of the conjunction. But it must be admitted that if the Babylonians were able to calculate the conjunctions of the moon, then the Egyptians must have known them also. Their civilization was so similar, and intercourse between the two lands so frequent, that such an important matter could not have been unknown in one country and well known in the other. It follows necessarily, then, if this hypothesis is correct, that the Egyptians celebrated their New-Moon Festivals on the days of the moon's conjunction and not one, two, or three days later, when the moon became visible. Lehmann's argument that the modern *A*rabs celebrate their New-Moon Festivals when the moon becomes visible is no proof whatever for the custom of the ancient Egyptians. These latter calculated the appearance of the *S*irius-star, and celebrated that festival on the calculated day, whether the *S*irius-star could be seen or was hidden by clouds. It is against reason that a whole people should delay the celebration of a well-known and necessary festival until they were able to see the moon—not only subjecting themselves to the uncertainties of the weather, but also failing to remember that in some months the moon could be seen on the first day, and in others only on the third day, even under favorable weather conditions. These festivals, indeed, were calculated beforehand, and set down in their calendars of feasts, and were celebrated on the day on which the moon passed the conjunction.

Mahler and Eisenlohr are therefore correct in looking for the real astronomical new moon on the twenty-first of *P*achon and the thirtieth of Mechir. Now it happens that in the year 1482 B. C., there was a new moon on the twenty-first of *P*achon, which corresponds to our May 16, and also a new moon on the thirtieth of Mechir the following year, corresponding to our February 24.

As the first of these dates fell in the twenty-third year of *Thutmose III*, and as he began to reign on the fourth of *P*achon, his coronation took place on May 4, 1504 B.C., and he died on March 18, 1450 B. C., having reigned 53 years, 10 months, 19 days.

C. EGYPTIAN CHRONOLOGY

Combining these *Sothic* and New-Moon dates with the data from the chronological material already presented, we shall now proceed to reconstruct the chronology of Egypt, and shall begin with

Dynasty XVIII

This dynasty began with *Ahmose* and ended with *Amenhotep IV* (*Ikhnaton*) and his successors. Then follows the Nineteenth Dynasty, the first ruler of which was *Haremhab*.

For the Eighteenth Dynasty we have the following certain dates:

1. *Amenhotep I* became king about 1556–1554 B. C.[1]
2. *Thutmose III* reigned from 1504–1450 B. C.[2]
3. *Amenhotep IV* (*Ikhnaton*) must have ascended the throne before 1405, because *Kuri-Galzu I*, of Babylonia, sent letters to him, and the death year of *Kuri-Galzu I* cannot be placed later than 1405 B. C.[3]
4. *Ramses I* began to reign in 1321 B. C.[4] He was preceded by *Haremhab*, who, according to Josephus, reigned 4 years, 1 month, i. e., he became king in 1325 B. C., which year would therefore mark the fall of the Eighteenth Dynasty.

If we now apply to this last year the dates furnished by Josephus concerning the reigns of *Amenhotep IV* and his successors, amounting to 82 years, 2 months, the accession of *Amenhotep IV* falls in 1407 B. C. This date is so strongly corroborated by the *Amarna Letters*, that we may regard it as established and correct. This fact tends to show that the dates of Josephus are practically correct, which is what we should expect in view of the fact that he gives minutely, not only the years, but also the months of each reign.

We shall therefore take Josephus' dates as a basis for our further calculations, and starting with 1407 B. C. we

---

[1] See above page 180.　　[3] *Ibid.*, p. 33.
[2] *Ibid.*, p. 184.　　[4] *Ibid.*, p. 177.

DYNASTY XVIII—COMPARATIVE CHART

Sakkara List	Abydos List	Josephus	Syncellus	Africanus	Eusebius
Dynasty XVIII					
47. Nebpeh(ti)re	66. Nebpeh(ti)re	1. Tethmosis (I) 25 y. 4 m.	1. Amosis and Tethmoris 26 y.	1. Amos	1. Amosis 25 y.
48. [Seserka]ye	67. Seserkare				
49. [Okheper]kare	68. Okheperkare	2. Khebron 13 y.	2. Khebron 13 y.	2. Khebros 13 y.	2. Khebron 13 y.
50. [Okheper]nere	69. Okhepernere	3. Amenophis (I) 20 y. 7 m.	3. Amenphes 15 y.	3. Amenophthis 24 y.	3. Amenophis 21 y.
		4. (Sister) Amesses 21 y. 9 m.	4. Amenses 11 y.	4. Amensis 22 y.	. . .
51. [Menkheperre]	70. Menkheperre	5. Mephres 12 y. 9 m.	5. Misphragmouthosis 16 y.	5. Misaphris 13 y.	4. Miphres 12 y.
52. [Okheperure]	71. Okheperure	6. Mephrimouthosis 25 y. 10 m.	6. Misphres 23 y.	6. Misphragmouthosis 26 y.	5. Misphragmouthosis 26 y.
53. [Menkheperure]	72. Menkheperure	7. Tythmosis (IV) 9 y. 8 m.	7. Touthmosis 39 y.	7. Touthmosis 9 y.	6. Touthmosis 9 y.
54. [Nebma(t)re]	73. Nebma(t)re	8. Amenophis (III) 30 y. 10 m.	8. Amenophis 34 y.	8. Amenophis 31 y.	7. Amenophis 31 y.
		9. Oros 36 y. 5 m.	9. Oros 48 y.	9. Oros 37 y.	8. Oros 36 y.
		10. Akerkheres (I) 12 y. 1 m.	10. Akhenkheres 25 y.	10. Akherres 32 y.	9. Akherkheres 16 y.
		11. Rathotis 9 y.	11. Athoris 29 y.	11. Rathos 6 y.	. . .
		12. Akerkheres (II) 12 y. 5 m.	12. Khenkheres 26 y.	12. Khebres 12 y.	10. Akherres 8 y.
		13. Akerkheres (III) 12 y. 3 m.	13. Akherres 8 or 30 y.	13. Akherres 12 y.	11. Kherres 15 y.

shall apply them in turn to the predecessors of *Amenhotep IV*. *Amenhotep III* would then have reigned from 1438–1407; *Thutmose IV* from 1447–1438; *Amenhotep II* from 1473–1447; *Thutmose III* from 1486–1473; *Hatshepsut* from 1508–1486 B. C. Here it should be noted that, according to Josephus, *Thutmose III* reigned only 12 years, 9 months, although his monuments indicate his reign as extending over almost 54 years. That Josephus is correct is, however, evident from the fact that the monuments indicate unmistakably that *Hatshepsut* was a coregent with *Thutmose III* for a long period, and that the first record of his receiving taxes from Syria falls in his fifteenth year, while his annals begin with his twenty-second year. A part of his long reign must therefore be assigned to a coregency with *Hatshepsut*, and Josephus' allotment of 1504–1486 as the period of this coregency is not only reasonable but evidently accurate. It is also certain from the monuments[1] that *Amenhotep II* was a coregent with *Thutmose III*, although the duration of his coregency is not clear; but when later on we return to this, we shall find that Josephus is correct even in this date. One thing is certain, the reigns of *Amenhotep II*, *Thutmose IV*, and *Amenhotep III* preceded 1407 B. C., and the only reasonable way of adjusting this is to accept the solution offered by Manetho and Josephus.

Prior to *Hatshepsut's* reign the dates of Josephus are confused. *Amenhotep I (Amenophis)* has been placed next before *Amenses (Hatshepsut)*, while he ought to have come before *Thutmose I*. This confusion can be accounted for by the fact that both *Ah-mose* and *Thut-mose* mean "child of the moon-god," and that both reigned about twenty-

[1] See Breasted, *ARE.*, Vol. II, §184.,

five years, with only one reign (that of *Amenhotep I*) between them. As *Ahmose* expelled the *Hyksos*, and as Josephus came to identify *Ahmose* with *Thutmose I*, the latter's reign came to head his Eighteenth Dynasty. *Khebron*, or *Thutmose II*, who was a coregent with his father, *Thutmose I*, came therefore to be recorded next to *Thutmose I*, and after them *Amenhotep I*. Josephus states that *Amenses (Hatshepsut)* was a "sister," evidently of the preceding king, who according to his list is *Amenhotep I*, but it is certain that she was the sister of *Thutmose II*, and this proves again that Josephus had placed *Amenhotep I* in the wrong place. The *Abydos-* and *Sakkara-Lists*, as well as all other monuments bearing on the case, indicate plainly that *Amenhotep I* preceded *Thutmose I*. *Thutmose I* would therefore have reigned from 1533–1508, and *Amenhotep I* from 1554–1533. The reign of *Ahmose* falls back of 1554.

The Feud of the Thutmosids

At the close of the reign of *Thutmose I* the succession of kings becomes very much confused, and a satisfactory explanation of the sequence of events in the succeeding period has not yet been given. Four persons, more or less interrelated, seem to have been kings of Egypt within a very short time: *Thutmose I*, *Thutmose II*, *Thutmose III* and Queen *Hatshepsut*. On several monuments of *Hatshepsut* her name has been erased and replaced by the names of *Thutmose I* and *II*. Again, it seems as though *Thutmose III* had reigned only for a short while and had then been superseded for a brief period by *Thutmose I* and *II*. Finally, it is held by some that *Thutmose III* at first ruled alone, and later associated with himself *Hatshepsut*, who then obtained the upper hand of the government until her death, when *Thutmose III* became sole ruler.

*S*ethe has endeavored to solve these difficulties, and his solution has been accepted by Breasted. These scholars hold: (1) that the king who inserted a royal name in the place of another name is none other than the king who bore the inserted name; (2) that because the names of *Thutmose I* and *II* are inserted in the place of the names of *Hatshepsut*, these kings made the erasures, and must have reigned some time after *Hatshepsut's* accession; (3) that *Thutmose III* was the husband of *Hatshepsut*, and he must therefore have reigned some time before the deaths of both *Thutmose I* and *II;* (4) that *Hatshepsut* was at first only "great king's wife" of *Thutmose III*, but later became coregent with him. From these premises *S*ethe offers the following solution of the problem: (1) *Thutmose III* reigned alone for a time; (2) *Hatshepsut* was forced upon *Thutmose III* as coregent; (3) about the sixth year of *Thutmose III*, *Thutmose I* and *II* together gained the throne. These latter were, however, not able to suppress *Thutmose III*, who, after the death of *Thutmose I*, became coregent with *Thutmose II*, who died in the eighth year of *Thutmose III;* (4) *Hatshepsut* ruled together with *Thutmose III* for twelve years more, when she died and *Thutmose III* became sole king.

Breasted admits, however, "that a number of difficulties beset any theory of the Thutmosid struggle," and that "the above reconstruction, in view of recent discoveries, is perhaps not to be regarded as finally demonstrated."

In reconsidering this question and attempting to solve its many difficulties the following facts should be considered:

1) It cannot be proved conclusively from the monuments that *Thutmose III* reigned before the death of *Thutmose I*.

2) *Thutmose III* was married to *Hatshepset*, not to *Hatshepsut*, and we may therefore assume that the great Queen *Hatshepsut* was another person than the Queen of *Thutmose III*.

3) *Thutmose III* bore a deadly hatred toward *Hatshepsut*, who stood between him and the throne, and *Thutmose III* therefore would most likely be the king who erased her name, and on monuments built before his accession he would insert the names of either *Thutmose I* or *II*, but on monuments built after his proclamation as king, he would insert his own name.

From these premises we shall now attempt to reconstruct the succession of these kings.

Thutmose I (throne-name: *O-kheper-ka-Re*) had two consorts, *Ahmose*, and his half-sister *Mutnofret*. By the first wife he had two daughters, *Khebt-noferu*, who died in youth, and *Hatshepsut*. By his second wife he had a son, who became King *Thutmose II*.

Thutmose II was coregent with his father *Thutmose I* for 13 years, and was married to his older half-sister *Hatshepsut*. He died a few months before the death of his father, in 1509, and therefore became coregent about 1522 B. C. After the death of *Thutmose II*, *Thutmose I* took steps to insure the succession for his daughter, the queen-widow, *Hatshepsut*, and on the New-Year's Day of the next year, 1508 B. C., she was crowned queen of Egypt. A few months[1] later *Thutmose I* died.

By the help of the priests of Amon at Thebes, *Thutmose*,

[1] About 6 months.

DYNASTY XVIII 191

a young priest of that temple and morganatic son of either *Thutmose I* or *Thutmose II*, succeeded in proclaiming himself king of Egypt, and as king *Thutmose III* he set up a counter-reign against *Hatshepsut*. After four years the court party supporting the queen effected a reconciliation on the terms that *Hatshepsut* should be the queen and ruler of Egypt, and that *Thutmose III* should be her successor.

When *Hatshepsut* died, in 1486 B. C., *Thutmose III* became sole king until he appointed his son *Amenhotep II* as his coregent in 1473 B. C., and died in 1450 B. C. According to this analysis, the chronology of the Eighteenth Dynasty would be as follows:

Ahmose	25 y.	ca. 1579–1554 B. C.
Amenhotep I	20 y., 7 m.	1554–1533 B. C.
Thutmose I	25 y., 4 m.	1533–1508 B. C.
(*Thutmose II*	13 y.	1522–1509 B. C.)
Hatshepsut	21 y., 9 m.	1508–1486 B.
Thutmose III, whole reign	53 y., 11 m.	1504–1450 B.
Sole King	12 y., 9 m.	1486–1473 B.
Amenhotep II	25 y., 10 m.	1473–1447 B.
Thutmose IV	9 y., 8 m.	1447–1438 B.
Amenhotep III	30 y., 10 m.	1438–1407 B.
Amenhotep IV	36 y., 5 m.	1407–1370 B.
Akerkheres I	12 y., 1 m.	1370–1358 B.
Tutenkhamon	9 y.	1358–1349 B.
Akerkheres II	12 y., 5 m.	1349–1337 B. C.
Akerkheres III	12 y., 3 m.	1337–1325 B. C.

Ahmose

This king expelled the *Hyksos*, and became the founder of the Eighteenth Dynasty. His highest year on the monuments is year 22, but it is probable that he reigned at least 25 years. Josephus, in identifying him both with *Thutmose I* and with the *Pharaoh* of the Exodus, assigns him 25 years. As his son, *Amenhotep I*, came to the throne in 1554, *Ahmose's* reign began about 1579 B. C.

The war against the *Hyksos* lasted for at least the first half of his reign, as it included three sieges of the city of Avaris, the stronghold of the *Hyksos*, a rebellion in Southern Egypt, a war against Nubia, and a siege of Saruhen which lasted not less than three, and perhaps six years. Josephus begins the Eighteenth Dynasty with the expulsion of the *Hyksos*, and assigns 245 years to the period between this event and the accession of *Ramses I*. As *Ramses I* became king in 1321 B. C., the expulsion of the *Hyksos* falls in 1566 B. C. And this date is in full accord with the monuments.

Amenhotep I

The *Sothic* date in the ninth year of *Amenhotep I* fixes the beginning of his reign to 1557/4 B. C. According to the chronology of Josephus, his accession year should be 1554 B. C. His highest date on the monuments is year 10, but Josephus assigns him 20 years, 7 months. This is probably correct, and he reigned accordingly from 1554–1534/3 B. C. He was succeeded by his son,

Thutmose I

Josephus assigns 25 years, 4 months, to *Thutmose I*, 1533–1508 B. C. In his second year he carried on a war against Nubia and later on he made a war-expedition against Naharina on the upper Euphrates. In this war is also included the conquest of Palestine, for he received tribute from the "sand-dwellers" (*Heriu-sha*).

DYNASTY XVIII 193

Thutmose II

This king was only a coregent with his father, *Thutmose I*. On his death *Thutmose I* appointed his daughter *Hatshepsut* to be his successor. *Hatshepsut* claims that her coronation took place on New-Year's Day, while her father was still living, but she does not make a single allusion to *Thutmose II*. *Thutmose I* died in 1508 B. C., and *Thutmose II* must therefore have died some time before this—not later than 1509, and possibly as early as 1511 B. C. Josphus assigns him 13 years, and he would then have become coregent in 1524 (or at the latest 1522 B. C.). The only events of his reign, known from the monuments, are a war in his first year against Nubia (Ethiopia), and, probably in the next year, a war against the *Shasu*, or Bedwin of Southern Palestine.

Hatshepsut

This remarkable woman was the daughter of *Thutmose I* and half-sister of *Thutmose II*, after whose death she became coregent with her father, and then, after his death, queen of Egypt, 1508 B. C. Her throne-name was *Maꜥt-ka-Re*, and her birth-name *Amen-Khnemet-Hatshepsut*, the first part of which Manetho rendered by *Amensis* or *Amessis*. Josephus assigns her 21 years, 9 months, and she would, therefore, have died in 1486 B. C. She was a highly talented woman, noble in character, energetic in carrying out her plans, and undoubtedly the most gifted woman of Egypt. Numerous monuments—among them her obelisks and the temples at Medinet *H*abu and Benihasan (*S*peos Artemidos)—testify to her artistic taste and lofty conceptions. Her great expedition to *P*unt is a strong testimony to her executive ability. The prosperous and peaceful years of her reign contributed to make Egypt the foremost power of the earth in that time.

Thutmose III

The monuments contradict each other in regard to the parentage of *Thutmose III*, some assigning T*hutmose I* and others *Thutmose II*. His mother was a royal concubine. While yet a boy, he was placed in the temple of *A*mon at *K*arnak, where he advanced rapidly, being first appointed priest, then prophet, and finally elevated to the honorable rank of "*Pillar of his mother.*" This position he used, supported by the mighty priesthood of *A*mon, to further his ambition and his own interests, and finally seized the throne of Egypt. After the death of *Thutmose I*, a woman sat on the throne of the *Pharaohs*, a fact that was almost a scandal in the eyes of the *A*mon priesthood, and especially so to *Thutmose.*

On a great *A*mon-feast in *K*arnak, in the year 1504 B. C., when the statue of *A*mon was carried in procession, the god stopped before T*hutmose*, who was standing in "the king's place," in the northern hypostyle, nodded to him and proclaimed him king. The whole proceeding was of course a prearranged plot on the part of the priests. *Thutmose* promptly laid claim to the throne, on the ground, not of rightful inheritance, but of divine appointment. He set up his rule in opposition to *Hatshepsut*, and we have monuments of his, dated in his second and fifth years. The court party, however, was loyal to *Hatshepsut* and a compromise was effected, by which T*hutmose III* was married to *Hatshepset*, a daughter of *Hatshepsut*, and made heir to the throne. We have therefore no monuments of *Thutmose III* for the following period until the death of *Hatshepsut* in 1486 B. C., except a record of receiving tribute from *P*alestine by T*hutmose III* in his fifteenth year, 1490 B. C. *Hatshepsut* was now very old, and she may have appointed him to superintend the foreign office. All other monuments of *Thutmose III*, which are very numerous, are dated after the death of *Hatshepsut*, i. e., after 1486 B. C. *Hatshepsut* had ruled both Egypt and the provinces with statesmanlike energy and wisdom, and was universally loved. *P*eace reigned over all her great empire. But immediately on her death *P*alestine and *S*yria revolted, and in 1483 B. C. T*hutmose III* had to march into *S*yria to quell the rebellion and force *S*yria to recognize him as king. Then began his long series of seventeen *S*yrian campaigns. In his annals he dates them after his first accession in 1504 B. C., and his first campaign is therefore dated in his twenty-second year, 1483 B. C. These campaigns lasted for twenty years, to 1463 B. C. Other campaigns were carried on in the south against Nubia, while great building operations went on at home, especially in the temple of Amon at *K*arnak. From the monuments we know that he reigned 53 years, 11 months, and his accession is fixed by his New-Moon dates as having taken place in 1504 B. C. He died therefore, in 1450 B. C., and was coregent with *Hatshepsut* until her death in 1486 B. C. The fact of his coregency is supported by the profound silence in which his monuments pass by the first twenty-one years of his reign. Manetho assigns him, however, only 12 years, 9 months, while his monuments make him carry on his wars in *S*yria until 1463 B. C. This discrepancy, referred to above, can, however, be explained on the assumption that he appointed his son as coregent in 1473 B. C.

Amenhotep II

Two facts in the reign of *Amenhotep II* deserve special notice: (1) the scarcity of monuments from his long reign of almost twenty-six years, and (2) the few war expeditions undertaken by him. If his long reign had been an entirely independent one, we should have expected to find a number of monuments erected by him, somewhat akin to the great undertakings of his father, *Thutmose III*. Even his son, *Thutmose IV*, who reigned only about nine years, erected obelisks and built temples, but of *Amenhotep II* we know only that he set up a few columns in the southern half of the hypostyle of *Thutmose I*, which was razed by *Hatshepsut* to make room for her obelisks.

In regard to his wars, we know that he made an expedition to Nubia in his third year, and that he had already at that time directed a campaign against *Syria*. This Syrian campaign was undoubtedly carried out in his second year. After a battle on the Orontes, he proceeded to Niy and Ikathi, and then returned to Egypt. But the Turra inscription of *Minhotep* shows that *Amenhotep II* had been in Naharina and there erected a tablet, although this is unnoticed in his own account of the war.

Now *Thutmose III* was in Naharina in the year 1472 B. C., on his great eighth campaign, and erected then and there his stela. Our assumption is that *Amenhotep II* became coregent in 1473 B. C., and his second year was 1472, i. e., the very year when *Thutmose III* made his great campaign in Naharina. The inference is that there were two Egyptian armies in the field that year, one led by *Thutmose III*, operating in Naharina, and another led by *Amenhotep II*, operating on the Orontes, and that the two armies finally joined each other somewhere near the

Euphrates. That this assumption is correct is shown by his *K*arnak stela, where his Asiatic campaign is recorded, for *Amenhotep* ends this inscription with the following words:

"*By the good god, lord of the Two Lands, lord of offerings,* [name lost], *beloved of Amon, protector of him who is in Thebes, celebrator of the feasts of the house of Amon, lord of Thebes,* [- - - -] *son of Re, Thutmose, given life forever.*"

This makes it certain that *Amenhotep II* was a coregent with T*hutmose III*, and it seems probable that the latter had added these lines to *Amenhotep's* inscription.

Thutmose (*III*) is here referred to as one "who is in Thebes." This is corroborated by another fact, namely, that T*hutmose III* always bears, in his later years, the title "ruler of Thebes," while *Amenhotep II* likewise and persistently calls himself "ruler of *H*eliopolis." These two titles are at once seen to be of great importance, for they indicate that while these two kings were coregents, one lived in Thebes and the other in *H*eliopolis. In the latter city we should naturally look, then, for the monuments of *Amenhotep II*, but as the monuments of that city have been destroyed, only a slight record has been left of his building undertakings.

Amenhotep II died in 1447 B. C., three years after the death of his father, *Thutmose III*, and this circumstance explains why so few events are recorded as dating from his reign, because it is only natural that all wars carried on in the lifetime of *Thutmose III* would be attributed to the latter king.

Thutmose IV

Amenhotep II was succeeded by one of his sons, *Thutmose IV*, but it is doubtful whether the latter was his oldest son. The only known monument which gives the names of the sons of *Amenhotep II* is a stela of *Heqerneheh*, but most of the names have been erased, probably by *Thutmose IV* himself. His highest date on the monuments is year 8, but Josephus assigns him 9 years, 8 months, i. e., 1447–1438 B. C., and this is undoubtedly correct.

Amenhotep III

Amenhotep III (throne-name: $Nib\text{-}ma^c(t)\text{-}Re$; in the *Amarna Letters: Nimmuria;* in Josephus: *Amenophis*) was the son of *Thutmose IV* and Queen *Mutemuya*. He built the beautiful temple of *Luxor* and the *Memnonion*, and was a great patron of art. In the latter part of his reign he made an expedition against *Syria*. His highest date on the monuments is his thirty-sixth year. Josephus, however, assigns him only 30 years, 10 months. It is quite probable that Josephus is correct, and that his last five years constituted a coregency with his son *Amenhotep IV* or *Ikhnaton*. This latter king built his residence-city at *Amarna* at the beginning of his reign. Among the *Amarna Letters* from the *Asiatic* princes are a number addressed to *Amenhotep III*, and evidently belong to the last years of his reign. As there have not been found in Amarna any other foreign dispatches addressed to other Egyptian kings of this dynasty, it is evident that these letters were sent to *Amenhotep III* after the city of Amarna was built, and as the foreign office was removed to this city, they were sent to that place. This proves indubitably that *Amenhotep III* was living after the city of Amarna was built, and he must then have associated his son *Ikhnaton* with him as coregent. The date of Josephus is therefore to be accepted as correct, indicating his sole reign from 1438–1407 B. C., and his date on the monuments suggests that he died in 1402 B. C., five years after the accession of his son. *Amenhotep III* also built a temple in Soleb, Nubia, and here *P*rofessor Breasted has lately discovered a city, *Gem-Aton*, dedicated to the same *Aton*-worship, for which *A*marna became celebrated. It seems therefore an open question, whether the kernel of this faith was not planted by *Amenhotep III* and his queen, T*eye*.

Amenhotep IV or Ikhnaton

Ikhnaton (throne-name: *Nefer-kheperu-Re-wa-n-Re;* birth-name: *Amenhotep IV, Ikhnaton;* Josephus: *Oros*) was the son of *Amenhotep III* and Queen T*eye*. His birth-name was *Amenhotep IV*, but after his introduction of the *Aton*-faith, or the worship of the Sun, he changed his name to *Ikh-n-itn* (or *Ikhnaton*), "the splendor of *Aton*." This new faith was of *S*emitic origin, for the Egyptian *Aton* corresponds to *S*emitic *Adonai*, Greek *Adonis*. On account of this change of faith, he built a new city, *Akhet-Aton*, modern *A*marna, as his capital. The Amon-priesthood of *K*arnak placed the new religion under ban. This led finally to an open break between the adherents of the new religion and the Amon priesthood. We are not now able to follow the development of this struggle, but it ended disastrously for the "heretics." The highest monumental date of *Amenhotep IV* is year 17, but Josephus assigns him 36 years, 5 months, and 46 years for his sons-in-law, who succeeded him. Only a few monuments of these successors of his have been preserved. Still, there is no cogent reason to doubt the correctness of Josephus, as these phenomena can be explained in a satisfactory manner.

As early as the time of *Amenhotep IV*, the monuments inform us of a powerful general, named *Haremhab*, and later on we meet with a king *Haremhab*, founder of the Nineteenth Dynasty. The identity of these two has not been established, but it is certain that King *Haremhab* reigned 59 years, 1380–1321 B. C. But Josephus assigns only 4 years, 1 month to *Haremhab*. I understand this to mean that Manetho regarded the sons-in-law of *Amenhotep IV* as legitimate rulers of Egypt, and that he accordingly ended the Eighteenth Dynasty with the overthrow of the last *Akenkheres* in 1325 B. C. This left only 4 years for *Haremhab*. The *Abydos-* and *Sakkara-Lists*, on the other hand, did not recognize *Amenhotep* and his successors as legitimate kings of Egypt, and therefore place *Haremhab* next after *Amenhotep III* in the succession of Egyptian kings. The inference is that *Haremhab* usurped a part of Egypt sometime in the period of the "heretics." The *Aton* worshipers maintained themselves for a while in *A*marna and in Nubia (Soleb), until *Rathotis* gave up the *Aton-*faith, assumed the name *Tut-enkh-Amon*, and was reconciled to the *A*mon priesthood of Thebes.

The rebellion led by the house of *Haremhab* spread in the meantime. In 1325 B. C. Thebes was occupied, and the kings of the Nineteenth Dynasty became the lawful rulers of Egypt.

Dynasty XIX

The Nineteenth Dynasty includes the period from *Haremhab* (*Harmais*) to the *S*yrian usurper (*O-ar-su, Osarsiph, Thouoris*). The *terminus a quo* is quite certain, as *Ramses I*, the second ruler of this dynasty, was ruling

DYNASTY XIX

in 1321 B. C., and *Haremhab*, who reigned 4 years over all Egypt, became king in 1325 B. C. The *terminus ad quem* is more difficult to ascertain. Eusebius' Canon, however, claims that *Ilion* was taken in the last year of *Thouoris*, the usurper, and also says that this happened 405 years before the first Olympiad (776 B. C.), i. e., in 1181 B. C.

Other Greek authors like Eratosthenes, Apollodor, *P*orphyry, Diodorus, Clemens Alexandrinus, Dionysius of *H*alicarnassus, Suidas, Solinus, and even Eusebius, in his other writings, assert that Troy fell 407 years before the first Olympiad, i. e., in the year 1183 B. C. This date is probably correct, and, on the authority of Eusebius and *A*fricanus, this was the last year of *Thouoris*, and therefore of the Nineteenth Dynasty, which extended over 142 years.

Africanus assigns seven kings, Eusebius five, and Syncellus only four, to this dynasty. From the monuments we know that nine kings reigned during this period, but *Siptah* and *Seti II* were probably only vassals, or ruled only over an insignificant part of Egypt, and the number given by *A*fricanus seems to be correct.

We know from the *Sakkara-List*, as well as from the monuments, that the order of succession of the first half of this dynasty was: *Haremhab, Ramses I, Seti I*, and *Ramses II*. We know also that *Seti I* was the (only) son of *Ramses I*, and *Ramses II* was a son, perhaps the oldest,[1] of *Seti I*. The relationship between *Haremhab* and *Ramses I* is, however, not exactly clear, but Manetho declares them to have been brothers.

Through some misunderstanding of Manetho, Josephus

---

[1] So Josephus. Breasted (*ARE.*, Vol. III, p. 123-31) contends that *Ramses II* had an older brother.

DYNASTIES XIX, XX—COMPARATIVE CHART

Sakkara List	Abydos List	Josephus	Syncellus	Africanus	Eusebius
		14. Harmais 4 y. 1 m.	14. Harmaios 9 y.	14. Armesis 5 y.	12. Armais 5 y.
		15. Ramesses (I) 1 y. 4 m.	. . .	15. Ramesses 1 y.	. . .
		16. Rampses (II) 66 y. 2 m.	15. Ramesses 68 y.	. . .	13. Ramesses 68 y.
		17. Amenophis 19 y. 6 m.	16. Amenophis 8 y.	16. Amenophath 19 y.	14. Amenophis 40 y.
		Total 333 y.°		Total 263 y.°	Total 348 y.[1]
Dynasty XIX					
55. Sezerkheperure-Setepnere	74. Sezerkheperure-Setepnere	Sethos and Ramesses 59 y.		**7 Thebans**	**5 Thebans**
56. Mnspeh(t)yre	75. Menpeh(t)yre	Rampses 66 y.		1. Sethos 51 y.	1. Sethos 55 y.
57. Menma(t)yre (= Seti I)	76. Menma(t)re (= Seti I)	Amenophis		2. Rapsakes 61 y.	2. Rampses 66 y.
58. Usermatre-setepnere (= Ramses II)		Sethos and Ramesses		3. Amenphthes 20 y.	3. Ammenephthis 40 y.
				4. Ramesses 60 y.	. . .
				5. Ammenemses 5 y.	5. Ammenemes 26 y.
			Thouoris 17 y.	6. Thouoris 7 y.	6. Thouoris 7 y.
				Total 209 y.	Total 194 y.
Dynasty XX				12 Thebans 135 y.	12 Thebans 178 y.

[1] This total includes also the reigns of the Eighteenth Dynasty.

identified *Seti I* and *Ramses I*.[1] Eusebius and Syncellus call them *Armais* and *Ramesses* (*Amesses* in Syncelli Eusebius). Josephus, quoting from the history of Manetho, makes *Ramses II* the immediate successor of *Ramses I*, assigning 1 year, 4 months, to the former and 66 years, 2 months, to the latter; but *Syncellus* and the *Sothis-Book* merge the two into one *Ramesses*, assigning him 68 years. In the *Epitomes* Josephus, Africanus, and Eusebius head the Nineteenth Dynasty with *Sethos* (*Seti I*), succeeded by *Ramesses Miamoun* (*Ramses II*). While the latter is credited with a reign of 66 years, Josephus assigns 59 years to *Sethos*, which Lepsius, however, corrects to 50 years, 9 months. As Africanus states it as 51 years, and Eusebius 55 years, the latter evidently included in it *Harmais'* reign of 4 years.

Josephus and Eusebius affirm also, that *Harmais* (*Haremhab*) was called *Danaus*, and *Sethosis-Ramesses* (*Ramses I*) *Aegyptus*, but that *Aegyptus*, having during his own war-expeditions to foreign lands placed Egypt under his brother *Danaus*, on his return expelled his brother, who fled to *Argos* and founded there the *Danaid Dynasty*, which succeeded that of *Inachos*. The monuments offer no serious objection to these stories, which evidently rest on a historical basis, and can readily be brought into harmony with the inscriptions.

In consideration of these data I would offer the following reconstruction of the Nineteenth Dynasty.

Haremhab

On the monuments from Amarna and of *Amenhotep IV* we find the mention of a certain nobleman named *Rames*.

[1] Σέθωσις (υἱὸς) (ὁ) καὶ 'Ραμέσσης—"Sethos (fil.) qui et Ramêsês" (Arm.).

Another name, *Suti* or *Seti*, occurs here also. It is possible that this *Rames* later became *Ramses I* or *Setos-Ramesses*.

Haremhab was a prominent general of *Amenhotep IV*, intrusted with the oversight of the Delta, and *Rames* may likewise have been an overseer of Nubia. This *Haremhab* is undoubtedly identical with king *Haremhab*, the founder of the Nineteenth Dynasty. It seems probable that in the disintegration of the empire, brought about by the *Amon*-priesthood in its opposition to the *Aton*-faith, *Haremhab* became practically independent. There is a legal document referring to his fifty-ninth year, but the highest date on his own monuments is the year 21. He may therefore have assumed the royal title in his own city, Alabastronpolis, as early as 1380 B. C., but proclaimed himself as king over Northern Egypt not earlier than about 1342 B. C. In 1325 B. C. he was crowned king over all Egypt in Thebes, and it is from this time that Manetho regards him as legitimate king of Egypt, for which reason Josephus assigns him a reign of 4 years, 1 month.

Ramses I

The accession of *Ramses I* in 1321 B. C. is certain from the fact that the *Sothic* cycle beginning in that year was called "the era of *Menophris*," but the only royal name of this time with which we can identify "*Menophris*" is *Men-peh(ti)-Re*, the throne-name of *Ramses I*, and as this king reigned only 1 year, 4 months, and must have been ruling when the great *Sothic* festival, heralding in the new era, was celebrated, *Haremhab* must have died or been expelled a few days or months before the New-Year's Day of 1321 B. C.

DYNASTY XIX

The few monuments of *Ramses I* of which we know bear witness that this king was chiefly interested in Nubia, and as *Amenhotep IV* had a great city, Gem-Aton in Soleb, Nubia, it seems possible that after the death of *Amenhotep IV* (1370 B. C.) *Ramses* proclaimed himself also king of Nubia and Southern Egypt, as his brother *Haremhab* did in Northern Egypt, and that the two brothers divided the power between them. It is also possible, as Josephus avers, that *Ramses* (called *Seti* by Josephus) was the chief administrator of the two, and that he, when *Haremhab* usurped all the royal prerogatives, marched against his brother with his army and expelled him from Egypt. This would then have happened in 1322/1 B. C. *Ramses I*, being the older of the two brothers, died, therefore, after a reign of 1 year, 4 months, i. e., in the first months of 1320 B. C.

Seti I

The monuments show that *Seti I* was coregent with his father. It is possible that he was such from the beginning of the dynasty in 1325, and that this is the reason why Eusebius assigns him 55 years. Africanus, who credits him with only 51 years, dates his reign from the beginning of *Ramses'* reign in 1321 B. C., and with this Josephus agrees, giving his reign as 50 years, 9 months (for 59 years). On the monuments, however, he began his dates with the death of *Ramses I*, 1320/19 B. C. In the latter year, 1319 (or 1318) B. C. *Ramses II* was born, according to the horoscope on the ceiling of the Ramesseum. Now, the reign of *Ramses II* began with his birth, i. e., he was made coregent as soon as he was born, for *Ramses II* asserts that he began to reign while he was yet "in the egg." This explains, then, why *Seti I* is not mentioned in the *Epitome* of Josephus, because his whole reign was one of coregencies. This is further corroborated by Syncellus and the *Sothis-Book*, where the two reigns of *Ramses I* and *Ramses II* are fused into one, and 68 years assigned to them. *Seti I* died in 1271 B. C.

The highest date of *Seti I* on the monuments is the year 9, but the high-priest, *Beknekhonsu*, states in his biography that he served in his youth for 12 years as chief of the training-stable of *Seti I*, and it seems probable that this period was the actual length of his reign from the death of *Ramses I* to the year when *Ramses II* took over the reins of the government.

Ramses II

As stated above, *Ramses II* was born in 1319 B. C., and became coregent with his father from his birth. He was only a "stripling," about twelve years old, when he took charge of the government of Egypt, about 1307 B. C. Although his whole reign covered 66 years, 2 months— 1319–1253 B. C.—his actual government over Egypt amounted in reality only to 54 years, he having begun to date his documents in the year 1307, when he had nominally been king for twelve years. I base this assertion on the celebrations of his *Sed*-jubilees. The first occurrence of this jubilee was celebrated on the thirtieth anniversary of his accession or coronation. *Ramses II* repeated them thereafter every third year, but only nine of these *Sed*-jubilees of his are recorded. Now, he celebrated his sixth jubilee in his forty-fourth year. The three last jubilees are undated, but it is probable that he celebrated them also at intervals of three years, i. e., the seventh in year 47, the eighth in year 50, and the ninth in year 53. We have no adequate explanation why he should not have celebrated another jubilee three years later, if he lived then, and if he lived thirteen years after his ninth jubilee, we should have expected him to have celebrated four more jubilees. But according to our calculation, his ninth jubilee was celebrated the year before his death, and as that jubilee would have been celebrated in his fifty-third year, we must assume that he began to number his years from his thirteenth year, when he actually took over the government from his father. All his dates on his monuments should therefore be counted from his thirteenth year, 1307 B. C.

Merneptah

Ramses II was succeeded by his son *Merneptah*, who reigned for 19 years, 6 months—1253-1234 B. C.

Amenmeses

After *Merneptah* came *Amenmeses*, and in his reign began the disintegration of the second empire. The data from the monuments are indeed scanty for this time, and the few quotations from Manetho help us scarcely any better. Eusebius avers that *Amenmeses* reigned for twenty-six years, Africanus states that his reign covered only five years. Perhaps both are correct, the five years applying to his unmolested reign, the remaining twenty-one years to his flight into Ethiopia.

From this reference to his flight I assume that he is identical with Josephus' *Amenophis*, who fled from Egypt before *Osarsiph*. This story is corroborated by the monuments, for *Ramses III* records in *Papyrus Harris* the following:

"The land of Egypt was overthrown from without, and every man was deprived of his right; formerly they had no 'chief mouth' for many years. The land of Egypt was in the hands of rulers of towns; they slew one another, great and small. There arose other conditions with empty years. ʿ-*ir-su*, a certain man from *Kharu*, was their chief. He made the whole land tributary to him; he united his companions and plundered the land, and made the gods of no repute, so that no offerings were presented in the temples."

Osarsiph

It is indeed possible that even the name ʿ-*ir-su* is identical with *Osarsiph; su* often corresponds with *siph*, and if we read the two first signs *ir-is(t)*,[1] they represent *Osiris* or *Osar*. In any event, this usurper is identical with *Osarsiph*. *K*haru was now in the hands of the *P*hilistines, against whom *Merneptah* fought in the early part of his reign, in order to ward them off from entering Egypt. Although they were defeated on that occasion, they soon succeeded in capturing *P*alestine, and the Bible asserts that they made Israel tributary for eighteen years, 1230–1212 B. C., after the death of *Jair*. Some of Manetho's "lepers" may very well have entered Egypt in the time of *Merneptah* and settled in *A*varis; these "lepers" being a part of the northerners, who then invaded Egypt. It is also quite probable that they called on their allies, who then ruled Jerusalem, and that *Osarsiph* headed an army which invaded Egypt in 1229 B. C., and captured *A*varis. *Ramses III* avers that the land of Egypt was in the hands of "town-rulers." *Amenmeses* may have con-

---

[1] The difference is quite slight between the ʿ-and the *ist*-signs, which might be a mistake on the part of the scribe of *Ramses III*.

tinued to rule some part of Upper Egypt for twenty-one years. Another such king was *Siptah*, who reigned at least six years, and a third was *Seti II*, who ruled at least two years. Finally *Osarsiph* succeeded in laying all Egypt under tribute to him.

Thouoris

In the *Epitomes* this *Osarsiph* is called *Thouoris*. Syncellus and the *Sothis-Book* assign him seventeen years, Eusebius and Africanus seven. Both Africanus and Eusebius assert that this *Thouoris* is identical with *H*omer's *Polybus*,[1] a man from Alkandra, and that in his last year Troja was captured. As this took place in 1183 B. C., *Thouoris*' reign over all Egypt dates from 1200 (or 1190) to 1183 B. C.

This great usurpation of Egypt by *Osarsiph-Thouoris* is only one wave in the ocean of great political upheavals that swept over Asia at that time. About 1235 B. C. *Ninib-apil-Êkur* established himself on the throne of Assyria and gave rise to the mighty dynasty that numbered among other kings *Ashur-dân I* and *Tiglath-pileser I*. In Babylonia the *Kassite Dynasty* fell in 1205, succeeded by the *Dynasty of Pashe*. The kingdom of *Mitâni* was then wiped out of existence. The mighty *Hittites* were made tributary to these invaders. Israel likewise lost its nominal independence. In *Lydia* the *Atys Dynasty* was succeeded by the *Heraclide Dynasty* in 1194 (or possibly 1210) B. C. Troja fell in 1183 B. C., and anarchy reigned in Egypt from 1229 to 1183 B. C. It was the signal for the entrance of the Aryan race into the politics of Western Asia.

[1] *Odyss.*, IV, 126.

Summarizing the above results, we obtain the following

Chronology of Dynasty XIX

Haremhab	4 years, 1 month	1325–1321 B. C.
Ramses I	1 year, 4 months	1321–1320 B. C.
Seti I	50 years, 9 months	1321–1271 B. C.
"	sole reign	1319–1307 B. C.
Ramses II	66 years, 2 months	1319–1253 B. C.
"	sole reign	1307–1253 B. C.
Merneptah	19 years, 6 months	1253–1234 B. C.
Amenmeses	5 years, sole king	1234–1229 B. C.
"	21 years, city lord	1229–1208 B. C.
Siptah	6 years,	1208–1202 B. C.
Seti II	2 years	1202–1200 B. C.
Thouoris (*Osarsiph*)	17 years	1200–1183 B. C.

Dynasty XX

The Twentieth Dynasty of Egypt was regarded as of so little importance, that *Africanus* and *Eusebius* omitted the list of kings and recorded only the years of the duration of this dynasty, the former assigning it 135, the latter 178 years. *Syncellus* credits it with 141 and the *Sothis-Book* with 133 years. The total of the minimum dates on the monuments amounts to 104 years.

By reckoning backward from the Twenty-sixth Dynasty, the Twentieth Dynasty fell about 1050 B. C., and as the *Sothis-Book*, with which *Africanus* practically agrees, accords it 133 years, I shall assume that date to be approximately correct. This dynasty lasted, therefore, from 1183–1050 B. C. The order of kings is known from the monuments, and the list is headed by

Nakht-set,[1] who reigned about two years, 1183–1181.

[1] For *Setnakht;* Syncellus' Νεχεψώs.

He was probably a descendant of *Amenmeses*, and began the war of liberty against *Thouoris*.

Ramses III, Josephus' *Rapsakes*, succeeded *Nakht-set*, and reigned thirty-one years, 1181–1150 B. C.

From the horoscope of the *Ramessides* it appears that *Ramses VI* was a son of *Ramses IV*, and was born in 1199/8 B. C. The monuments indicate that *Ramses IV* reigned six years, *Ramses VI* at least four years, *Ramses IX* nineteen years, and *Ramses XII* at least twenty-seven years. On the basis of these scanty data I would suggest the following

Chronological Table of Dynasty XX

Nakht-Set	2 (?) years	1183–1181 B. C.
Ramses III	31 years	1181–1150 B. C.
Ramses IV	6 years	1150–1144 B. C.
Ramses V	10 (?) years	1144–1134 B. C.
Ramses VI	4 (?) years	1134–1130 B. C.
Ramses VII *Ramses VIII*	17 (?) years	1130–1113 B. C.
Ramses IX	19 years	1113–1092 B. C.
Ramses X *Ramses XI*	17 years	1092–1077 B. C.
Ramses XII	27 years	1077–1050 B. C.

Dynasty XII

We found above from the *Sothic* date in a *Kahun* papyrus that the seventh year of *Sesostris III* fell in 1881 B. C., and his accession year must therefore be 1887 B. C. From this date we can now count backward to the beginning of this dynasty, and forward to its end. The monumental material for this period is comparatively abundant, and it is held that of all Egyp-

DYNASTY XII—COMPARATIVE CHART

Turin Papyrus	Sakkara List	Abydos List	Africanus	Eusebius	Monuments
Dynasty XII			Ammenemes 16 y.	Ammenemes 16 y.	
Amenemhet I [1]9 y.	39. Sehetepibre	59. Sehetepibre	7 Thebans	7 Thebans	Amenemhet I 30 y.
Senwosret I 45 y.	40. Kheperkare	60. Kheperkare	1. Sesogkhosis 46 y.	1. Sesogkhosis 46 y.	Sesostris I 44 y.
Amenemhet II 30[+8] y.	41. Nubkare	61. Nubkaure	2. Ammanemes 38 y.	2. Ammenemes 38 y.	Amenemhet II 35 y.
Senwosret II [19] y.	42. Khekheperre	62. Khekheperre	3. Sesostris 48 y.	3. Sesostris 48 y.	Sesostris II 19 y.
Senwosret III 30[+3] y.	43. Khekare	63. Khekaure	4. Lakhares 8 y.	4. Lamares 8 y.	Sesostris III 33 y.
Amenemhet III 40[+8] y.	44. Nemare	64. Nemare	5. Ameres 8 y.	Their Successors 42 y.	Amenemhet III 46 y.
Amenemhet IV	45. Makhrure	65. Makhrure	6. Ammenemes 8 y.	Total 245 y.	Amenemhet IV 9 y.
9 y. 3 m. 27 d.					
Sebeknefrure	46. Sebekkare	. . .	7. Skemiophris 4 y.		Sebeknefrure 4 y.
3 y. 10 m. 24 d.			Total 160 y.		
Total 213 y. 1 m. 17 d.					

tian chronological data those of the Twelfth Dynasty are most complete, and so fully given that an absolutely certain chronology of this dynasty can be built thereon.

Manetho's figures for this dynasty, are, however, entirely discredited,[1] but so much more reliance is placed on the *Turin Papyrus*. This document has been assumed to be correct, at least in its summary, (213 years, 1 month, 17 days,) of the whole dynasty, and it has been compared with the monuments, which are supposed to corroborate it.

It is further held that the monuments show that several coregencies existed in this period, e. g., ten years of *Amenemhet I* with *Sesostris I*;[2] at least three years of *Sesostris I* with *Amenemhet II*;[3] and at least three years of *Amenemhet II* with *Sesostris II*.[4] Breasted[5] and Meyer[6] have, therefore, on the basis of these data, constructed the following chronology of the Twelfth Dynasty:

Amenemhet I	30 years	2000–1970	2000–1980 alone / 1980–1970 with his son
Sesostris I	45 years	1980–1935	1980–1970 with his father / 1970–1938 alone / 1938–1935 with his son
Amenemhet II	35 years	1938–1903	1938–1935 with his father / 1935–1906 alone / 1906–1903 with his son
Sesostris II	19 years	1906–1887	1906–1903 with his father / 1903–1887 alone
Sesostris III	38 years	1887–1849	Uncertain period with son
Amenemhet III	48 years	1849–1801	Uncertain period with father
Amenemhet IV	9 years	1801–1792	
Sebeknefrure	4 years	1792–1788	

[1] Meyer, *Aeg. Chron.*, pp. 58–60; Breasted *ARE.*, Vol. I., pp., 35, n. 6, 36, 37.

[2] Stela of *Intef* at Cairo: "*Year 30 of Amenemhet I, year 10 of Sesostris I.*"

[3] Stela of *Upwaweto* at Leyden: "*Year 44 of Sesostris I=year 2 of Amenemhet II.*"

[4] Inscription of *Hapu* at Assuan: "*Year 3 of Sesostris II=year 35 of Amenemhet II.*" The monuments also indicate that *Sesostris III* and *Amenemhet III*, as well as *Amenemhet III* and *Amenemhet IV*, were coregents for uncertain lengths of time.

[5] *ARE.*, Vol. I, p. 222.   [6] *Chron. of Eg.*, p. 57.

According to this scheme the Twelfth Dynasty extended over a period of 212 years, while the *Turin Papyrus* states it as 213 years, and thus it must be admitted that a slight error has been made at some point in this scheme. The dates of the *Turin Papyrus* have been restored by these scholars to read:

	Breasted's and Meyer's Dates	My Restoration
Amenemhet I	[2] 9 y	[1] 9 y . . . .
Sesostris I	45 y	45 y. [11 m.]
Amenemhet II	[35 y . . . .]	[37 y., 7 m.]
Sesostris II	[19 y . . . .]	[19 y. . . . .]
Sesostris III	3[8 y . . . .]	3[0 y., 10 m.]
Amenemhet III	4[8 y . . . .]	4[7 y., 8 m.]
Amenemhet IV	9 y., 3 m., 27 d.	9 y., 3 m., 27 d.
Sebeknefrure	3 y., 10 m., 24 d.	3 y., 10 m., 24 d.
Total	228 y., 2 m., 21 d.	213 y., 2 m.

Ed. Meyer assumes that the *Turin Papyrus* has recorded the full length of each reign, including coregencies, but in the total of the dynasty only its actual duration. This assumption is based on the fact that this papyrus assigns 45 years to *Sesostris I*, while his reign from his accession to that of *Amenemhet II* covered only 42 years, according to the stela of *Upwaweto*. But if that part of his reign was only 42 years, then, on the same principle, the sole reign of *Amenemhet III* must be less than 49 years, for he was for some time coregent with his son; and if that be accepted, then it is impossible to reach the total of 213 years. This shows that the same untrustworthiness applies to the *Turin Papyrus* as is alleged to attach to the dates of Manetho, or else we must reinvestigate the inscriptions on the monuments, which are held to prove the coregencies referred to above.

Turning our attention first to the inscription of *Hapu* at Assuan, which is supposed to establish the coregency of *Sesostris II* with his father *Amenemhet II* in the thirty-third year of the latter's reign, we find on examination that this inscription does not support such a deduction, and its syntactical construction excludes it. This inscription reads:

"*Made in the third year of the Majesty of Horus: Seshmutawy* (=*Sesostris II*). *In* (*ḥft*) *the thirty-fifth year of the Majesty of Horus: Hekenemat* (=*Amenemhet II*) *came the - - kf³-yb- officer, Hapu, to inspect the fortresses of Wawat.*"

It is true that the Egyptian preposition *ḥft* sometimes means "contemporary with," but its original meaning is "in face of," "opposite," and corresponds to Assyrian *ina tarṣi, ištu tarṣi*, "in the time of," "since the time of," orig. "in the opposite of," "from the opposite of." The first number refers to the year when this inscription was cut on the rocks of Assuan. If the second date be referred to the same verb, "made," the last sentence becomes exceedingly awkward and unintelligible. *Hapu* evidently meant that he came to Assuan *in*, and had been there *since, the thirty-fifth year of Amenemhet II*, until he now, *in the third year of Sesostris*, made this inscription, which therefore gives no clue whatever to the coregency of these two kings.

This does not exclude the fact that coregencies existed at that time, for that fact is well attested by the monuments; but we have as yet no means of knowing at what time these coregencies began. We know from the *Lists*, as well as from other monuments, both the order of the kings of this dynasty and their number. Africanus also has eight kings, although he places the first of them *Ammenemes* (=*Amenemhet I*) by himself, between the Eleventh and Twelfth Dynasties.

At the same time it would seem that Africanus and Eusebius have fused *Sesostris II* and *Sesostris III* into one king, *Sesostris*, assigning him 48 years. And this view is supported by the fact that according to a *Kahun* papyrus, *Sesostris II* reigned only 19 years.

Amenemhet III reigned 48 years, according to my restoration of the *Turin Papyrus*. Year 46 is his highest date on the monuments. Eusebius assigns only 8 years to *Lamares* (for N-$m^{\circ}c.t$-Re, throne-name of *Amenemhet III*).

Africanus assigns 160 years from the accession of *Sesostris I* to the beginning of the *Hyksos* rule. For this reason he places the reigns of *Amenemhet IV* (*Ammenemes*) and *Sebeknefrure* (*Skemiophris*) as actual coregencies with that of *Amenemhet III*, whose reign he shortens to 16 years (*Lakhares* 8 years, *Ameres* 8 years).

As the *Hyksos'* rule began in 1826 B. C., *Sesostris I* began to rule in 1986 B. C., according to Africanus, and his reign was preceded by that of *Amenemhet I*. Manetho assigns only 16 years to the latter reign, while the *Turin Papyrus* evidently meant [1]9 years, for the stela of *Intef* at Cairo makes his thirtieth year correspond with that of the tenth year of *Sesostris I*. This discrepancy between the *Turin Papyrus* and Manetho can, however, be harmonized by assuming that *Mentuhotep IV*, of the Eleventh Dynasty ruled 3 years after the accession of *Amenemhet IV*.

On the basis of the results achieved by these inquiries,

THE HYKSOS

let us now compare the list of Africanus and the *Turin Papyrus* with the monuments:

	Africanus		Turin Papyrus		Monuments	
Amenemhet I........	(16)	2002–1986	19	2006–1987	20	2006–1986
Sesostris I..........	46	1986–1940	46	1987–1941	42	1986–1944
Amenemhet II.......	38	1940–1902	38	1941–1903	38	1944–1906
Sesostris II ⎫	48	1902–1854	19	1903–1884	19	1906–1887
Sesostris III ⎭			30	1884–1854	33	1887–1854
Amenemhet III ⎫			48	1854–1806	46	1854–1808
Amenemhet IV ⎬	44		9	1806–1797		
Sebeknefrure ⎭			4	1797–1793		
Totals..........	176		213			

The differences between Manetho on the one hand and the *Turin Papyrus* and the monuments on the other hand are therefore to be ascribed to a different viewpoint, rather than to real discrepancies.

Chronological Table of Dynasty XII

Amenemhet I	30 years	2006–1976	⎧ 2006–2002 with *Mentuhotep IV* ⎨ 2002–1986 alone ⎩ 1986–1976 with his son
Sesostris I	46 years	1986–1940	⎧ 1986–1976 with his father ⎨ 1976–1944 alone ⎩ 1944–1940 with his son
Amenemhet II	42 years	1944–1902	⎧ 1944–1940 with his father ⎨ 1940–1906 alone ⎩ 1906–1902 with his son
Sesostris II	19 years	1906–1887	⎰ 1906–1902 with his father ⎱ 1902–1887 alone
Sesostris III	33 years	1887–1854	
Amenemhet III	48 years	1854–1806	
Amenemhet IV	9 years	1806–1797	
Sebeknefrure	4 years	1797–1793	

The Hyksos

Josephus assigns six kings and 259 years, 10 months, or in round numbers 260 years, to the rule of the *Hyksos* kings; and this period ends with their expulsion and the rise of the Eighteenth Dynasty in 1566 B. C. The *Hyksos*

THE HYKSOS KINGS—COMPARATIVE CHART

JOSEPHUS		SYNCELLUS		AFRICANUS		EUSEBIUS	
1. Salatis	19 y.	1. Salitis	19 y.	1. Saites	19 y.	1. Saites	19 y.
2. Bnôn	44 y.	2. Baion	4 y.	2. Bnôn	44 y.	2. Bnôn	40 y.
3. Apakhnan	36 y. 7 m.	3. Apakhnas	36 y.	3. Pakhnan	61 y.	. .	.
4. Apophis	61 y.	4. Apophis	61 y.	4. Staan	50 y.	. .	.
5. Iannas	50 y. 1 m.	5. Sethos	50 y.	5. Arkhles	49 y.	3. Arkhles	30 y.
6. Aseth	49 y. 2 m.	6. Kertos	44 y.	6. Aphobis	61 y.	4. Aphophis	14 y.
Total	259 y. 10 m.	Total	254 y.	Total	284 y.	Total	103 y.
		Dyn. XVIII. Aseth	20 y.				

rule would then have begun in 1826 B. C. This date falls within the reign of *Amenemhet III*, but we noticed above that Josephus' expression ἡμῖν Τιμαίος was probably a corruption of the name *Amenemhet*. The monuments indicate distinctly that the *Hyksos* rule began before the end of the Twelfth Dynasty. Josephus, Africanus, and the *Sothis-Book* agree that there were six great *Hyksos* kings. They also agree that the first two of them were *Salitis* and *Bnôn* (or *Baiôn*), the former reigning 19 years, the latter 44 (Eusebius gives only 40). These two names form a group by themselves, and these dates can hardly be disputed:

Salitis, 19 years, 1826–1807 B. C.
Bnôn, 44 years, 1807–1763 B. C.

Eusebius adds that these two kings were brothers, foreigners from Phoenicia, and that at that time *Joseph* appeared in Egypt and began to rule there. Josephus and Eusebius also aver that *S*ais was their capital, superseding that of Memphis, where the *Hyksos* rule began.

The following two kings—*Apakhnan* and *Apophis*—seem also to form a group by themselves. Josephus assigns 36 years, 7 months, the *Sothis-Book* 36 years, to *Apakhnan*. *Apophis* is credited with 61 years by Josephus, Africanus, and the *Sothis-Book*. Africanus, however, has placed *Apophis* last among the *Hyksos* kings, and transferred the years of his reign to *Apakhnan*. Eusebius gives the name of *Arkhles* instead of *Apakhnan*, crediting him with 30 years, and then follows *Apophis* with only 14 years. Africanus, on the other hand, places *Arkhles* fifth among these kings, and assigns him 49 years. These discrepancies, however, are not so serious as they may appear to be at first sight.

There were several dynasties ruling Egypt at this time, and it appears that Africanus has here attempted to give the kings of the *Pakhnan Dynasty*. This *Pakhnan* or *Apakhnas* is well known from the monuments, where he is called *Kha-y-an*, "the Canaanite," and the form *Pakhnan* is the same name with the Egyptian definite article *pa* prefixed to it.

The monuments know no less than three kings with the name *Apophis*, and it is possible that Manetho included them all under the name *Apophis*, assigning 61 years to their reigns. The name reminds us of the Midianite or *Kenite* name, *Hobab*. These two reigns should then be dated:

Apakhnan, 36 years, 7 months, 1763–1726 B. C.

Apophis, 61 years, 1726–1665 B. C.

Clement of Alexandria states that the Exodus took place 345 years before the *Sothic* period (1321 B. C.) i. e., in the year 1665 B. C. This seems corroborated by other evidence. Chron. Barb. mentions a *Bubastite Dynasty*, known by him as the Twelfth Dynasty, which lasted for 153 years. We know that Bubastis was the capital of *Kha-y-an* and the *Apophises*, and it is very probable that a Canaanitic or Midianitic migration entered Egypt about 1818 B. C. and settled around Bubastis, and that their kings became supreme lords over Egypt at the death of *Bnôn* in 1763 B. C. But Chron. Barb. records also a *Tanite Dynasty*, which lasted for 184 years. This dynasty is also known from the monuments, its kings being named after the *Tanite* divinity *Set*. To these kings belong *A-seth* or *Sethos*, of the Manethonian lists. These *Tanites* evidently represent another *S*emitic migration, which entered Egypt about 1750 B. C. After having ruled in Tanis to 1665 B. C., they succeeded in acquiring supreme lordship over Egypt, which seems to have caused the Bubastites to migrate from Egypt and settle in Southern Palestine, and it is this migration or exodus to which Clement of Alexandria refers as having taken place 345 years before the beginning of the *Sothic* period of 1321/0 B. C.

The last two *Hyksos* kings of Josephus and the *Sothis-Book* belong, therefore, to a new dynasty, the *Tanite*. Josephus calls them *Iannas* (or *Annas*) and *Aseth*, assigning them 50 years, 1 month, and 49 years, 2 months, respectively. The *Sothis-Book*, on the other hand, calls them *Sethos* (50 years), and *Kertos* (44 years), after which it begins the Eighteenth Dynasty with *Aseth*, who is credited with 20 years, and then follows *Amosis*. It is possible that *Iannas* and *Sethos* represent the same king, one being the throne-name, the other the birth-name. But it is also possible that the order has been confused by Josephus, and that *Aseth* should precede *Iannas*, for *Aseth* and *Sethos* seem in reality to be the same name.

Greek authors[1] allude to calendar reforms introduced by the *Hyksos* kings. We know now from the monuments that not only were calendar reforms inaugurated by them, but one of them introduced a new era, called

Era of O-peh(ti)-Set

Seti, a high official of *Ramses II*, was commissioned to erect a stela in honor of *Seti I* at Tanis. He carried out his commission, and took the opportunity to erect a stela of his own at the same time. On this second stela *Seti* records the following:

"*His Majesty commanded me to make a great stela of*

[1] *Schol. Plat.*, Vol. II, p. 424.

granite, in the great name of his fathers, in order that the name of his father('s) father, King Menmare, son of Re, Seti (I)-Merneptah, might be exalted, enduring, and abiding forever, like Re."

"*In the year 400, in the fourth month of the third season, on the fourth day, of (the reign of) the King of Upper and Lower Egypt: ꜥꜣ-phty-St, son of Re, his beloved, Nubti, whom Harakhte desires to live forever and ever, came the hereditary prince, governor of the residence city, vizier - - - - Seti,*" etc.

We know that Tanis was a *Hyksos* capital, and was rebuilt by the *Hyksos*. In the Bible this city is called Zoan, of which it is said that "*Hebron was built seven years before Zoan in Egypt*" (Num. 13:21).

It is evident that the only *Hyksos* names with which we can compare the ꜥꜣ-*ph(ti)-Set*, are *Sethos* or *Aseth*. The first one became king in 1665, the second one in 1615, and 400 years deducted from these dates carry us to 1265 and 1215 B. C. respectively. Only the first of these dates falls within the reign of *Ramses II*, who died in 1253 B. C., and this stela was therefore set up in the year 1265 B. C. This date falls six years after the death of *Seti I*, and it was therefore a time well suited for the erection of this memorial.

The new era of Tanis presupposes that the kings of Tanis came to power at the inauguration of this era, and also that these kings, although of *Hyksos* blood, were not descendants of the other *Hyksos* kings who ruled Egypt from Bubastis or *Sais*. The dates of the last two *Hyksos* kings are then:

Iannas or *Sethos*, 50 years, 1 month, 1665–1615 B. C.
Aseth (Kertos), 49 years, 2 months, 1615–1566 B. C.

Hyksos

Salatis	19 years	1826–1807 B. C.
Bnôn	44 years	1807–1763 B. C.
Apakhnan	36 years, 7 months	1763–1726 B. C.
Apophis	61 years	1726–1665 B. C.
Jannas (Sethos)	50 years, 1 month	1665–1615 B. C.
Aseth (Kertos)	49 years, 2 months	1615–1566 B. C.

Dynasties XIII–XVII

With the *Hyksos* kings we have filled up the entire gap between the Twelfth and Eighteenth Dynasties. What are we then to do with the intervening Thirteenth to Seventeenth Dynasties, and the long lists of their kings, appearing in the *Turin Papyrus*, the *Karnak-List*, and on the monuments? The only reasonable answer is that these dynasties and kings represent contemporary dynasties in different large cities, subordinate to the great *Hyksos* kings.

Petrie argues that we should accept the lists of Africanus and push back the Twelfth Dynasty a whole *Sothic* cycle of 1,460 years.

Breasted calls attention to the scarcity of monuments in this period, and avers that "two hundred years is ample for the whole period," and he adds: "The proposal to push back the said *Sothic* date (of the Twelfth Dynasty) by a whole *Sothic* cycle, thus lengthening the above period between the Twelfth and Eighteenth Dynasties by 1,460 years, is hardly worthy of a serious answer. It involves the assumption that nearly fifteen hundred years of history have been enacted in the Nile Valley without leaving a trace behind! It is like imagining that in European his-

DYNASTIES XIII–XVII—COMPARATIVE CHART

Africanus	Eusebius	
Dynasty XIII 60 Diospolitans 453 y.	60 Diospolitans 453 y.	XII Dyn. of Bu
Dynasty XIV 76 Khoite Kings 184 y.	76 Khoite Kings 184 y.	XIII Dyn. of T
Dynasty XV 6 Shepherd Kings 284 y.	Diospolitans 250 y.	XIV Dyn. of : nitos
Dynasty XVI 32 other Shepherds 518 y.	5 Thebans 190 y.	XV Dyn. of Me
Dynasty XVII 43 other Shepherds and 43 Thebans 151 y.	4 Shepherds 103 y.	XVI Dyn. of opolis
Dynasty XVIII Diospolitans 263 y.		XVII Dyn. of polis

tory we could insert at will a period equal to that from the fall of Rome to the present!"[1]

There are two lists of dynasties for this period, one in Chron. Barb., the other furnished by Africanus. Meyer assumes that these two lists are practically identical, the differences arising from distortion or miscopying of the numbers. I cannot share this opinion, because the discrepancies apply not only to the numbers, but also to the names of the dynasties. It seems to me, therefore, that we have here two entirely separate lists of dynasties, and we must assume that they represent local dynasties of different cities of Egypt.

The list in Chron. Barb. reads:

Dynasty XI	*Diospolitans*	60 years
Dynasty XII	*Bubastites*	153 years
Dynasty XIII	*Tanites*	184 years
Dynasty XIV	*Sebennites*	224 years
Dynasty XV	*Memphites*	318 years
Dynasty XVI	*Iliopolitans*	221 years
Dynasty XVII	*Ermupolitans*	260 years

Ed. Meyer assumes that Dynasty XI in Chron. Barb. corresponds to Manetho's Twelfth Dynasty, and emends its 60 years to 160, which is the number that Africanus gives for the length of the Twelfth Dynasty. This assumption and emendation is perhaps not necessary. Africanus gives 43 years as the length of the Eleventh Dynasty, to which he adds the 16 years of *Amenemhet I*. These numbers make a total of 59 years, lacking only one year of the number given in Chron. Barb. for the Eleventh Dynasty.

[1] *ARE.*, I, p. 36, note.

The *Bubastite* and *Tanite Dynasties* have been considered above.[1]

The *Sebennitos Dynasty* reigned 224 years, from 1793–1569 B. C., i. e., from the fall of the Twelfth Dynasty to the fall of *Sebennitos*.

The *Memphis Dynasty* lasted 318 years, from 1887–1569 B. C., the last year being probably the one in which *Ahmose* captured Memphis.

The *Iliopolis Dynasty* of *Heliopolis* reigned 221 years, from 1793–1574 B. C., which would represent the time from the fall of the Twelfth Dynasty until the *Hyksos* people lost control of *H*eliopolis.

The *Ermupolis Dynasty*,[2] with its 260 years, I assume to be the latter part of *A*fricanus' Thirteenth Dynasty, and to have reigned from 1793–1533 B. C.[3]

The List of Africanus reads:

Dynasty XII	*Diospolitans*	160 years
Dynasty XIII	*Diospolitans*	453 years
Dynasty XIV	*C*hoites	184 years
Dynasty XV	*S*hepherds	284 years
Dynasty XVI	32 other *S*hepherds	518 years
Dynasty XVII	43 other *S*hepherds and 43 Thebans	151 years

The Twelfth Dynasty lasted, according to *A*fricanus, for 160 years, from *Sesostris I*, 1986 B. C., to the rise of the *Hyksos* in 1826 B. C.

---

[1] Pp. 220 f.

[2] Marquart identifies this with *Hermopolis* and assumes it to be identical with the Eighteenth Dynasty, which would then have ruled from 1581 to 1321 B. C., and must have included the reign of *Haremhab*, of the Nineteenth Dynasty.

[3] See below, pp. 228 ff.

In the *Turin Papyrus* the Thirteenth Dynasty appears as the immediate successor of *Amenemhet I*. Africanus assigns it 453 years and 60 kings, whom he calls *Diospolitans*. The latest discoveries in the Fayûm district make it evident that the kings of this dynasty resided somewhere near that oasis,[1] and were therefore close neighbors of the kings of the Twelfth Dynasty, who resided at Ithit-Tawy. If we then subtract 453 from the year 1986 B. C., when *Sesostris I* was appointed coregent by his father *Amenemhet I*, we come down to the year 1533 B. C., which is the accession year of *Thutmose I*. This fact is remarkable, and explains a number of obscure questions in the Egyptian history of this period. First of all, the Thirteenth Dynasty is contemporary with both the Twelfth Dynasty and the *Hyksos* kings. Secondly, we have found that Manetho placed *Amenemhet I* by himself, while the *Turin Papyrus* (and the royal *Lists*) place him in the Twelfth Dynasty. From the above it is evident that Manetho was correct, because *Amenemhet I* was the founder of two lines of kings, represented by the Twelfth and Thirteenth Dynasties, and although he and the Twelfth Dynasty kings were supreme rulers of Egypt, and he therefore, strictly speaking, belonged to the Twelfth Dynasty, still he belonged in a certain sense also to the Thirteenth Dynasty, and Manetho could therefore with perfect right place him alone. Thirdly, this fact sheds light upon the origin of the *Thutmose* family. It has been generally assumed that *Thutmose I* was not of royal blood, but inherited the throne of Egypt through his marriage with princess *Aahmes*, daughter of *Amenhotep I*. Still *Thutmose I* calls himself "*king's son of a king's son*,"[2] showing

[1] King and Hall, *History of Egypt*, p. 337.   [2] L. D. III 18.

that he was descended from a royal line. As *Africanus* ends the Thirteenth Dynasty with the accession of *Thutmose I*, there is justification for assuming that *Thutmose I* was a descendant of the Thirteenth Dynasty kings, and that by his marriage with *Aahmes* two royal houses of Egypt were united. *Africanus* regards both the Twelfth and Thirteenth Dynasties as *Diospolitan*, but if they were contemporary, they could hardly have resided in the same city. While the kings of the Twelfth and the earlier kings of the Thirteenth Dynasty were buried near Fayûm or Crocodilopolis, the *Turin Papyrus* makes it certain that the Twelfth Dynasty kings resided in Ithit-Tawy, which probably is identical with or lay near *Hermopolis Parva*. It seems therefore possible that the Thirteenth Dynasty kings resided in *Hermopolis Magna*, halfway between Fayûm and Thebes. They would then use the Fayûm district as their burial place until the fall of the Twelfth Dynasty, when the *Hyksos* took possession of this rich oasis region, and they then transferred their burial place to the region of the southern Crocodilopolis. *Thoth* was the god of *Hermopolis*, and it is possible that *Africanus'* Dios-polis is a corruption of Thoth-polis. It is certain from a number of references[1] that *Hermopolis* had royal palaces, indicating that it had been a residence city. The Seventeenth Dynasty of Chron. Barb. is called *Hermopolitan*, and lasted for 260 years, but the space from the fall of the Twelfth Dynasty in 1793 B. C. to the accession of *Thutmose I* in 1533 B. C. is exactly 260 years. It is therefore possible that this dynasty is identical with the latter part of *Africanus'* Thirteenth Dynasty. From the time of *Thutmose I*, the name *Thoth*, god of *Hermopolis*, is borne

---

[1] Cf. my references to Hermopolis in Breasted, *ARE*. Vol. V, Index VI.

by four kings, bearing the name *Thutmose*, who interchanged with four kings, named *Amenhotep*, descendants of the *S*eventeenth Dynasty kings of Thebes.

The Fourteenth Dynasty of Africanus and Eusebius is *Khoite*, consisting of 76 kings, who reigned 184 years. I assume that it is identical, or at least contemporary, with the Thirteenth Dynasty of Barbarus, which he calls *Tanite*, lasting from 1750–1566 B. C.

The Fifteenth Dynasty of Africanus is the great *Hyksos Dynasty*, 1826–1566 B. C. Africanus assigns it 284 years, because, contrary to the testimony of Josephus and *S*yncellus, he attributed 61 instead of 37 years to *Apakhnan*.

The "32 other Shepherd kings" in Africanus' Sixteenth Dynasty, ruling for 518 years, must be referred to the invasion in the time of *Mentuhotep I*, for if we add 518 to 1566 B. C., the year of the expulsion of the *Hyksos*, we reach the year 2084 B. C., which is the most reasonable date for that king, in whose time an Asiatic invasion of Egypt is recorded.

The *S*eventeenth Dynasty of Africanus is called *Theban*, consisting of 43 kings, who reigned 151 years, together with "43 other *S*hepherd kings." Now, the *Karnak-List* makes the kings of the *S*eventeenth Dynasty the immediate successors of *Sesostris I*, and as in the case of the Thirteenth Dynasty of *Diospolis*, so must we regard this dynasty as contemporary with the Twelfth Dynasty. The Twelfth Dynasty kings descended from the *Intefs* of the Eleventh Dynasty, but in the *S*eventeenth Dynasty we again find a number of *Intefs* ruling in Thebes, and closely associated with the *Sesostres* kings of the Twelfth Dynasty. Thus we find a doorpost, erected at Coptos by

Sesostris I, and inscribed by an *Intef* (*IV*), whose thronename was *Nub-kheper-Re*. This shows that Steindorf is correct in claiming that not all *Intefs* belonged to the Eleventh Dynasty, but on the other hand, it does not follow necessarily that all the later *Intefs* were subsequent to the Twelfth Dynasty. As the Thirteenth Dynasty arose with the accession of *Sesostris I*, so it seems probable that the Seventeenth Dynasty arose with the accession of *Amenemhet II* in 1944 B. C. If we subtract therefrom 151, which represents Africanus' number of years of the duration of this dynasty, we come down to the year 1793 B. C., which marks the fall of the Twelfth Dynasty, and here begins Barbarus' Seventeenth Dynasty of Hermopolis. The large number of kings—43—for the short period of 151 years, giving an average of $3^1/_2$ years to each king, is fully substantiated by the *Turin Papyrus*, and thus we find again how correct Africanus is. The Seventeenth Dynasty of Thebes lasted, therefore, from 1944 to 1793 B. C.

Dynasty XI

Africanus assigns 43 years to the Eleventh Dynasty. Chron. Barb. agrees substantially with this statement when it assigns 60 years to the same dynasty, because it placed the 16 years of the reign of *Amenemhet I* between the Eleventh and Twelfth Dynasties, and if these 16 years be added to Africanus' 43 years, we obtain 59 years. And since Chron. Barb. may have included fractions of years in the three reigns, the number 60 may be taken as perfectly correct.

The *Turin Papyrus* assigns 6 kings and 160[1] years to this dynasty, and the names of the last two kings, *Neb-*

---

[1] The unit is lost; it lasted somewhere between 160 and 169 years.

DYNASTIES X, XI—COMPARATIVE CHART

Turin Papyrus	Sakkara List	Abydos List	Africanus	Eusebius	Monuments
Dynasty X			19 Herakleopolitans 185 y.	19 Herakleopolitans 185 y.	
Dynasty XI . . . . Nebhepetre . . Sankhkare . . Total 160+y.	. . . . 37. Nebhepetre 38. Sankhkare	. . . . 57. Nebhepetre 58. Sankhkare	16 Thebans with Ammenemes 43 y. 16 y. Total 192 Kings 2300 y. 70 d. from Menes to end of XI dynasty.	16 Thebans with Ammenemes 43 y. 16 y. Total 192 Kings, 2300 years, 7 d.	Nebhepetre 46 y. Sankhkare 8 y.

hepet-Re (= *Mentuhotep III*) and *Sankh-ka-Re* (= *Mentuhotep IV*),[1] are preserved. The *Sakkara-* and *Abydos-Lists* verify this, and the reigns of these two kings therefore correspond to the 43 years of Africanus.

It is certain that *Nebhepetre-Mentuhotep*, whom we shall designate as *Mentuhotep III*, united all Egypt under his scepter, and that his capital was in Thebes. His highest date on the monuments is the year 46.

He was succeeded by his son *Sankhkare-Mentuhotep*, whom we shall designate as *Mentuhotep IV*, and he reigned at least 8 years. He died in 2002 B. C., being succeeded by *Amenemhet I* of the Twelfth Dynasty, but as the *Turin Papyrus* and the *Intef* stela at Cairo assign to *Amenemhet I* a reign of 19 years before the accession of *Sesostris I*, we must assume that he was a rival king to *Mentuhotep IV* for three or four years, 2006-2002 B. C. The end of the Eleventh Dynasty falls, however, in the latter year, 2002 B. C., and from that date we should reckon the length of this dynasty, 43 years, that is to say, the Eleventh Dynasty ruled all Egypt from 2045 to 2002 B. C.

But *Mentuhotep III* had been king of all Egypt for some time before he succeeded in overpowering the *Heracleopolitan* kings of the Tenth Dynasty. If we assume that he reigned 50 years, and his son 10 years, we obtain the following dates:

Mentuhotep III, 50 years, 2062-2012 B. C.
Mentuhotep IV, 10 years, 2012-2002 B. C.

The *Turin Papyrus* assigns at least 160 years to this

---

[1] Ed. Meyer and Breasted contend that a seventh king, *Nebtawire-Mentuhotep* should be added, and that he was the last king of this dynasty, but this has been successfully refuted by Sethe, *ZÄ.*, Vol. XLII, pp. 132-34.

DYNASTY XI

dynasty, in which should be included at least two *Intef* kings and two *Mentuhoteps*, who preceded the two *Mentuhoteps* mentioned above. But it is incontrovertibly certain that no one of the *Intefs*, nor *Nibhotep-Mentuhotep*, whom we shall designate as *Mentuhotep I*, ruled all Egypt, the rule of the *Intefs* never extending further north than Thinis. *Mentuhotep II* had to face a great invasion of Egypt, as well as a rebellion, and there is nothing to show that his kingdom was even as large as that of the *Intefs*.

Sethe[1] has lately offered a hypothesis, according to which all the *Intefs* were vassals of *Mentuhotep III*. He bases this on the assumption that the son of *Neb-tep-nefer-Intef*, whose *H*orus-name began with *Sankh* - - - , is identical with *Sankhkare-Mentuhotep IV*. This can hardly be admitted. The *Intefs* bear the title *Suten-Bity*, "kings of Upper and Lower Egypt," and they could not very well do this if they were only vassals of a king, who ruled only Upper Egypt and perhaps a small part of Lower Egypt. Then again, Thebes was the residence city both of the *Intefs* and of the last two *Mentuhoteps*, and we cannot assume that both the king and his vassals lived in the same city. The *Turin Papyrus* presupposes that *Sankhkare-Mentuhotep IV* is a son of *Nebhepetre-Mentuhotep III* and not of *Intef III*.

It seems therefore that this king, whose *H*orus-name began with *Sankh* - - - - was the last *Intef*, who was deposed by a *Mentuhotep*. This *Mentuhotep* can hardly be any other than (*Nibhotep-*)*Mentuhotep I*.

Inscribed blocks from a temple of *Mentuhotep I* at Gebelên tell us that this king smote an enemy, who was "*chief of Tehenu*" (=Libya), but the *Intefs* were of

[1] *ZÄ*., Vol. XLII, pp. 132–34.

Libyan or Berber descent, as the dog stela of *Wahanekh-Intef* plainly indicates. Another block bears the inscription: "*Son of Hathor, mistress of Dendera, Mentuhotep*," showing that this *Mentuhotep II* was not descended from a king, and therefore claimed his royal prerogatives on account of divine birth, and that Denderah probably was his native home. This inscription says also that *Mentuhotep I* slew four enemies, the first of them unnamed, but the relief shows him to be an Egyptian, and the three other enemies were: "*Nubians, Asiatics (sttyw), Libyans.*" Over the whole is an inscription, reading: "*Binding the chiefs of the Two Lands (=Egypt?), capturing the South and the Northland, the Highlands, and the Two Regions, the Nine Bows and the Two Lands.*"

The Nubians and the Asiatics must be invaders from Ethiopia and Southern Palestine. The Libyans may be the *Intef*-people who held Thebes. The Egyptians may include the people both of Upper and Lower Egypt, i. e., the people formerly governed by the *Intef* kings of Thebes (Upper Egypt) and the people of the Northland or the Delta. No reference is made to Middle Egypt, or to the kingdom of Heracleopolis.

This war cannot be dated as late as 2045 B. C., when the Theban kings overthrew the Tenth Dynasty of Heracleopolis, for that was done by *Mentuhotep III;* and *Kheti II* of Siût, who spent the larger part of his life in the service of the kings of Heracleopolis, became, at the close of his life, a vassal of *Mentuhotep III*, indicating that Siût and Heracleopolis came under Thebes in the reign of that king.

The monuments furnish us with information of still another king, *Nebtawire-Mentuhotep*, whom I shall designate as *Mentuhotep II*. His Hammamat-inscriptions show that he collected an army from the northland or Delta, and that peace seems to have reigned in his time. The fact of his having mustered his army in the Delta does not necessarily imply, however, that he also ruled over Middle Egypt or *H*eracleopolis, the kingdom of which extended principally on the western bank of the Nile. This *Mentuhotep* may, therefore, have been the successor of *Nebhotep-Mentuhotep I*, and predecessor of *Nebhepetre-Mentuhotep III*, and the last four kings of this *Theban Dynasty* were then all *Mentuhoteps*.

This leaves us two kings for the beginning of this dynasty, and these kings must be *Intefs*. *H*ere the monuments again fully sustain our contention, for, while the monuments mention four *Intefs*, only two of them were kings.

The first *Intef* was never king, being only a monarch of Thebes. The *Intefs* were of foreign *L*ibyan descent, and it seems probable that this *Intef* invaded Egypt and captured Thebes in the beginning of the Tenth Dynasty of *H*eracleopolis. He did not become independent, however, but acknowledged the suzerainty of the kings of *H*eracleopolis.

He was succeeded by his son *Wahanekh-Intef*, whom we shall designate as *Intef I*. This king rebelled against his superiors of *H*eracleopolis, and succeeded in establishing at Thebes a kingdom, that extended from Elephantine ("Door of the *S*outh") to Thinis or Abydos ("Door of the North"). His reign lasted at least fifty years, for he set up his "dog stela" in the fiftieth year of his reign, and on this stela he claims that he had carried on a war to establish his southern boundary at

Thinis, and his enemy can hardly have been anyone else than a king of *H*eracleopolis.

Intef I was succeeded by his son, *Nakht-neb-tep-nefer-Intef*, whom we shall designate as *Intef II*. This king, whose reign does not seem to have been of long duration, was succeeded by an *Intef* who, however, never became recognized as king, or who, at any rate, ruled only for a short time,[1] being dispossessed by a *Mentuhotep*, whom I assume to be *Mentuhotep I*, with the throne-name of *Nebhotep*.

The *Turin Papyrus* states that the Eleventh Dynasty lasted at least 160 years. Now a *Thinite* official, *Intef-yoker*, erected a stela in the thirty-third year of *Sesostris I*, and stated thereon that his great-grandfather had been appointed to the same office as his (field-scribe) by *Intef I*. As this stela was erected in 1954 B. C., and assuming forty years to a generation, this date carries us to about 2114 B. C., which should fall within the time of *Intef I*. If, according to the *Turin Papyrus*, we add 160 years to

---

[1] I have assumed that this *Intef* is identical with the king whose Horus-name began with *Sankh* - - - -. It is possible that this name was *Sankh-ka-re*. Syncellus avers that his Sixteenth Dynasty ended with a king, *Konkharis*, who reigned 5 years, and at whose death, which came 700 years after the *Sothic* period, the *Hyksos* rule began. It is possible that this *Konkharis* is a miscopying of *Sonkharis*. Seven hundred years from the beginning of the Sothic cycle bring us to the year 2081 B. C., but we found above that Africanus' Sixteenth Dynasty of *Hyksos* kings began in 2084, or, according to Josephus, in 2077 B. C. *Mentuhotep I*, who overthrew this *Intef*, fought an invading army of Asiatics, and these data seem to indicate that our date of *Mentuhotep I* as given below is approximately correct.

The Twelfth Dynasty is said (*Turin Papyrus*) to be from *Ithit-tawy*, and probably descended from these *Intefs*, who were overthrown by the *Mentuhoteps*. *Sesostris I* regarded the monarch *Intef* as his "father," and this is evidently not an empty term, but a recognition of his having descended from the *Intefs*. *Ithit-tawy* was presumably a *Tehenu*-settlement in the Delta, and the *Tehenu* (Libyan or Berber) origin of the *Intefs* may be regarded as certain.

DYNASTY X   237

2002 B. C., when the Eleventh Dynasty ended, we come to the year 2162 B. C., and as *Intef I* reigned at least 50 years, he died about 2112, which coincides admirably with the data on the stela of *Intef-yoker*.

The period from 2112 B. C. to about 2062 B. C. is then to be filled in by the reigns of *Intef II*, *Mentuhotep I*, and *Mentuhotep II*. I would, therefore, propose the following approximate

Chronological Table of Dynasty XI

Intef I	50 years	2162–2112 B. C.
Intef II	26 years	2112–2086 B. C.
Intef III	5 years	2086–2081 B. C.
Mentuhotep I	9 years	2086–2077 B. C.
Mentuhotep II	15 years	2077–2062 B. C.
Mentuhotep III	50 years	2062–2012 B. C.
Mentuhotep IV	10 (?) years	2012–2002 B. C.

Dynasty X

The Eleventh Dynasty was preceded by the *S*econd Dynasty of *H*eracleopolis, known as Dynasty X, which lasted 185 years.[1] This number has not been doubted, so far as I am aware, but the question is, where it should be applied. Breasted and Ed. Meyer assign the Heracleopolitan rule to a period wholly preceding that of the Eleventh Dynasty, but it is incontrovertibly certain that the *Intefs* and some of the *Mentuhoteps*, reigning in Thebes, were contemporaries of the kings of Heracleopolis, and from the monuments of *Kheti II* of *S*iût it appears that the *H*eracleopolitan kingdom was overthrown in the time of *Nebhepetre-Mentuhotep III*.

[1] Africanus and Eusebius. Chron. Barb gives 204 years.

The date of Africanus and Eusebius, giving 43 years to the Eleventh Dynasty, seems so reasonable, that I cannot hesitate to accept it as correct. Here again we see the danger of an uncritical following of the *Turin Papyrus*, the object of which was to give the dates of reigns in each dynasty, without taking into account the existence of partially or completely contemporary dynasties.

The Tenth Dynasty was therefore overthrown in 2045 B. C., and as it lasted for 185[1] years, it came to power about 2230 B. C. At its accession it ruled all Egypt and continued to do so until (*Wahanekh-*) *Intef I* made himself independent in Thebes about 2162 B. C.

Dynasties VII–IX

The Tenth Dynasty was preceded by another dynasty of Heracleopolis, known as Dynasty IX. Eusebius states that this dynasty lasted for 100 years. Africanus, on the contrary, assigns to it 409 years. The date of Eusebius interests us especially, because it offers a valuable comparison with another date. For Eusebius also assigns 100 years to the Eighth Dynasty of Memphis.

This seems to indicate that we are here dealing, not with two successive, but with two contemporary dynasties, one ruling in Memphis, and the other in Heracleopolis, both beginning in 2330 and lasting to 2230 B. C.

The date, 409 years, assigned by Africanus for the Ninth Dynasty of Heracleopolis, may indicate that vassal kings had ruled that city for 309 years before, i. e., 2639–2330 B. C. The Sixth Dynasty was also Memphitic, and

---

[1] The nineteen years overlapping in Chron. Barb. may indicate that the last king of Heracleopolis continued to reign as a vassal under *Mentuhotep III* for that space of time.

DYNASTIES VII–IX—COMPARATIVE CHART

Turin Papyrus	Sakkara List	Abydos List	Africanus	Eusebius
Dynasty VII			70 Memphites 70 days	5 Memphites 75 days
Dynasty VIII		41. Menkare	27 Memphites 146 y.	5 Memphites 100 y.
1. . . .		42. Neferkare		
2. . . .		43. Neferkare-Neby		
3. Neferkare		44. Dedkare-Shema		
4. Kheti		45. Neferkare-Khendu		
5. S-h-				
6. . . .		46. Merenhor		
7. Mer . .		47. Sneferka		
8. Senti .		48. Nekare		
9. H . .				
10–14.		49. Neferkare-Tereru		
15. Nitaqerti		50. Neferkahor		
16. Neferka		51. Neferkare-Pepy-seneb		
17. Neferes		52. Sneferka-Anu		
18. Yeb		53. [. . . .]kaure		
		54. Neferkaure		
		55. Neferkauhor		
		56. Nefererkare		
Dynasty IX			19 Herakleopolitans 1. Akhthoes Total 409 y.	4 Herakleopolitans 1. Akhthoes Total 100 y.

when that dynasty was overthrown, about 2330 B. C., a new dynasty arose, Dynasty VII, which lasted only 70 days. This change of government in Memphis gave an opportunity to the nomarchs of *H*eliopolis to declare themselves independent, and when the new dynasty of Memphis, Dynasty VIII, established itself, Egypt was rent in twain, the Eighth Dynasty ruling the Delta from Memphis, and the Ninth Dynasty ruling Middle and *S*outhern Egypt from *H*eracleopolis.

After 100 years, i. e., about 2230 B. C., the new dynasty of *H*eracleopolis, Dynasty X, extended the rule of that city over all Egypt, until the *Intefs* rebelled in Thebes.

*A*fricanus assigns 146 years to the Eighth Dynasty of Memphis, and the overlapping 46 years may represent a vassal rule in Memphis under the first kings of the Tenth Dynasty of *H*eracleopolis.

The dark period between the *S*ixth and Twelfth Dynasties is then an exact counterpart of the *Hyksos* rule and the numerous vassal dynasties that intervened between the Twelfth and Eighteenth Dynasties. Instead of extending the *Hyksos* rule and the Thirteenth to the *S*eventeenth Dynasties over a period of 1500–1700 years, we found that the 260 years of the *Hyksos* rule was all that could be conceded to that dark period. *S*imilarly we find again that the dark period between the *S*ixth and Twelfth Dynasties, instead of extending over some 900 years,[1] is amply covered by allotting it 328 years.

The problem of the chronology of this dark period has resolved itself into the question of a number of coregencies.

---

[1] Africanus: Eighth Dynasty, 146 years; Ninth Dynasty, 409 years; Tenth Dynasty, 185 years; *Turin Papyrus:* Eleventh Dynasty, 160 years, total, 900 years.

Memphis	Heracleopolis	Thebes
Dynasty VIII, 2330–2230 B. C.	Dynasty IX, 2330–2230 B. C. Dynasty X, 2230–2045 B. C.	Dynasty XI, 2162–2002 B. C.

The *Abydos-List* gives the names of sixteen kings (N^{os}41–56), from the end of the Sixth Dynasty to *Mentuhotep III* of the Eleventh Dynasty. The *Turin Papyrus* offers a similar list, and its name, *Kheti*, may be one of the *Khetis* of Siût, but more probably *Akhthoes* of the Ninth Dynasty of *H*eracleopolis. A period of 330 years seems to be very reasonable for these sixteen kings in the *Abydos-List*. Its names may be those of the kings of *H*eracleopolis, or they may represent a dynasty of nomarchs in Abydos or Thinis, and in that case we would have to add another contemporary dynasty to those mentioned above.

Dynasties V and VI

The year 2330 B. C. marks the beginning of the Eighth and Ninth Dynasties. As the Seventh Dynasty lasted only 70 days, this year marks also the end of the Sixth Dynasty. This dynasty is also Memphitic. *A*fricanus assigns it 6 kings, Chron. Barb., 8. Eusebius regards it as an Elephantine dynasty, corresponding to the Fifth Dynasty of Africanus, and consisting of 31 kings, and makes its last ruler, Queen Nitokris, to be the only representative of the Sixth Dynasty. Eratosthenes assigns it 5 kings, the *Abydos-List* 7, the *Sakkara-List* only 4, but the *Turin Papyrus* has 13 kings of this dynasty, although it seems as if it regarded only the first 6 of its kings as really legitimate rulers.

DYNASTIES V, VI—COMPARATIVE CHART

Turin Papyrus	Sakkara List	Abydos List	Africanus	Eusebius	Monuments
Dynasty V			8 Kings from Elephantine		
32. [User]kaf 7 y.	25. Userka[f]	26. Userka	1. Ouserkheres 28 y.	. . .	Userkaf 7 y.
33. [Sahure] 12 y.	26. Sahure	27. Sahure	2. Sephres 13 y.	. . .	Sahure 13 y.
34. [Neferkare] x y.	27. Neferkare	28. Kakai	3. Nefercheres 20 y.	. . .	Neferkare 10 y.
35. [Shepseskare] 7 y.	28. Shepseskare	29. Neferefre	4. Sisires 7 y.	. . .	Shepseskare 7 y.
36. [Akauhor] x y.	29. Khemeferre	.	5. Kheres 20 y.	. . .	Khemeferre
37. [Nuserre] 30 + x y.	.	30. Nuserre	6. Rathoures 44 y.	. . .	Nuserre 30 y.
38. Menkahor 8 y.	30. Menkahor	31. Menkauhor	7. Menkheres 9 y.	. . .	Menkauhor 8 y.
39. Ded(kare) 28 y.	31. Dedkare	32. Dedkare	8. Tankheres 44 y.	. . .	Dedkare 28 y.
40. Unas x y.	32. Unas	33. Unas	9. Onnos 33 y.	. . .	Unas 30 y.
Total of the Kings from Menes unto			Total 248 y.	Total 448 y.	
Dynasty VI			6 Memphites	31 Kings from Elephantine	
41. [Atoti] x y.	33. Atoti	34. Atoti	1. Othoës 30 y.	1. Othoës y.	Teti x
42. [. . .]	.	35. Userkare	.	.	Userkare
43. [Pepi] 20 y.	34. Pepy	36. Merire	2. Phios 53 y.	. Phios	Pepi I 20 y.
44. [Mernere] 4(?) y.	35. Mernere	37. Mernere	3. Methousouphis 7 y.	.	Mernere I 4 y.
45. [Pepi] 90+x y.	36. Neferkare	38. Neferkare	4. Phiops 94 y.	4. Phiops 94 y.	Pepi II 90 y.
46. [. . .] 1 y.	.	39. Mernere-zefamsaf	5. Menthesouphis 1 y.	.	Mernere II 1 y.
		40. Neterkare	6. Nitokris 12 y.	Dyn. VI. Nitokris	
Total 181 y.			Total 203 y.	Total 203 y.	
Total since Menes 955 y.					
10+x d.					

DYNASTIES V AND VI

It is the fragment No. 61 of the *Turin Papyrus* which gives the list of the kings of this dynasty, contained in the

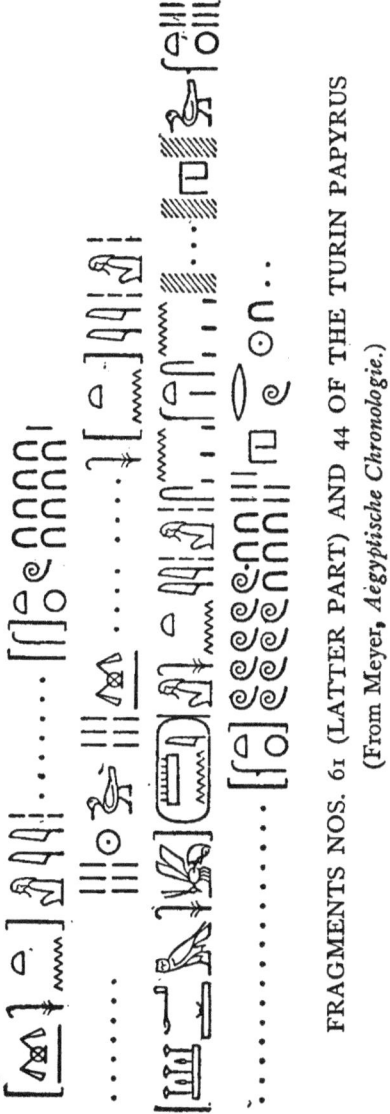

FRAGMENTS NOS. 61 (LATTER PART) AND 44 OF THE TURIN PAPYRUS
(From Meyer, *Aegyptische Chronologie*.)

first 13 lines; in the 14th line follows the total of the years, 181, which is of the utmost importance for the chronology of this period. Manetho gives 203 years as its length, but the total of the reigns sums up only 197 years. Now, the *Turin Papyrus* adds in the next line a mutilated note to the effect that "*16[1] years are not to be counted.*" If we add these 16 years to the total 181, we obtain 197 years, which is the total of the reigns in the list of Africanus. We may therefore regard it as certain that this dynasty lasted 181 years, from 2511 to 2330 B. C. The *Abydos-List* mentions *Userkare* as the second king, but this king is omitted by the *Sakkara-List*, and by Manetho and Eratosthenes. The probability is that he was only a coregent with his father. The "*16 years not to be counted*" may represent the first period of *Teti's* (*Athoe's*) reign, being contemporary with the latter part of the Fifth Dynasty. If this be admitted, the list of Africanus coincides with the total given in the *Turin Papyrus*, and we obtain then the following

Chronological Table of Dynasty VI

Teti (Athoes)	30 years	(2527–)2511–2497 B. C.
Userkare		
Pepi I (Phios)	53 years	2497–2444 B. C.
Mernere I	7 years	2444–2437 B. C.
Pepi II (Phiops)	94 years	2437–2343 B. C.
Mernere II	1 year	2343–2342 B. C.
Nitokris	12 years	2342–2330 B. C.

Dynasty V

For the dates of the Fifth Dynasty we must rely upon Africanus, who assigns 9 kings to this dynasty, and this number is also given by the *Turin Papyrus*. The *Sak-*

---

[1] Read 10+6 instead of "*Sun*"+6.

kara- and *Abydos-Lists* mention only 8 kings, but the former has omitted *Nuserre* and the latter His predecessor, *Khaneferre*, and the number 9 is thus correct. Africanus gives 248 years as the length of this dynasty, but the total of the reigns amounts only to 218 years, which I am inclined to accept as correct. The separate reigns can partly be checked by the *Palermo Stone* and the *Turin Papyrus*, and the indications are that the dates given by Africanus are at least approximately correct. Accepting them as they are given, we obtain the following

Chronological Table of Dynasty V

Userkaf	28 years	2729–2701 B. C.
Sahure	13 years	2701–2688 B. C.
Neferirkare	20 years	2688–2668 B. C.
Shepseskare	7 years	2668–2661 B. C.
Akauhor (Khaneferre)	20 years	2661–2641 B. C.
Nuserre	44 years	2641–2597 B. C.
Menkauhor	9 years	2597–2588 B. C.
Dedkare	44 years	2588–2544 B. C.
Unas	33 years	2544–2511 B. C.

Dynasties I–IV

The Fifth Dynasty is regarded as Memphitic by Africanus, as Elephantine by Eusebius. *Papyrus Westcar* presents the legend of the birth of its first three kings. According to this story, these three kings were brothers, and sons of the high-priest of *H*eliopolis. There is a historical truth embodied in this story, for the fifth Egyptian royal title, *Sa-Re*, "Son of Re," is introduced by the kings of this dynasty, and although they may have resided in Memphis, or were buried in the sacred

DYNASTIES I, II—COMPARATIVE CHART

TURIN PAPYRUS	SAKKARA LIST	ABYDOS LIST	AFRICANUS	EUSEBIUS
Dynasty I			8 Thinites	8 Thinites
1. Menes	. .	1. Menes	1. Menes 62 y.	1. Menes 60 y.
2. Af[ôti]	. .	2. Atôti	2. Athothis 57 y.	2. Athothis 27 y.
3. [. . .]	. .	3. Atôti	3. Kenkenes 31 y.	3. Kenkenes 39 y.
4. [Atôti]	. .	4. Atôti	4. Ouenephes 23 y.	4. Ouenephes 42 y.
5. Usaphais	. .	5. Usaphais	5. Ousaphais 20 y.	5. Ousaphais 20 y.
6. Miebis	1. Miebis	6. Miebis	6. Miebis 26 y.	6. Miebais 26 y.
7. [. . .]	. .	7. Semempses	7. Semempses 18 y.	7. Semempses 18 y.
8. [Qebhu]	2. Qebhu	8. Qebhu	8. Bienekhes 26 y.	8. Oubienthis 26 y.
			Total 253 y.	Total 252 y.
Dynasty II			9 Thinites	9 Kings
9. Bau[nuter]	3. Baunuter	9. Bazau	1. Boethos 38 y.	1. Bokhos
10. [Ka]kau	4. Kakau	10. Kakau	2. Kaikhos 39 y.	2. Kekhbos
11. [Ba]nuter	5. Banuteru	11. Banuier	3. Binothris 47 y.	3. Biophis
12. [. . .]	6. Uznas	12. Uznas	4. Tlas 17 y.	4. } Three Others
13. Send	7. Sendi	13. Senda	5. Sethenes 41 y.	5. }
14. Neferka[re]	8. Neferkare	. .	6. Khaires 17 y.	6. }
15. Neferkasoker 8 y.	9. Neferkasoker	. .	7. Nepherkheres 25 y.	7. The Seventh
16. Huzefa 11 y.	10. Huzefa	14. Zazay	8. Sesokhris 48 y.	8. Sesokhris 48 y.
17. Beby 27 y.	11. Beby	. .	9. Khenephes 30 y.	9. The Ninth
			Total 302 y.	Total 297 y.

cemeteries west of Memphis, the dynasty is undoubtedly Heliopolitan in origin.

Of the first four dynasties, the first two are styled *Thinite* by Manetho, the third and fourth *Memphitic*. The totals of the years, given by Africanus, are $253+302+214+277=1,046$ years, but the first three are given by Eusebius as $252+297+198$, while the Fourth and Fifth Dynasties are accorded 448 years. If we subtract from that 218 years for the Fifth Dynasty, it leaves 230 years for the fourth, and the total of the first four dynasties in Eusebius amounts, therefore, to 977 years. The first two dynasties are declared to embrace 555 years by Africanus, and 549 by Eusebius. The Third and Fourth Dynasties total 491 years in Africanus, but only 428 years in Eusebius.

Eratosthenes differs remarkably from Africanus and Eusebius, assigning only 17 kings and 501 years for the first four dynasties. It should be admitted that no great reliance can be placed on Eratosthenes for chronological purposes, but the fact remains that Manetho also ascribes 17 kings to the two *Thinite Dynasties*, and the same number to the *Memphite Dynasties*.

The length of this period, 501 years, seems also to be approximately correct. Seyfarth and Ed. Meyer[1] have shown that fragment No. 44 of the *Turin Papyrus* fits admirably after fragment No. 61, and belongs therefore to the end of the Sixth Dynasty. In this fragment, No. 44, the total from *Menes* is given as 955 years, which means, therefore, that the time from the accession of *Menes* to the fall of the Sixth Dynasty was 955 years. The arguments of these scholars in favor of placing fragment No. 44 after

[1] *Chron.*, pp. 165, 166.

DYNASTIES III, IV—COMPARATIVE CHARTS

Turin Papyrus		Sakkara List	Abydos List	Africanus		Eusebius		Monuments	
Dynasty III.				9 Memphites		8 Memphites			
18. Nebka	19 y.	. .	15. Nebka	1. Nekherophes	28 y.	1. Nekherokhis			
19. Zoser	19 y.	12. Zoser	16. Zoser	2. Tosorthros	29 y.	2. Sesorthos			
. .	.	. .	. .	3. Tureis	7 y.	3.			
. .	.	. .	. .	4. Mesokhris	17 y.	4.			
. .	.	. .	. .	5. Souphis	16 y.	5. ⎫ The Six Others			
20. Zoserti	6 y.	13. Zoser-Atoti	17. Atoti	6. Tosertasis	19 y.	6. ⎬			
. .	.	14. Nebkare	. .	7. Akhes	42 y.	7. ⎭			
21. [. . .]kefa	6 y.	. .	18. Sezes	8. Sephouris	30 y.	8.			
22. Huni	24 y.	15. Huni	19. Neferkare	9. Kerpheres	26 y.	Total	198 y.		
				Total	214 y.				
Dynasty IV.				8 Memphites		17 Memphites			
23. Snofr[u]	24 y.	16. Snofru	20. Snofru	1. Soris	29 y.	1.		Snofru	29 y.
24. [Cheops]	23 y.	17. Khufu	21. Khufu	2. Souphis	63 y.	2.		Khufu	23 y.
25. [Dede]re	8 y.	18. Dedefre	22. Dedefre	.		.		Dedefre	8 y.
26. Kheu[fre]	x y.	19. Kheufre	23. Khefre	3. Souphis	66 y.	3. Souphis		Khefre	18 y.
27. [Mykerinos]	x y.	20. . .	24. Menkaure	4. Menkheres	63 y.	.			
28. [. . .]	x y.	21. . . ⎫	. .	5. Ratoises	25 y.	.			
29. [Shepseskaf]	8 y.	22. . . ⎬ destroyed	25. Shepseskaf	6. Bikheris	22 y.	.		Shepseskaf	4 y.
30. [. . .]	4 y.	23. . . ⎭	. .	7. Seberkheres	7 y.	.			
31. [. . .]	2 y.	24. . .	. .	8. Thamphthis	9 y.	.			
				Total	277 y.				

No. 61 seem convincing, and we have then in this fragment a date of extraordinary value for Egyptian chronology, since it places the accession of *Menes* at about 3285 B. C. As we have assigned 181 years to the Sixth Dynasty and 218 years to the Fifth Dynasty, there are left only 556 years for the first four dynasties. If, on the contrary, we accept the full dates of Africanus, 248 years for the Fifth and 203 (or 197) years for the Sixth, there would be left only 504 years for the first four dynasties, which comes surprisingly near the 501 years which Eratosthenes assigns to these four dynasties.

Assuming, however, that we are correct in assigning only 181 years to the Sixth Dynasty, as this date is given in the *Turin Papyrus*, and 218 years to the Fifth Dynasty, there remain 556 years for the first four dynasties. Can this number be brought into harmony with the Manethonian lists? This seems impossible, for the first two dynasties of *Thinis* alone amount to 555 years, i. e., they practically cover the whole period from *Menes* to the rise of the Fifth Dynasty. But this very fact may point out the way to the solution of this difficulty, namely, that we are dealing here either with contemporary reigns or contemporary dynasties.

The *Sakkara-List* begins with *Miebis*, the sixth king of the First Dynasty, and archaeological evidence[1] indicates that he was the first king of Egypt, residing in or ruling Memphis. The *Sakkara-List* represents him with the crown of *Lower* Egypt, and it is a peculiarity of this list that its kings alternate as kings of Upper and *Lower* Egypt, while a few of them are represented as only "*H*onorables."

[1] See Hall, in *History of Egypt*, Vol. XIII, pp. 91 ff.

On the *Palermo Stone* differentiation is constantly made between "*the Kings of Lower Egypt*" and "*the Kings of Upper Egypt*," and it is not until the Fifth Dynasty that the kings bear constantly the full title "*King of Upper and Lower Egypt.*"

On the other hand it should be remarked that the *Turin Papyrus* assigns far shorter reigns to the kings of the first four dynasties than do the Manethonian lists, but the *Turin Papyrus* is so mutilated, that, with the exception of a very few cases, we cannot rely upon it for ascertaining the exact lengths of the reigns of this period.

The historical material of this early period is yet, however, entirely too insufficient to enable us to construct anything like an exact chronology. Meanwhile, we may gratefully accept two well-assured dates—the accession of *Menes* about 3285 B. C., and the fall of the Fourth Dynasty, about 2729 B. C. New discoveries increase our knowledge of this period almost daily, and we may hope that the uncertainties that still confront students of early Egyptian history will shortly be entirely cleared away.

D. PREDYNASTIC AND PREHISTORIC KINGS OF EGYPT

The sources for the history of Egypt before the foundation of the united kingdom consist of a few records in the classical authors, the *Turin Papyrus*, and the *Palermo Stone*.[1] To these can now be added the opinions of modern scholars based on the results achieved by recent excavations and discoveries in Egypt, bearing on the prehistoric period.

The classical authors, in referring to the predynastic period, mainly followed the records of Manetho, but in

---

[1] For the predynastic kings of Lower Egypt on the *Palermo Stone*, cf. above, p. 172.

some instances it is evident that other material must have been at their disposal.

Syncellus

Thus Syncellus avers that the Egyptians possessed a "*certain tablet called the Old Chronicle, containing thirty dynasties in 113 descents, during the long period of 36,525 years. The first series of princes was that of the Auritae, the second was that of the Mestraeans, and the third that of the Egyptians.*"

This historian then goes on to divide the whole history of Egypt into five periods:

1. *Hephaistos* (*Ptah*). No definite time is assigned to this period.
2. *Helios*, the son of *Hephaistos*, reigned 30,000 years.
3. *Kronos* and the other twelve gods reigned 3,984 years.
4. The eight demigods reigned 217 years.
5. The thirty dynasties of kings reigned 2,324 years.

The total is 36,525 years for predynastic and dynastic Egypt, and Syncellus claims that this total equals 25 Sothic cycles of 1,461 years each, for "*it relates to the fabled periodical revolution of the zodiac among the Egyptians and Greeks, that is, its revolution from a particular point to the same again, which point is the first minute of the first degree of that equinoctial sign which they call Aries, as it is explained in the Genesis of Hermes and in the Cyrannian books.*"

The *Auritae* of Syncellus may represent the *Horites* or *Horus* people. *Mestraeans* may be a form of *Mizraim* (= Egypt).

The fabulous length of the duration of the Egyptian kingdom is somewhat reduced by

Eusebius

He divides the prehistoric dynasties into seven periods:

I. Dynasty of gods.
  1. *Hephaistos* (*Ptah*).
  2. *Helios.*
  3. *Sosis* (*Shu*).
  4. *Keb* (*Kronos*).
  5. *Osiris.*
  6. *Typhon.*
  7. *Horus,* son of *Isis.*

II. "*After them, the kingdom descended by a long succession until Bidi, for a space of 13,900 years, reckoned, I say, in lunar years of thirty days to each; for even now they call the month a year.*"

III. "*After the gods, the dynasty of the demi-gods reigned for 1255 years.*"

IV. "*Then again other kings reigned for 1817 years.*"

V. "*After these, thirty other kings from Memphis, for 1790 years.*"

VI. "*After them, ten other kings of Thinis, for 350 years.*"

VII. "*Finally, a dynasty of shades (Manes)[1] and the demi-gods, for 5813 years.*"

Eusebius' remark that he was dealing with lunar years brings these fabulous dates within possible limits.

Manetho and Panodorus

But Manetho and Panodorus have reduced this period still further, for they know of only two prehistoric periods, viz.,

[1] νέκυες.

PREDYNASTIC KINGS

		Manetho	Panodorus
I.	GODS.		
	1. *Hephaistos*	9,000	727¾
	2. *Helios*	992	80⅙
	3. *Agathodaemon*	700	56½
	4. *Kronos*	501	40½
	5. *Osiris* and *Isis*	433	35
	6. *Typhon*	359	29
		11,985	969
II.	DEMIGODS.		
	1. *Horus*	100	25
	2. *Ares*	92	23
	3. *Anubis*	68	17
	4. *Herakles*	60	15
	5. *Apollo*	100	25
	6. *Ammon*	120	30
	7. *Tithoes*	108	27
	8. *Sosus*	128	32
	9. *Zeus*	80	20
		858	214½

The dates of Panodorus seem reasonable. The gods and demigods may in fact represent ancient rulers of Egypt.

The Turin Papyrus

The prehistoric period, during which Egypt was governed by gods and demigods, is also recognized in the *Turin Papyrus*, which devotes the first eleven lines of Col. 2 to this period:

1. [. . . . .] their [years] *1000* [. . . . . .].
2. [. . . . .] *20*, their years *1110*, months [. . . . .].
3. [. . . . .] *10*, they carried on their dynasty [. . . . .].
4. [. . . . .] *their* [*years*] *330*, [*their life*] *time* [. . . . .].
5. *10, their dynasty, their reign 1000* [. . . . .] *years*.

6. these [.....] of Memphis 19, 11 years, 4 months, 22 days.

7. honorables from the Northland 19, 2100 [+ .....] years.

8. [.....] after his father, 7 ladies, their years and reigns [.....].

9. [.....] honorables, Followers of Horus, 13420 [+ .....] years.

10. the reigns until the Followers of Horus, 23200 [+ .....] years.

11. [.....] the majesty of the king of Upper and Lower Egypt, Menes [.....].

The Horus Period

The *Turin Papyrus* evidently divided this prehistoric time into three periods. The first of these is covered by the first seven lines, dealing with dynasties in different cities. This period corresponds to the dynasty of the gods in the classical authors, and undoubtedly indicates that Egypt was governed at that time by seven contemporary dynasties, each ruling in one of the ancient cities under the protection of the tutelary deity of his particular city or city-district.

The Two Goddesses

The second period is the one covered by line 8, and corresponds to the second period of Mestraeans of Syncellus, when the different nomes had been united into two kingdoms, placed under the tutelage of the goddesses of Hieraconpolis and Buto. It is possible that this period began with seven city-kingdoms, each protected by a goddess, as the *Turin Papyrus* plainly indicates, but that these seven city-kingdoms were in the course of time united into two independent realms, under the kings of Hieraconpolis and Buto. It is the period characterized by the introduction of the matriarchal institution.

Followers of Horus

The third period is the one of the "Followers of *H*orus," referred to in the ninth line of the *Turin Papyrus*, and which corresponds to the dynasty of demigods, or shades, i. e., to a period when ancestral worship was introduced, and the king was protected by his deified ancestor. This period marks the beginning of the patriarchal institution and the introduction of astronomical observations based on the zodiacal signs. The "Followers of *H*orus" are often mentioned in the inscriptions, and their rule precedes that of the united kingdom.

Archaeological Discoveries

These legends of prehistoric times have been corroborated in the main by recent archaeological discoveries in Egypt. Ten years ago, Egyptian history, properly speaking, began with *Snofru* and the pyramid builders. *Menes* and the kings of the first three dynasties were regarded as legendary and mythological figures. All this has now been changed. The myths of Egypt and of the *H*omeric poems, as well as the folk-tales of Greece and Rome dealing with ancient heroes, have, by discoveries in Egypt, Cyprus, Mycenae, and Crete, been found to rest upon a historical basis, and it seems safe to predict that within the next ten years new discoveries in *P*alestine will dispel the last doubt concerning the biblical patriarchs, whom a deceptive criticism of the past forty years has attempted to relegate to the shadows of myth and legend.

The discoveries in Egypt are of the highest interest and value. Prehistoric Egypt has been resuscitated by the tireless labors of famous specialists in various branches of archaeology, and a long chapter in the world's history has been written anew in the light of results yielded by recent excavations.

De Morgan was the first to adduce scientific proof of the prehistoric date of a large class of antiquities discovered by him in Egypt in 1894 and 1895. He was followed, shortly after, by the renowned Egyptian explorer Petrie, who in his *Sequence-dates*, has furnished us with an admirable system for the chronological classification of the prehistoric monuments of Egypt. The labors of these explorers have been supplemented by those of a host of other specialists, among whom may be mentioned Quibell, Garstang, Randall, MacIver, Breasted, Reisner, Hall, Pitt-Rivers, Wilkin, Amélineau, Budge, Maspero, Lythgoe, and Beadnell. The results obtained by these scientists may be grouped and arranged under the following "ages."

The Palaeolithic Age

The most ancient period of Egyptian civilization is that now known as the palaeolithic age, i. e., the age of flint tools and flint implements. These flint implements have been found in large quantities on the desert plateaus along the Nile from Kawâmil to Edfu, where the workshops for their manufacture were located. They have also been found near the cultivated land on the western bank of the Nile, showing that the primitive Egyptians cultivated the Nile Valley, in some form or other, as early as the palaeolithic period.

Palaeolithic man of Egypt was most probably contemporary with the cave-man of Europe. We do not know to what race he belonged, as no skeletons dating from this period have been found, but he may have been indigenous to the Nile Valley. Nor have we any means of estimating the duration of this period. Flint and stone weapons were used in Egypt as late as in the time of the Twelfth Dynasty, when the palaeolithic age had already long disappeared.

The religion of palaeolithic man was evidently the worship of spirits embodied in the animals with which he was familiar. Traces and survivals of this primitive worship lingered among the Egyptians down to the Christian era, and occupy a conspicuous place in that mixed religion whose systematic study has proven so difficult.

We know nothing of the social culture of the period, except that the division of the country into nomes may possibly reach back to this age, for the nomes were representative of the sacred animals whose habitat they were, and to which they gave their names.

The Neolithic Age

The palaeolithic age was followed by the neolithic The study of this period has been facilitated by the discovery of a large variety of pottery and of a number of graves.

The pottery of prehistoric neolithic Egypt belongs to three different periods. The most ancient type is a red polished ware with a black top. Next comes a red or black ware bearing geometrical white lines, incised in designs of rude basket-work. This type was probably a development of the earlier plain pottery. The latest variety is a buff ware with red wavy lines, concentric circles, and elaborate drawings from life on and along the Nile.

The mortuary customs of the age are characterized by the placing of the body on the left side in a contracted position, the knees being drawn up to the chin. The bodies were surrounded by flint or stone implements and wares of the black-on-red or red-on-buff types. Embalming was not practiced. The graves were usually of an oval form, near together, and close to the surface. Sometimes the body lies in an earthenware coffin, but more often on a mat. Elaborate carvings of ivory and fine gold have also been found, dating from these periods of the neolithic age. The stone implements display careful designing and beautiful workmanship.

The Chalcolithic Age

The bronze or copper age follows the neolithic period, and was introduced not long before the dynastic period. The pottery of this time exhibits clumsy forms and imperfect coloring, but the process of glazing dates from this period, and fine specimens of light-blue glazed *faïence* of this age have been discovered.

The burial customs are changed. The body lies extended on the back, embalmed. Brick graves, which developed during the early dynasties into the *mastabas* and brick pyramids, appear at this time.

Stone implements are found together with bronze tools, and in the older graves of this period are found almost exclusively. The period therefore marks the introduction of the bronze age, properly speaking. It should be observed, however, that bronze, or rather copper, implements have been discovered in the earliest graves of the neolithic age, and the demarkation between these periods depends more on the development of the earthenware than on the presence or absence of copper.

Legends of Egyptian Settlements

Two ancient Egyptian legends or folk-tales attempt to explain how the country was first settled.

One of these legends assumes that the invaders came from the northeast, crossing the Isthmus of Suez, and, after conquering Lower Egypt, spread in a southerly direction.

The other declares that the incoming tribe or tribes reached Egypt by way of the Red Sea, through Wady *H*ammamat, entering the Nile Valley in the vicinity of Coptos.

These divergent stories may embody historical facts. There may have been two distinct invasions of Egypt in prehistoric times. These settlements may have given rise to the neolithic and the chalcolithic periods, and they may have occurred in the order indicated.

Egyptian Royal Titles

Every Egyptian king after the Fourth Dynasty was entitled to five names, one for each royal title belonging to him as king of all Egypt.

(1) "Majesty of *Horus*" was the first royal title, and was employed to designate the king as a successor of *Horus*, one of the gods who ruled Egypt before the demi-gods and the dynastic kings. The sign for this title is the *Horus*-hawk.

(2) "Majesty of the Two Goddesses" was the second title. The sign for it is the vulture and the uraeus, the former being the sign of the goddess *Nekhbet*, the latter that of the goddess *Buto* or *Uzet*, *Nekhbet's* abode was the city of Nekhbet (Greek, *Eileithyaspolis;* Latin, *Lucinae*) the capital of the third nome of Upper Egypt.

Uzet's abode was the city of Buto, the capital of the seventh nome of *L*ower Egypt. *Nekhbet* was the bestower of the white (silver) crown of Upper Egypt, and *Uzet* the giver of the red (golden) crown of *L*ower Egypt. The vulture and the uraeus signs designate the whole land as Upper and *L*ower Egypt. The biblical "Mizraim" ("the two lands of Egypt") corresponds to this twofold name. The value of the vulture-sign is $Mu(t)$, and it was used to signify "mother." The value of the uraeus-sign is unknown, but it is possible that it may have been *zir* or *ṣir*, which is the value of the *S*umerian sign for "serpent." If this be true, the two signs were actually read *mut-Zir*, the dual character of which was expressed by the *H*ebrew equivalent $Mi(u)zraim;$ *A*ssyrian, *Muzur* and *Mizir*. Syncellus' *Dynasty of Mestraim* evidently refers to this name. The origin of the title belongs to the period intervening between the reigns of the gods and demigods.

(3) "Majesty of the Golden *Horus*" was the third title of the Egyptian kings. Its sign is the *Horus*-hawk, sitting upon the gold (*nub*) sign. It has been suggested, however, that it represents *Horus* as victor over *Set*. The origin of the title belongs to the period of the demigods.

(4) "Majesty of the *K*ing of Upper and *L*ower Egypt" was the fourth royal title, and was first assumed by *Menes*, when he united all Egypt under his rule. The signs for it are the *reed* of *S*outhern Egypt and the *bee* of the Delta, signifying respectively *S*outhern and Northern Egypt.

(5) "Majesty of the Son of *Re*" (the sun-god) was the fifth royal title of Egypt, and was introduced by the kings of the Fifth Dynasty of *H*eliopolis. It represents the king as a physical son of the sun-god *Re*, and is designated by the *goose* (="son") and *Sun* (*Re*) signs.

On the basis of these data I would offer the following hypothesis in explanation of the prehistoric development of Egypt:

The Horus Period

The palaeolithic period was brought to a close by an invading people who brought with them the culture of the neolithic age. There is a marked cultural affinity between the first neolithic period of Egypt and the so-called Mediterranean period. There are numerous traces of this latter in Palestine, and several scholars have accordingly concluded that the first neolithic people of Egypt entered the country from Southern Palestine across the isthmus of Suez.

I would identify this period with the legendary dynasty of the gods. Seven gods are said to have ruled Egypt at this time. They are all solar divinities. Chief among them was *Horus*, who represents the Semitic *Êl* or *Anu*, the sky-god, (Greek *Ur-anus*). The seven gods may represent seven contemporary city-dynasties of Egypt, over whom *Horus* of Edfu, i. e., the king of Edfu, exercised a kind of sovereignty.

The people of this *Horus* are called *Mesniu*, "smiths," and by their assistance *Horus* subdued the country. The *Qenites* were an ancient race of southern Palestine, but *Qenites* means "smiths," and it is thus possible that the people of the first neolithic period were related to these "smiths" of Southern Palestine.

Palestine, the Sinaitic peninsula, and Arabia were long known to the Egyptians as the "land of the gods," which may be reminiscent of the fact that the "gods" who first ruled Egypt had come from this region.

The Period of the Two Goddesses

The period of red and black pottery was followed by that of buff ware, and a high development of its manufacture was reached.

Almost exactly the same kind of pottery has been found by De Morgan in Elam, especially at Mussian, on the eastern bank of the river Tib.

In Anzan, the northern part of Elam, survivals of serpent-worship have been discovered. Serpent-worship also existed in Muzazir of Kurdistan, but Muzazir was most probably a settlement from Anzan.

The second of the royal titles of Egypt was that of the "Majesty of the Two Goddesses," symbolized by the vulture and the uraeus. The vulture symbol is conspicuous in the reliefs at Telloh (cf. the Stele of Vultures). Serpent-worship was also characteristic of the Sumerian religion. The Sumerians, however, entered Babylonia from an eastern mountain, and *Anzan* would be the nearest equivalent.

It seems possible, therefore, that a great migration from Anzan, a fore-runner of the Sumerian invasion, crossed the Syrian desert and entered Egypt from the isthmus of Suez. This people, which may even have been related to the former invaders, conquered the seven kingdoms. Now the *Turin Papyrus* avers that the period of the gods was succeeded by a dynasty of seven ladies. This is quite possible, but in course of time these seven kingdoms were reduced to the "Two Lands of Upper and Lower Egypt," under the tutelage of the goddesses *Nekhbet* and *Buto*.

The culture of the second neolithic age of Egypt closely resembles that of prehistoric Elam, and the ornamentations on the vases are surprisingly similar.

The Period of Demigods

The appearance of the chalcolithic age in Egypt marks the entrance of a new race into the country. In all probability they came through the *H*ammamat Valley from the Red Sea, which they had crossed on their way from Southern Arabia. The original home of this people was undoubtedly Babylonia, whence they had been driven out by the *S*emitic settlers of pre-*S*umerian times. This people must have been a branch of the *H*amitic race, who, together with the *P*unt (biblical Puṭ) people, left the Sealand and migrated to Arabia. From *A*rabia they crossed the Red Sea, one group penetrating as far south as Ethiopia (*K*ush) and Somali-land (*P*unt); the other entering Egypt.

The Egyptian settlers of this period are known in the inscriptions as the "Followers of *Horus*."

It seems evident that this race was in some way related to Babylonia. The pottery of the chalcolithic age of Egypt resembles that of ancient Babylonia, especially that of the oldest strata of *S*usa, and the civilization of *S*usa probably followed the same line of development as that of prehistoric Babylonia. *Min*, the god of Coptos and *H*ammamat, is evidently identical with *Ea* of Eridu. *Osiris* corresponds to *Asir-Tammuz* of Abzu, and *A*bydos itself recalls the Southern Babylonian *Ab-zu* (for *Zu-ab*).

The burial of the dead in coffins, the bodies recumbent, is characteristic both of the chalcolithic period of Egypt and of ancient Babylonia. The practice of embalming and mummifying, introduced in this period, was certainly in use before the *S*umerians entered Babylonia, and even in later times the Babylonian inscriptions speak of the "royal oil" which was poured over the dead body. The graves of this period were often lined with brick, and this custom points unmistakably to Babylonia. The hieroglyphic system of writing has been referred above to an Old Babylonian origin.

The chalcolithic period corresponds to the dynasty of the demigods of Egypt. The *Osiris* story may have been an Egyptian version of the Babylonian Tammuz legend, but it may also reflect the early struggles of this people, when the city of *A*bydos endeavored to gain supremacy over Egypt and was defeated by the king of some northern Egyptian city under the tutelage of *Set*. De Morgan discovered a slate relief, showing seven cities, fortified according to the Babylonian manner, being besieged and captured by seven clans. It is possible that this slate records the conquest of the old heptarchy by the invading race.

*S*yncellus calls this people "Egyptians." The name goes back to Coptos, and the god of Coptos was *Min*, chief divinity of the *H*amitic race. The three dynasties mentioned by *S*yncellus, *Auritae, Mestraeans*, and *Egyptians*, correspond, accordingly, to the dynasties of the "gods," "the two goddesses" and "the demigods;" or, following archaeology, to the two neolithic and the chalcolithic periods; or, again, according to my suggestion, the Mediterranean race, the Mizraim race from Anzan, and the *H*amites from the Sea-land.

*A*fter the struggles between Abydos and the Northland cities, it seems probable that *Horus* of Edfu, now supported by the "Followers of *Horus*," succeeded in gaining a degree of supremacy over all Egypt, and this continued until *Menes*, king of Thinis, united all Egypt under his scepter, and added to his titles that of king of Upper and *L*ower Egypt.

The Invasion of the Sun-Worshipers

In the time of the Fourth Dynasty a new Semitic wave poured into Palestine and Egypt, coming from the east, from Middle Babylonia or Ki-en-gi, which had been conquered at this time by the Sumerians. A tribe of this Ki-en-gi or Canaanite people, probably from the sun-city of Larsa, entered Egypt by way of Wady Tumilat, and, capturing Heliopolis, made that city their capital. Since the time of the "smiths," Heliopolis had been the center of sun-worship, but its sun-god was then known as *Tum* or *Atum* (Sumerian, *Tam*.) This new people brought with them the worship of the sun-god *Re*, which replaced that of *Tum* or *Atum*.

The Fifth Dynasty of Egypt was Heliopolitan, and introduced the title *Sa-Re*, "son of the sun-god." It is possible that this is a purely Egyptian name, but it is equally probable that it represents the Semitic *shar*, "king," originally, "the shining one," for this idea is indigenous to Egyptians and Semites alike. The Old Babylonians of the Sargon period and of *Dynasty A of Babylon* regarded the king as divine, and often appended the god-determinative to his title.

The *Re*-worship soon became highly popular in Egypt, and almost every faith of that land was colored by it. Even the separate gods were finally regarded as nothing but manifestations of the Sun-god in some particular form. In order to signify this, the name of *Re* was added to the names of the other gods, and we therefore find *Ammon* worshiped as *Amon-Re*, *Sebek* as *Re-Sebek*, not to speak of *Re-Atum* and *Re-Harakhte*.

Ikhnaton's introduction of the *Aton*-faith was therefore a natural development of the *Re*-worship, for the *Aton-*

faith was not a worship of the sun disk, as is so often claimed by modern scholars, but was a manifestation of the henotheistic worship of Apollo, appearing under the symbol of *H*elios. But *Aton* is identical, in name and nature, with the *H*ebrew *Adonai*, the Greek *Adonis*, and *Ikhnaton's Aton*-faith was Egypt's inheritance from the *H*yksos-*H*ebrew civilization, as that had been preserved and developed in *H*eliopolis.

SYNCHRONISTIC TABLE

SYNCHRONISTIC TABLE

	SEA-LAND	BABYLONIA	
1	**Dynasty of Kish**		
2		**Dynasty of Ki-en-gi**	
3		*Enshagkushanna*	
4		**Dynasty of Telloh**	
5		*Engilsa*	
6	*Manishtusu ca.* 3050	*Urukagina I*, ca., 3050	
7	*Mesilim*	*Enkhegal*	
8	*Lugaldak*	*Gursar*	
9	*Alzuzua*		
10	*Urzaguddu*	*Gunidu*	
11	*Lugaltarsi*	*Ur-Ninâ*	
12	*Urumush*	*Akurgal*	Assyria set
13	**Dynasty of Gishkhu**	*Eannadu*	Semites
14	*Ush*	*Enannadu I*, ca. 2800	
15	*Enakalli*	*Entemena*	
16	*Ili*	*Enannadu II*	
17	*Ukush*	*Enliltarzi*	
18	**Dynasty of Erech**	*Lugalanda*	
19	*Lugalzaggisi, ca.* 2675	*Urukagina II, ca,* 2675	
20			
21	*Lugalkigubnidudu*		
22	*Lugalkisalsi*		

SYNCHRONISTIC TABLE

Biblical Dates	Egypt	
Birth of *Arpachshad*, 3324	Predynastic kings	Hamitic migratio
	Dynasties I–IV 3285–2729	
Birth of *Cainan*, 3191		
Birth of *Shelah*, 3062		Sumerian migrati
Birth of *Eber*, 2933		
Death of *Shem*, 2826		Semitic migratio from Babylon
Birth of *Peleg*, 2800		Semitic settlemen Lydia Semitic settlement Kara Eyuk
Death of *Arpachshad*, 2762 Death of *Cainan*, 2733	**Dynasty V** *Userkaf*, 2729–01	Canaanitic migrat
	Sahure, 2701–2688	Temple of Bêl at built, 2730
Birth of *Reu*, 2671	*Nefererkare*, 2688–68	
Death of *Shelah*, 2604	*Shepseskare*, 2688–61 *Akauhor*, 2661–41 *Nuserre*, 2641–2597	

	Sea-Land	Babylonia	
23			
24	**Dynasty of Agade**		
25	Sargon, ca. 2550	Lugalushumgal	Kikia
26			
27	Narâm-Sin, ca. 2515	Ur-Ê	
28		Ur-Ba'u	
29		Nammakhni	
30	Bingani ca. 2485		
31	**Dynasty of Ur**	Gudea	Aushpia
32	Ur-Engur, 2477–59		
33	Dungi, 2459–01	Urningirsu	
34	Bur-Sin I, 2401–2392	Urninsun	
35	Gimil-Sin, 2392–85	Lukani	
36	Ibi-Sin, 2385–60	Khalalama	
37	**Dynasty of Isin**	Urkal	
38	Ishbi-Ura, 2360–28		
39	Gimil-ilushu, 2328–18		
40	Idin-Dagan, 2318–2297		
41	Ishme-Dagan, 2297–77		
42	Libit-Ishtar, 2277–66		
43	Ur-Ninib, 2266–38	**Dynasty A of Babylon**	
44	Bur-Sin II, 2238–17	Sumu-abi, 2233–18	Ilu-shuma,

SYNCHRONISTIC TABLE

	EGYPT	MISCELLANEOUS	
	Menkauhor, 2597–88		23
	Dedkare, 2588–44		24
erug, 2540	*Unas*, 2544–11		25
	Dynasty VI .		26
	Teti, 2511–2497		27
	Userkaf, 2497–81		28
	Pepi I, 2497–44		29
		Elamite migration	30
			31
eleg, 2463			32
	Mernere I, 2444–37		33
ber, 2431	*Pepi II*, 2437–2343		34
ihor, 2411			35
	Mernere II, 2343–42		36
eu, 2334	*Nitokris*, 2342–30	Armenian migration	37
	Dynasty VII, 2330		38
		Urartean migration	39
	Dynasty VIII		40
	of Memphis, 2330–2230		
		Kudur-Nankhundi of Elam	41
	Dynasty IX	Joqtanide migration	42
	of *H*eracleopolis, 2330–2230		
		Ninus and *Semiramis* found Nineveh	43
erah, 2233	**Dynasty X**		44
	of Heracleopolis 2230–2043		

	Sea-Land	Babylonia	
45	Itêr-ka-sha, 2217–12	Sumu-la-ilu, 2218–2183	Eris
46	, 2212–05		
47	Sin(?) - - -, 2205–04		Ikur
48	Bêl-bâni, 2204–2180		Dyna
49	Zame - -, 2180–77	Zabu, 2183–69	Shar
50	, 2177–72		
51	Ea - - -, 2172–68		
52	Sin-mâgir, 2168–57	Apil-Sin, 2169–51	
53	Dâmiq-ilushu, 2157–35	Sin-muballit, 2151–31	Bêl-i
54	Sin-muballit, 2135–31	Sin-muballit vassal, 2131–21	Bêl-i
55	Eri-Aku, 2131–2079	Hammurabi, vassal, 2121–09	
56	**Dynasty B of Sea-Land**	Hammurabi, king, 2109–2066	Shar 21
57	Ilu-ma-ilu, 2079–19	Samsu-iluna, 2066–31	
58			
59			
60			
61			
62		Abeshu, 2031–06	
63	Ki-an-ni-bi, 2019–1963		

BIBLICAL DATES	EGYPT	
Death of *Serug*, 2212		
		Belus conquers Ass
Birth of *Abram*, 2165	**Dynasty XI** *Intef I*, 2162–2112	*Kudur-Mabug*, c 2140
Death of *Nahor*, 2106		*Chedor-Laomer* o Elam
Death of *Terah*, 2090	*Intef II*, 2112–2086	
Abram in Canaan, 2090		First *Hyksos* se ment, 2084
Abram in Egypt, 2084–81	*Intef III*, 2086–81	Kassite invasion Babylonia, 205
Battle of Dan, 2080	*Mentuhotep I*, 2086–77	Dyn. XVI of Sh herds, 2084–15
Birth of *Ishmael*, 2078	*Mentuhotep II*, 2077–62	
Birth of *Isaac*, 2065	*Mentuhotep III*, 2062–12	
Marriage of *Isaac*, 2046		Fall of Dynasty 2043
Death of *Sarah*, 2022	*Mentuhotep IV*, 2012–02	

	Sea-Land	Babyloni...
64		
65		*Ammi-ditana*, 1981
66		*Ammi-zadugga* –60
67		
68	*Damqi-ilishu*, 1963–37	
69	*Qadushshi*, 1937–22	*Samsu-ditana*, 29
70	*Milkipal*, 1922–1898	
71		
72		
73	*Gulkishar*, 1898–43	
74		
75		
76		
77	*Kir-gal-dara-bar*, 1843–1793	
78		
79		
80		
81		
82	*Adara-kalama*, 1793–65	

SYNCHRONISTIC TABLE

Biblical Dates	Egypt	Miscellan
Birth of *Jacob*, 2006	**Dynasty XII** *Amenemhet I*, 2006–1986	
Death of *Abraham*, 1990	*Sesostris I*, 1986–1940	Dyn. XIII of Dio 1986–1533
Marriage of *Esau*, 1967		
Death of *Ishmael*, 1943	*Amenemhet II*, 1944–02	Dyn. XVII of Th 1944–1793
Jacob in Paddan-Aram, 1931		*Hittites* in Babylo
Marriage of *Jacob*, 1924		
Birth of *Joseph*, 1917		Birth of *Sebek-k* 1917
Jacob in Canaan, 1911	*Sesostris II*, 1906–1887	
Joseph sold to Egypt, 1901		Asiatics visit *Khn hotep II*, 1901
Joseph vizier of Egypt, 1887	*Sesostris III*, 1887–54	Dyn. XV of Me phis, 1887–156
Jacob in Egypt, 1877		
Death of *Jacob*, 1860		
Death of *Joseph*, 1807	*Amenemhet III*, 1854–06	
		Hyksos Kings *Salatis*, 1826–07
	Amenemhet IV, 1806–1797 *Sebeknefrure*, 1797–1793	*Bnôn*, 1807–1763

	SEA-LAND	BABYLONIA	
83		**Dynasty C of Kassites**	
84		*Gandish,* 1782–66	
85	*Ê-kur-ul-anna,* 1765–39	*Agum-shi,* 1766–44	
86	*Melamma,* 1739–31	*Bitil-iashu I,* 1744–22	*Ashir-rabi*
87	*Ea-gâmil,* 1731–11	*Dushi-ashu,* 1722–14	*Ashir-nirar*
88		*Agum (Adumetash),* 1714–	*Ashir-rîm-n*
89	**Kassite Dyn. of Sea-Land**	*Tashzigurmash*	
90	*Ulam-Buriash*	*Agum-kakrime*	
91			
92		*Zibir*	
93	*Burna-Burariash*		
94	*Ula-Burariash*	*Adad-shum-nâzir*	*Ashur-nirar*
95			*Nabû-dâni*
96			
97			
98			
99			

SYNCHRONISTIC TABLE

	EGYPT	MISCELLANEOUS	
	Dynasty XIV of Sebennitos 1793–1569.	Hebrew migration, *ca.* 1750	83 84
		Apakhnan, 1763–26	85
	Dynasty XVI of Iliopolis 1793–1579	*Apophis*, 1726–1665	86 87
		Midian migration, *ca.* 1650	88 89
	Dynasty XVII of Ermupolis 1793–1533	*Iannas*, 1665–15	90
		Aseth, 1615–1566 Expulsion of *Hyksos*, 1566	91 92
ders, 1566–	**Dynasty XVIII**		93
	Ahmose, 1579–54 *Amenhotep I*, 1554–33		94 95
ishathaim,	*Thutmose I*, 1533–08	War in Syria, 1523–2	96
oses, 1526	*Thutmose II*, 1522–09		97
523–1483	*Hatshepsut*, 1509–1486		98
ht to Mid-6	*Thutmose III*, 1486–73	Wars in Syria, 1483–62	99

	Sea-Land	Babylonia
100		
101		
102		Kara-Indash, 1.
103		35 Kadashman-Bêl
104		1435–20 Kuri-Galzu I, 1. 05
105		Burna-Buriash, 1405–1380
106		Kara-Khardash, 1380–77
107		Kadashman-Khi I, 1380–77
108		Nazibugash, usi 1377
109		Kuri-Galzu II, 1 53
110		Nazi-Maraddas 1353–27
111		
112		
113		
114		Kadashman-Tu: 1327–10
115		Kadashman-Bêl 1310–04
116		Kudur-Bêl, 130 1296

SYNCHRONISTIC TABLE

BIBLICAL DATES	EGYPT	
Eglon of Moab, 1483–65	*Thutmose III*, whole reign, 1504–1450	
Exodus, 1447	*Amenhotep II*, 1473–47	**Kings of Mitani**
Ehud, 1465–1385	*Thutmose IV*, 1447–38	*Artatama*, ca. 1450
	Amenhotep III, 1438–02	*Shutarna*, ca. 1420
		Dushratta, ca. 1390
Death of *Moses*, 1407	*Amenhotep IV*, 1407–1370.	**Hittite Kings**
Leadership of *Joshua* 1407	(*Ikhnaton*)	*Seplel*, ca. 1370
Jabin of Hazor, 1385–65		
Death of *Joshua*, 1365	*Akerkheres*, 1370–58	
Deborah and *Barak*, 1365–25	*Tutenkhamon*, 1358–49	
	Akerkheres II, 1349–37	*Merasar*, ca. 1340
	Akerkheres III, 1337–25	
	Dynasty XIX	
Midian oppression, 1325–18	*Haremhab*, 1325–21	
	Ramses I, 1321–20	
Gideon, 1318–1278	*Seti I*, 1321–1271	War in Syria, 131

	SEA-LAND	BABYLONIA	
117		*Shagarakti-Shuriash*,	7
		1296–83	
118		*Bitil-iashu II*, 1283–	
		75	
119		*Bêl-shum-iddin*,	
		1275–73	
120		*Kadashman-Kharbe*	
		II, 1273–2	
121		*Adad-shum-iddin*,	
		1272–66	
122		*Adad-shum-uzur*,	A
		1266–36	
123			T
124			B₁
125		*Meli-shipak*, 1236–	
		21	
126		*Marduk-apil-iddin*,	A.
		1221–08	
127		*Zamama-shum-iddin*,	
		1208–7	
128		*Bêl-shum-iddin*,	
		1207–5	
129		**Dynasty D of Pashe**	
130		*Marduk - - -* , 1205–	
		1187	
131			
132		- - - - -, 1187–81	

SYNCHRONISTIC TABLE

	EGYPT	MISCELLANEOUS	
	Ramses II, 1319–1253	Mutallu, ca. 1310	117
, 1278–5		Khatasar, ca. 1280	118
5–52		Kidinkhutrash of Elam	119
		Hittite treaty, ca. 1275	120
			121
			122
2–30	Merneptah, 1253–34	Philistine migration, ca. 1250	123
			124
oppression,	Amenmeses, 1234–08		125
			126
1212–06			127
	Siptah, 1208–1202		128
6–1199	Seti II, 1202–1200	Heraclide Dynasty of Lydia, ca. 1190	129
9–89	Thouoris, 1200–1183	Fall of Troy, 1183	130
89–81	**Dynasty XX**	Expulsion of the Lepers, 1183	131
oppression,	Nakhtset, 1183–81	Khattusar of Qummukh, 1175	132

	Sea-Land	Babylonia	Assyr
133		Three unknown kings, 1181–46	
134			Ashur-rêsh-i 1160–25
135		Nebochadrezzar I, 1146–30	
136		Bêl-nâdin-aplu, 1130–16	Tiglath-pile 1125–108
137		Marduk-nâdin-akhê, 1116–1094	
138		Marduk-akhê-erba, 1094–3	
139		Marduk-shâpik-zêr-mâti, 1093–81	
140		(Adad-apil-iddin, 1081)	Ashur-bêl-k 65
141	**Dynasty E of Sea-Land**	Nabû-nâdin, 1081–73	
142	Simmash-shipak, 1073–55		
143	Bêl-mukîn, 1055–4		
144	Kashshû-nâdin-akhê, 1054–1		Shamshi-Ad 1065–50

SYNCHRONISTIC TABLE

DATES	EGYPT	MISCELLANEOUS	
	Ramses III, 1181–50		133
	Ramses IV, 1150–44		134
41–21	*Ramses V*, 1144–34		135
81	*Ramses VI-VIII*, 1134–13	Shadi-Teshup, ca. 1125	136
	Ramses IX, 1113–1092		137
			138
	Ramses X-XI, 1092–77		139
			140
pression,			141
			142
1–49	*Ramses XII*, 1077–50		143 144

INDICES

INDICES

INDEX A
CLASSICAL AUTHORS

Africanus, 165, 201
Agathias, 21, 144, 146, 148
Alexander Polyhistor, 21, 77
Apollodorus, 201
Aristotle, 21, 76

Barbarus, 145, 165, 220
Berossos, 21, 77 ff.

Calisthenes, 21, 76 f.
Castor, 21, 145
Censorinus, 176 f.
Chalcidius, 178
Clement of Alexandria, 178, 201, 220

Diodorus, 21, 145 f., 201
Dionysius of Halicarnassus, 201

Ephorus, 8
Eratosthenes, 167, 201, 241, 247
Eusebius, 21, 77 f., 165, 201 *et passim*, 252

Herodotus, 8, 21, 145
Homer, 209, 255
Flavius Josephus, 7, 17 f., 153–164, 178, 185, 192
Justin, 8
Ktesias, 21, 145, 148
Manetho, 152 *et passim*
Manilius, 178
Menander of Ephesus, 78
Moerbeka, 76
Panodorus, 252
Pliny, 178
Porphyry, 21, 76, 201
Claudius Ptolemaeus, 1
Simplicius, 21, 76, 78 f.
Solinus, 201
Suidas, 201
George Syncellus, 21, 77 f., 165, 251
Trogus, 7 f.

INDEX B
BIBLICAL REFERENCES

Gen. 10:10.	108	Gen. 47:28.	10	Num. 19:10.	15
10:23.	105	50:26.	10	35:15.	15
10:30.	105	Exod. 7:7.	11	Deut. 34:7.	10, 11
11:10–26.	11	12:19.	15	34:9.	11
12:4.	9	12:40, 41.	9	Josh. 17:11.	16
14:1, 9.	20, 75, 78	12:49.	15	24:29.	11
16:16.	9	20:23–23:33.	14	Judg. 2:7.	18
17:17.	9	21:2.	15	2:8.	11, 13
17:24.	9	23:9.	15	3:8.	18
21:5.	9	Lev. 16:29.	15	3:11.	18
23:1.	9	17:8, 10, 12, 13, 15.	15	3:14	18
25:7.	10	18:26.	15	3:30, 31.	18
25:20.	9	20:2.	15	5:31.	18
25:26.	9	22:18.	15	6:1.	18
26:34.	10	24:16.	15	8:28.	18
30:25.	10	24:22.	15	9:22.	18
31:41.	10	Num. 9:14.	15	10:12,	3.18
35:28.	10	13:21.	222	11:26.	19
37:2.	10	15:14, 15, 16, 26, 29, 30.	15	12:7.	18
41:46.	10			12:9, 10, 11.	18
47:9.	10			12:14.	19

Judg. 13:1. 19	I Kings 2:11. 19	I Kings 22:51. 5
15:20. 19	6:1. 7, 9, 11,	II Kings 3:1. 5
I Sam. 4:18. 19	12, 13, 17	17:30. 103
7:2. 19	11:42. 7, 19	I Chron. 7:21, 22. 16
7:6. 17	22:1–37. 5	Acts 13:19, 20. 19
8:1, 5. 17	22:40. 5	13:21. 18, 19.
10:1. 17		

INDEX C
INSCRIPTIONS

A. CUNEIFORM

Adad-Nirari I, tablet, 146
Adad-Nirari III, 138
Adad-shum-nâzir I, letter, 64
Agum-kakrime, 64
Amenhotep III, letter, 32
Ashir-rîm-nishêshu, cylinder, 143
Ashurnazirpal III, annals, 64
Ashur-uballit, letter, 32
Bêl-nâdin-aplu, boundary stone, 82–84
Burna-Buriash, letters, 33
Chronicle A, 44–47
Chronicle K1, 47–51
Chronicle K2, 51–54
Chronicle K3, 53, 55–58
Chronicle P, 39–44
Chronological Table, 107–9
Date Lists, 29–31, 81, 91
Esarhaddon, Monolith of Zenjirli, 144
Expedition-Lists, 2
Hammurabi, Code of, 74, 93, 94
Irishum, brick, 140
Kadashman-Bêl I, 33
King-List A, 24–28
King-List B, 22–24
Kudur-Mabug, Kanephore, 97
——, votive inscription, 97, 98
Limmu-Lists, 1 ff.
Marduk-nâdin-akhê, 62
Nabû-ushabshi, letter, 118

Nabonidus, Sippara inscription, 67, 74, 108, 110
Sennacherib, Bavian inscription, 60, 61
Shagarakti-Shuriash, seal-inscription, 71, 72
Shalmaneser I, building-inscriptions, 140, 141
Shalmaneser II, Monolith, 4
——, Obelisk, 4
Shamshi-Adad I, brick, 137
Synchronistic History, 33–38
Tiglath-pileser I, cylinder, 134, 135
Ula-Burariash, 87

B. HIEROGLYPHIC AND HIERATIC

Abydos-List, 169 ff.
Amenhotep II, Karnak stela, 197
Hapu, Assuan inscription, 213, 215
Intef, stela at Cairo, 213
Kahun Papyrus, 179, 211
Karnak-List, 169 f., 174.
Palermo Stone, 168, 172, 250
Papyrus Ebers, 180, 181
Ramses III, Papyrus Harris, 208
Sakkara—List, 171
Seti, stela at Tanis, 221 f.
Turin Papyrus, 168 f., 171, 173 f., 213 ff., 243, 250, 253 ff.
Upwaweto, stela at Leyden, 213

INDEX D
MISCELLANEOUS

A

ʿam, Egyptian and Hebrew name of the old inhabitants of Palestine, 15
Aahmes, 227
Aahmose, queen of Thutmose I, 190
Abdon, judge of Israel, 19
Abeshu, king of Babylonia (Dynasty A), 24, 29 ff., 45; war with Ilu-ma-ilu, 53; reign of, 75; coregency of, 80
Abi, Mesopotamian god, 104
Abijah, king of Judah, 6
Abimelech, Hebrew king, 18
Abram or Abraham, the patriarch, 9 ff. 20, 151, 155

INDICES   289

Abydos, city of Egypt, 127, 171, 235, 241, 262
Abydos-List, 169 f., 174, *et passim*
Abzu, ancient name of the Sea-Land, 127–263
Achencheres I, 157, 186
Achencheres II, 157, 186
Achencheres III, 157, 186, 200
Adarakalama, king of Sea-Land (Dynasty B), 24, 26, 82
Adad, 71; god of Ekallâte, 60; of Ashur, 134
Adad-apil-iddin, son of Esagil-shaduni, called Nabû-nâdin after his accession to the throne of Babylonia (Dynasty D), 38, 55, 135.
Adad nirari I, king of Assyria, 36, 40, 59, 132 f., 146
Adad-nirari II, king of Assyria, 55, 59
Adad-nirari III, king of Assyria, 33, 138
Adad-shum-iddin, king of Babylonia, (Dynasty C), 28, 44, 66, 73
Adad-shum-nâzir, king of Babylonia (Dynasty C), 64 f., 131
Adad-shum-uzur, king of Babylonia (Dynasty C), 28, 36, 44, 66, 73, 134
Adasi, father of Bêl-ibni, 144
Adonai, 199, 266
Adonis, 199, 266
Adumetash (= Agum ?), king of Babylonia (Dynasty C), 26, 65, 86 f.
Ae (= Ea), 81, 93
Ae-aplu-uzur, king of Babylonia (Dynasty G), 55
Agade, city near Sippara in Northern Babylonia, 48, 95, 109, 114 f., 118; boundaries of, 48; dynasty of, 101 ff.; manner of dating in, 29
Age, the Heroic, 12
Agathodaemon, 253
Agum (= Aumetash), 53, 65, 87
Agum-kakrime, king of Babylonia (Dynasty C), 63 ff.
Agum-shi, king of Babylonia (Dynasty C), 26, 65, 87 ff.
Ahab, king of Israel, 3 f., 6
Ahaziah, king of Israel, 5 f.
Ahaziah, king of Judah, 6
Ahmose I, king of Egypt (Dynasty XVIII), 171, 185 ff., 191 f.
Ai, consort of Shamash, 74
Akar-sallu, city and land east of the lower Tigris, 36, 38

Akauhor, king of Egypt (Dynasty V), 245
A-kha-ab-bu (= Ahab), 4
Akhi, Mesopotamian god, 104
Akkadi, Babylonian goddess, 117
Akkad(!), southern part of Middle Babylonia, 38, 44, 53, 60, 71, 117 f.
Akurgal, king of Telloh, 122
Akurulanna, king of Sea-Land (Dynasty B), 24, 26, 82
Alabastronpolis, city of Egypt, 204
Alexander the Great, 1, 21, 76 ff.
Alisphragmuthosis, 155 f.
Alkandra, 209
Allamu, patesi of Telloh, 123
Alliances, 34, 38, 40, 55
Alzazua, king of Kish, 123
Amarna Letters, 15, 21, 32, 63, 151, 185, 198
Amenemhet I, king of Egypt (Dynasty XII), 212 ff., 225, 227, 232
Amenemhet II, king of Egypt (Dynasty XII), 212 ff.
Amenemhet III, king of Egypt (Dynasty XII), 153, 210 ff., 219
Amenemhet IV (Dynasty XII), 153
Amenhotep I, king of Egypt (Dynasty XVIII), 180, 185 ff., 192
Amenhotep II, king of Egypt (Dynasty XVIII), 186 ff., 196
Amenhotep III, king of Egypt (Dynasty XVIII), 21, 32 ff., 131 f., 151, 186 ff.
Amenhotep IV (= Ikhnaton), 157, 171, 185, 204 f.
Amenmeses, King of Egypt (Dynasty XIX), 207
Amenophis (= Amenmeses), 160 ff.
Amenophis (= Amenhotep I), 156
Amenophis (= Amenhotep III), 157
Amenophis (= Merneptah), 157
Amenophis, son of Papis, 161 ff.
Amenses and Amesses (= Hatshepsut), 157, 187, 193
Ammenemes (= Amenemhet I), 216
Ammi, Mesopotamian god, 104
Ammi-ditana, king of Babylonia (Dynasty A), 24, 30 f., 45, 79 f.
Ammi–Zadugga, king of Babylonia (Dynasty A), 24, 29 f., 45, 79 f. 101
Amorites, 103
Amon, god of Thebes, 190, 194, 199, 253
Amon-Re, 265
Amraphel (= Hammurabi), 20, 75, 78

INDICES

Amurru, land on the western bank of of the Euphrates, 96; mârê—, 103
Animals, Sacred, 257
Annalists, Hebrew, 6 f.
Anti-Lebanon, 4
Antoninus, 177
Anu, chief god of Sippara and Northern Babylonia, 81, 87, 92 ff., 134
Anubis, Egyptian divinity, 253
Anunnaki, 93
Anzan (=Northern Elam), 87, 105, 262
Anzan-Susunka (=Elam), 104
Apachnas, Hyksos king, 154, 219 ff.
Apil-Kishshu, early Babylonian king, 45
Apil-Sin, king of Babylonia (Dynasty A), 24, 30, 45, 79, 90 f., 95, 104
Apirak, city east of Babylonia, 48
Apis, the sacred bull of Memphis, 163
Apollo, 253
Apophis, Hyksos king, 154, 219 ff.
Arabia, 102, 262 f.; dialects of, 101; kings of, 77, 79
Aram (=Syria), 5; people of, 55, 57; 101, 105
Aram Damaseq (=Damascus), 5
Aramessis, 163
Ararat, kingdom of, 105
Arbaya, 106
Archon, Greek, 2
Argos, 159, 178, 203
Aries, 253
Aries, era of, 112; zodiacial sign of, 2, 112, 251
Arik-dîn-ilu, king of Assyria, 57, 59, 132 f.
Arkhles, Hyksos king, 219
Armais (=Haremhab), 157 f., 203 f.
Arman-akarsallu, 36
Armenian migration, 105
Armesses-Miamoun (=Ramses II), 157, 201, 203
Arpachshad, 11 f.
Aryan language, 126; race, 209
Arzukhina, 38
Asa, king of Judah, 6
Aseth, Hyksos king, 221 f.
Asher, tribe of, 16
Ashima, god of Hamath, 103
Ashir-nirari I, patesi of Assyria, 143
Ashir-nirari II, patesi of Ashur, 143
Ashir-rabi, patesi of Ashur, 143
Ashir-rîm-nishêshu, patesi of Ashur, 143

Ashur, chief god of the city of Ashur, 71
Ashur, city of, 106
Ashurbanipal, king of Assyria, 105, 118
Ashur-bêl-kala, king of Assyria, 38, 55, 59, 135 f.
Ashur-bêl-nishêshu, king of Assyria, 34, 64, 131
Ashur-dân I, king of Assyria, 36, 59, 134 ff., 209
Ashur-dân II, king of Assyria, 59
Ashur-nâdin-akbê, king of Assyria, 32, 131 f.
Ashurnazirpal I, king of Assyria, 44, 64, 73, 134
Ashurnazirpal III, king of Assyria, 64
Ashur-nirara III, king of Assyria, 64, 131
Ashur-rêsh-ishi, king of Assyria, ·36, 38, 59, 85, 135 f.
Ashur-uballit, king of Assyria, 32, 34, 40, 57, 131 f.
Asia, 156
Asianic Calender, 8
Asiatics, 234
Asir, 263
Asosi, king of Egypt, 169
Assis, Hyksos king, 155, 221 f.
Assuan, 215
Assyria, 3 ff., 79, 89, 130–148, 154, 156, 158
Athalia, queen of Judah, 6
Aton, Egyptian god, 199 f., 266; faith of, 203, 265
Attila, city of Zamua, 64
Atum, Egyptian god, 265
Atys, king of Lydia, 209
Augustus, era of, 177
Auritae, 251, 264
Aushpia, 140
Avaris, Hyksos stronghold, 154, 156, 162 f., 208
Avatarae, 112

B

Baal, god of Canaan, 129
Ba'alira'si, mountain in Syria, 4
Baasha, king of Israel, 6
Babel, 118
Babylon, 1 ff., 20, 22–24, 29–31, 38, 44 f., 48, 57, 60, 71, 76 f., 88, 90 ff., 99 ff.
Balikh, river of Mesopotamia, 104, 106, 115
Barak, Hebrew judge, 16, 18

INDICES

Barzi, 91
Bavian inscription, 60-62, 133
Bazi, dynasty of, 47
Bazu, city west of the Euphrates, 91, 99
Bebti, king of Egypt (Dynasty II), 171
Bedwîn, 193
Beknekhonsu, 206
Bêl, god of Ki-en-gi, 81, 87, 92 ff., 109, 129
Bêl-Marduk, 44, 48, 57, 88
Bêl-bâni (=Bêl-ibni), king of Isin, 108, 144, 146 f.
Bêl-ibni, ancient king, 51, 144 ff.
Bêl-iqbi, patesi of Ashur, 139
Bêl-kabkabu, 138
Bêl-kudur-uzur, king of Assyria, 36, 134
Bêl-mukin, king of Babylonia (Dynasty E), 28; also known as Ea-mukîn-zêr, 47, 63
Bêl-nâdin-aplu, king of Babylonia (Dynasty D), 62, 82-85
Bêl-nirari, king of Assyria, 34, 57, 132, 146
Bêl-shum-iddin, king of Babylonia (Dynasty C), 28, 44, 66, 73
Bêl-tâbi, patesi of Assyria, 139, 143, 148
Beletaras, 144
Beleous, 144
Belochus, 144
Belus, ancient king, 146
Benihasan, 193
Beon, Hyksos king, 154, 219
Berber tribes, 234, 236
Bibeiashu, 70; see Bitil-iashu
Bidi, 252
Bingani (—sharali), king of Agade, 108, 113
Biratu, city in land of Kharkhar (Media), 40
Bitil-iashu I, king of Babylonia (Dynasty C), 53, 65, 87
Bitil-iashu II, king of Babylonia (Dynasty C), 28, 31, 36, 44, 66, 70, 73
Blackhead race, 94
Bnôn, Hyksos king, 219
Borsippa, 57, 91 f., 95
Boundary, settling of, 34, 36, 40
Boundary stones, 62, 83-84
Brick graves, 258, 263
Brick making, 127
Bronze age, 258
Brutus, Roman consul, 177
Bubastis, 154

Buntakhtun-ila, king of Sippara, 119
Bur-Sin I, king of Ur, 108, 122
Bur-Sin II, king of Isin, 92, 116
Burial customs, 258 f., 263 f.
Burna-Burariash, king of the Sea-Land, 87, 89
Burna-Buriash, king of Babylonia (Dynasty C), 31 ff., 69 f., 74 f., 80, 131 f.
Buto, Egyptian goddess, 259 f., 262
Buto, city of, 254, 260
Buzur-Ashur, king of Assyria, 34, 132

C

Calendar, Asianic, 8; Egyptian, 175 ff.
Calendar reforms, in Babylonia, 2, 112 ff., in Egypt, 221
Cainan, 11 f.
Calneh, 118, 120
Canaan, 9 f., 14 ff., 129
Canaanites, origin of, 128; migration of, 129, 265; dialect of, 101 f.
Canon, the Ptolemaic, 1 ff.
Cappadocia, 102, 106 f.
Carthage, 7
Caspian Sea, 105, 129
Cavalry, Babylonian, 38
Chalcolithic age, 258, 263
Chaldea, 104; kings of, 77, 79
Chebron, see Khebron
Chedor-laomer, king of Elam, 105
Chronicle A, 44 ff.
Chronicle K1, 47 ff., 141 f., 144
Chronicle K2, 51 ff., 86, 88, 144
Chronicle K3, 53 ff.
Chronicle P, 32, 39-44, 63, 69 f., 89, 130 ff.
Chronicle S, 44
Chronicle, The Old, 251
Chronicle, Parian, 8
Chronicon Barbari, 225; *Eusebii*, 165
Chronology, Assyrian, 130-48; Babylonian, 60-130; Egyptian, 149-266; Hebrew, 1-19
Circumcision, 9
Codes, biblical, 14 f.; Deuteronomic, 14; Elohistic, 14; Levitical, 14 f.; of Hammurabi, 14, 74
Comagene, land west of the upper Euphrates, 106
Consul, Roman, 2, 177 f.
Contra Apionem, 153-64
Copper implements, 258
Coptos, 229, 259, 263 f.
Cornelius, Cn; Roman consul, 178
Country of the West (=Martu), 48

INDICES

Crete, 255
Crocodilopolis, 228
Crown, the red, 260; the white, 260
Cuneiform script, 111, 124 ff., 127
Cushan-Rishathaim, 17 ff.
Cynicus (the Dog star), 178
Cyprus, 158, 255
Cyrannian books, 251.
Cyrus, king of Persia, 77, 79, 145

D

Dadi, 91
Damascus, 4 f.
Dâmiq-ilushu, king of Isin, 47, 108
Damqi-ilishu, king of Sea-Land (Dynasty B), 24, 26, 82
Danaus (=Haremhab), 158 ff., 178, 203
Date-Lists, see Lists
David, 13, 19
Deborah, 16, 18
Dedkare, king of Egypt (Dynasty V), 245
Delta, 260
Demigods, 251, 253, 263 f.
Denderah, 234
Deuteronomic code, 14
Dilbat, 91 f.
Din-Tir, ancient name of a quarter of Babylon, 127
Diolectian, era of, 177
Diorite, 87
Diospolis, 224, 227 ff.
"Dog stela," 235
Dog star, 175 ff.
Door of the North, 235
Door of the South, 235
Dungi, king of Ur, 48, 108, 111, 114, 118, 121 ff.
Dushiashu, king of Babylonia (Dynasty C), 26, 65, 87
Dûr-Ea, 53
Dûr-ilu, 44, 55, 118
Dûr-Kurigalzu, 38
Dynasties of Babylonia:
— A of Babylon, 22, 29 ff., 45, 90, 73–81, 100, 121, 130, 140 ff., 265
— B of Sea-Land, 24, 26, 45, 51, 81–89, 121, 130
— C of the Kassites, 26–28, 63–73, 81, 130, 209
— D of Pashe, 28, 53, 60–63, 85, 130, 209
— E of Sea-Land, 28, 45, 47, 63, 130
— F of Bazi, 47
— G of Elam, 47

— I of Babylon, 21, 64
— of Agade, 100, 108–21, 129, 265
— of Erech, 120 f., 129
— of Dâmiq-ilishu, 47
— of Gishkhu, 121 f.
— of Isin, 51, 107 f., 130, 144
— of Ki-en-gi, 124
— of Kish, 100, 123 f.
— of Telloh, 122 f.
— of Ur, 108, 121, 129
Dynasties of Egypt:
I–IV, 245–48
V, 129, 172, 244 f., 260, 265
VI, 171, 241–44
VII–IX, 171, 238–41
X, 171, 234, 237 f.
XI, 171, 225, 230–37
XII, 31, 171, 211–17
XII, of Bubastis, 220 ff.
XIII, of Diospolis, 224 ff.
XIII, of Tanis, 220, 224 ff.
XIV, of Khois, 224 ff.
XIV, of Sebennitos, 224 ff.
XV, of Memphis, 224 ff.
XV, of Shepherds, 217–24
XVI, of Iliopolis, 224 ff.
XVII, of Thebes, 224 ff.
XVII, of Ermupolis, 224 ff.
XVIII, 20, 171, 191, 185–200
XIX, 20, 171, 200–10
XX, 210 f.
XXVI, 210
Dynasties of Lydia:
— of Atys, 209
— of Heracles, 209

E

Ê=Temple: Ê-Barra, 74, 108; Ê-kharsag-kurkura, 140; Ê-kur, 138; Ê-kur-igi-gal, 140; Ê-nun-makh, 97; Ê-sagila, 44, 48, 57, 73; Ê-Sharra, 138; Ê-Ulmash, 67; Ê- - -uruna, 53; Ê-zida, 57
Ê-Mutpal, 81 f., 91, 97, 100, 105, 122
Ê-Ulmash-shâkin-shum, king of Babylonia (Dynasty F), 47, 55
Ea, god of Sea-Land, 53, 81, 87, 263
Ea-gâmil, king of Sea-Land (Dynasty B), 24, 26, 53, 82, 87
Ea-mukîn-zêr, son of Kashmar, and king of Sea-Land (Dynasty E), 47; cf. Bêl-mukîn
Eannadu, patesi of Telloh, 121 f.

INDICES 293

Eber, 11 f.
Eber-hannahar, 106
Ebir-nâri, 106
Eclipse, 3
Edfu, 256, 262
Eglon, king of Moab, 18
Egypt, 1, 8 ff., 15; hieroglyphs of, 126
Egyptus (=Sethos), 158, 160, 203
Ehud, Hebrew judge, 16, 18
Ê-kur-ul-anna, see Akur-ul-anna
Eileithyaspolis, 259
Êkallâte, 60
Êl, Semitic god, 261
Elah, king of Israel, 6
Elam, 44, 53, 82, 87 ff., 90, 104 f., 115, 122, 129, 262; dynasty of, 47; see Dynasty G of Babylonia
Elders, Hebrew, 18
Eleazar, 104
Elephantine, 180, 235, 245
Eli, judge of Israel, 13, 19
Elohistic Code, 14
Elon, judge of Israel, 18
Embalming, 258, 263
Enannadum I, patesi of Telloh, 122
Enannadum II, patesi of Telloh, 122
Enakalli, patesi of Gishkhu, 121
En-kid, or En-lil, god of Nippur, 129
Enmennunna, early Babylonian king, 45
Enneugin, King of Kish, 123
Enshagkushanna, lord of Ki-en-gi, 124
Entemenna, patesi of Telloh, 122
Epagomene, 180
Ephesus, 7
Epitomes, 152, 156, 165, 206
Ephraimites, 16
Equinox, vernal, 2, 113
Era, of Aries, 112; Augustus, 177; Diocletian, 177; Gemini, 112; Menophris, 177, 204; Nabonassar, 2; Opeh(ti)set, 221 f., Sargon, 112 f.; Taurus, 112.
Erba-Marduk, king of Babylonia (Dynasty I), 57
Erba-Sin, father of Simmash-Shipak, 45, 55
Erech, 91, 118; dynasty of, 120 ff.
Eri-Aku, king of the Sea-Land, 81, 86, 130; king of Larsa, 51, 120; king of Ur, 51; king of Ê-Mutpal, 81; king of Babylonia, 30 f., 80, 91, 94, 96 f., 90 f., 148
Eridu, 48
Erishu, patesi of Ashur, 140 ff., 147 f.

Ermupolis, 225 f.
Esagil-shaduni, father of Adad-apil-iddina, 38; also known as Itti-Marduk-balatu
Esarhaddon, king of Assyria, 139, 144 ff., 148.
Esau, 9 f.
Ethiopia, 101, 164, 234, 263
Etil-Marduk, 47
Euphrates, 4, 95 f., 96, 99, 104, 106, 117, 192, 197
Exodus, 9, 12 f., 16 f., 192
Expedition-Lists, 2
Ezuab, patesi of Gishkhu, 122

F

Faïence, 258
Fayûm, 227 f.
Field-scribe, 236
Finnish lanugage, 124
Flint tools, 256
Flood, the, 11, 77 f.
Folk-tales, 255
Followers of Horus, 254 f., 263 f.
Fortress, 36
Four Regions, 94; king of, 88, 100; kingdom of, 117 f.

G

Gaddash, 88
Galukani, patesi of Telloh, 123
Galutu, patesi of Gishkhu, 122
Gande, 86, 88
Gandish, king of Babylonia (Dynasty C), 26, 65, 86, 88
Gare, land in Benjamin, 15
Gath, 16
Gebelên, 233
Gem-Aton, 199, 205
Gemini, zodiacal sign of, 112; era of, 112
Genealogies, Assyrian royal, 57, 59, 130, 133
Genesis of Hermes, 251
Ger, "the stranger," 15
Gera, land of "the strangers," 15
Gideon, judge of Israel, 18
Gimil-ilishu, king of Isin, 107
Gimil-sin, king of Ur, 108
Gir-ki-shar, king of Sea-Land (Dynasty B), 82, 85
Gir-su, 117, 124
Gish-ám-me-ti, 68
Gishkhu, land east of the Tigris, 121
Gold, implements of, 258
Graves, form of, 258, 263

Greece, archon office of, 2
Gudea, patesi of Telloh, 114, 123
Gulkishar, king of Sea-Land (Dynasty B), 24, 26, 82, 85
Gunammide, patesi of Gishkhu, 121
Gungunu, king of Ur, 120
Gunidu, patesi of Telloh, 122
Gursar, patesi of Telloh, 122
Gutium, land in Kurdistan, 115

H

Habor, river of Mesopotamia, 106
Hamath, city of Syria, 103; Hamathites, 128, 264
Hammamat, 235, 259, 263
Hammurabi, king of Babylonia (Dynasty A), 24, 29 f., 45, 51, 74 ff., 80 ff., 89 ff., 111 f., 116, 119, 121, 137 f., 141, 148; vassal of Eri-Aku, 30, 99; code of, 14, 74, 93, 137, 141; letters of, 137
Hapu, 215
Haran, city of Mesopotamia, 104, 148
Haremhab, king of Egpyt (Dynasty XIX), 171, 178, 185, 200 ff.
Hathor, Egyptian goddess, 234
Hatshepsut, queen of Egypt (Dynasty XVIII), 171, 186 ff., 193
Hauran, mountains in Syria, 4, 105 f.
Hazael, king of Damascus, 4
Hebrews, 14 ff.; annalists of, 6; dialects of, 101 f.; documents of, 8; original home of, 106; settlements in Egypt, 155, 266
Heliopolis, 127, 129, 162, 164, 240, 260, 265 f.
Helios, Greek divinity, 251 ff.
Hephaistos, Greek divinity, 251 ff.
Heqerneheh, stela of, 198
Heracleopolis, 171, 234 ff., 238 ff.
Heracles, Greek divinity, 253
Heriusha, 192
Hermes, Genesis of, 251
Hermeus (=Haremhab), 160, 203
Hermopolis, 226, 228, 230
Hermopolis Magna, 228
Hermopolis Parva, 228
Heroic Age, 12
Hieraconpolis, 254
Hieroglyphs, Egyptian, 126, 263; Hittite, 126
Hindu chronology, 112
Hiram I, king of Tyre, 8
Hittites, hieroglyps of, 126; invasion of Babylonia by, 53, 88; conquest of Mitani by, 209

Hobab, Qenite king, 220
Homeric poems, 255
Honorables, 249-254
Horus, Egyptian divinity, 251 ff., 261 ff.; Followers of, 254 f., 261; smiths of, 261; majesty of, 259; period of, 254, 261
Horus-hawk, 259
Hyksos, 179, 191, 226, 228, 236, 240, 266; history of, 154-164; meaning of name of, 155; kings of 154 f., 217 ff., 223; expulsion of, 17, 160, 192, 217

I

Ibzan, judge of Israel, 18
Ibi-Sin, king of Ur, 108
Idin-Dagan, king of Isin, 107
Igigi, 94
Igur-kakbabu, patesi of Ashur, 137
Ikhnaton, king of Egypt (Dynasty XVIII), 21, 32 f., 66, 131 f., 151, 185, 265. See Amenhotep IV
Ikunum, patesi of Ashur, 140, 142 f., 147 f.
Ilion, 201
Iliopolis, 225 f.
Ilu-illati, early Babylonian king, 45
Ilu-ma-ilu, king of Sea-Land (Dynasty B), 24, 26, 53, 82, 121
Ilu-shûma, king (?) of Assyria, 51, 139 ff., 147 f.
Immerum, king of Sippara, 95, 119
Inachus, ancient king of Argos, 178, 203
Ini, king of Egypt, 169
Intef, the count, 169, 235
Intef I, king of Southern Egypt, (Dynasty XI), 235 f., 238
Intef II, king of Southern Egypt (Dynasty XI), 235
Intef III, king (?) of Southern Egypt (Dynasty XI), 233
Intef IV, 230
Intef-yoker, 236 f.
Intercalary days, 180
Interregnum, in Babylonia, 57
Irishu, patesi of Ashur, 139 f.
Irria, city east of the Tigris, 36
Isaac, 9 f., 152
Ishbi-Ura, king of Isin, 107
Ishme-Dagan, king of Isin, 107, 120
Ishme-Dagan I, patesi of Ashur, 143
Ishme-Dagan II, patesi of Ashur, 136
Ishmael, 9 f.

INDICES

Ishtar of Agade, 48; of Nineveh, 117; of Mitani, 117; of Eredu, 117
Isin, city of Akkad, 29, 40, 90 f., 96, 99, 114; dynasty of, 51, 90, 96
Isis, Egyptian goddess, 252 f.
Israel, 6 f., 15, 18 f.
Issachar, tribe of, 16
Itêr-ka-sha, king of Isin, 107
Ithit-Tawy, 227 f., 236
Itti-Marduk-balatu, identical with Esagil-shaduni, 55
Ivory, implements of, 258

J

Jabin, king of Canaan, 18
Jacob, 9 f., 152
Jannas, Hyksos king, 155, 221
Jair, judge of Israel, 18 f., 208
Ja-u-a, 4
Jehoram, king of Israel, 5 f.
Jehoshaphat, king of Judah, 6
Jehu, king of Israel, 4 ff.
Jephthah, judge of Israel, 18 f.
Jeroboan I, king of Israel, 6 f.
Jerusalem, 6 f., 156, 160, 163, 208
Jews, 160
Joqtanides, 105
Joram, king of Israel, 4
Joram, king of Judah, 6
Joseph, 10, 152
Joshua, 11 ff., 15 f., 152
Joshua, Book of, 14
Jubilees, of Ramses II, 206 f.
Judah, land of, 1, 6 f., 156, 160
Judah, tribe of, 14
Judges, Book of, 12–14, 16, 18
Judges, Hebrew, 12

K

Kadashman-Bêl I, king of Babylonia (Dynasty C), 32 f., 65, 70
Kadashman-Bêl II, king of Babylonia (Dynasty C), 26, 31, 66, 69
Kadashman-Kharbe I, king of Babylonia (Dynasty C), 32, 40, 65, 69, 70, 131 f.
Kadashman-Kharbe II, king of Babylonia (Dynasty C), 28, 66, 73
Kadashman-Turgu, king of Babylonia (Dynasty C), 31, 66, 69
Kahun Papyrus, 179, 211
Kalama, 118, 120
Kanephore, 97
Kâr-Duniash, Kassite name of Middle Babylonia, 34, 36, 38, 40, 44, 64, 71, 86, 89, 130

Kâr-Ishtar, 36
Kâr-Tukulti-Ninib, 44
Kara-Indash, king of Babylonia (Dynasty C), 33 f., 65, 131
Kara-Indash (=Kara-Khardash), 34
Kara-Khardash, king of Babylonia (Dynasty C), 32, 34, 40, 65, 69 f., 131
Karashtu, 38
Karnak, 194 f.
Karnak-List, 169 f., 174
Kashmar, 47
Kashshu, region of, 88, 146
Kashshû-nâdin-akhê, king of Babylonia (Dynasty E), 28, 47, 63
Kassites, 34, 40, 53, 63, 86, 88 ff.; dynasty of, 26 ff., 63 ff.
Kawâmil, 256
Kazallu, 48, 91 f., 95
Keb, Egyptian divinity, 252
Khabire (=Hebrews), 15 f.
Khalalama, patesi of Telloh, 123
Khalamba, old Babylonian king, 91
Khaneferre, king of Egypt (Dynasty V), 245
Khani-rabbat, 106
Kharkag, city and land in Media, 40
Kharsag-Kalama, city on the eastern bank of the Lower Tigris, 44, 118
Kharu, southern Palestine, 208
Khatti (=Hittite), land of, 53
Khayan, Hyksos king, 220
Khayu, prehistoric king of Lower Egypt, 172
Khebron, throne-name of Thutmose II, 156, 188
Khebt-noferu, 190
Kheti, 241
Kheti II, prince of Siût, 234, 237
Khois, 224, 229
Khumri (=Omri), 4
Ki-an-ni-bi, king of Sea-Land (Dynasty B), 24, 26, 45, 82
Kidinkutrash, king of Elam, 44
Kikia, patesi of Ashur, 143
Ki-en-gi, old name of Middle Babylonia, 116 ff., 124, 128 f., 265
Ki-Mash (=Masius), 105
Kinakhkhi or Kinakhna, 129
"King of the Four Regions," 116, 128
"King of Isin," 90, 116
"King of Kalama," 120
"King of Kish," 124
"King of Shumir and Akkad," 90, 97, 99 f., 116
Kings, Books of, 14
King-Lists, see Lists

Kish, 91 f., 95, 100, 121
Kir-gal-dara-bar, king of Sea-Land (Dynasty B), 24, 26, 82
Konkharis, king of Egypt, 179, 236
Kronus, Greek divinity, 251 ff.
Kudur-Bêl, king of Babylonia (Dynasty C), 26, 31, 66 ff.
Kudur-Mabug, prince of Ê—Mutpal, 96 ff., 130
Kudur-Nankhundi, king of Elam, 105
Kullar, 36
Kurdistan, 105, 262
Kuri-Galzu I, king of Babylonia (Dynasty C), 36, 65 f., 70, 111, 185
Kuri-Galzu II, king of Babylonia (Dynasty C), 31 ff., 40, 66, 69, 131 f.
Kurkhi, 105
Kush, 263

Lakhares, 216
Lamares, 216
Lapis-lazuli, seal of, 71
Larsa, 265; kings of, 96 f., 120, 127
Laws, Hebrew, 14 f.
Lebanon, 4
Legends of Settlements in Egypt, 259
Lepers, 161 ff., 208; leprosy, 160
Letters, 32 f., 64, 137; the Amarna, 15, 21, 32 f.
Libit-Ishtar, king of Isin, 107
Libya, 233 f., 236; Libyans, 233 f.
Licinus, Roman consul, 178
Limmu, office of, 2 f.; lists of, 1 ff.;
Lists, Babylonian king-lists, 22–30. Egyptian king-lists, 168–72, date-lists, 22, 29–31, 80 f., 90; see also Abydos, Karnak, and Sakkara-lists.
Livitical Code, 14
Lord of All, 55
Lower Egypt, 172 ff., 259
Lucinae, 259
Lugalanda, patesi, of Telloh, 122
Lugaldak, king of Kish, 123
Lugalkigubnidudu, king of Erech, 120
Lugalkisalsi, king of Erech, 120
Lugalshuggur, patesi of Telloh, 122
Lugaltarsi, king of Kish, 123
Lugalushumgal, patesi of Telloh, 114, 123
Lugalzaggisi, king of Erech, 120, 122
Lulumê, land east of Assyria, 36
Lummadur, patesi of Telloh, 122
Lunar year, 252
Lupdi, 38

Luxor, 198
Lydia, 8, 209

M

Ma^ɔin, 101
Magan, 48
Majesty of the Golden Horus, 260
Majesty of Horus, 260
Majesty of the king of Upper and Lower Egypt, 260
Majesty of the Son of Re, 260
Majesty of the Two Goddesses
Matkare, 193
Makh, prehistoric king of Lower Egypt, 172
Malga, 91, 99
Man, kingdom of, 105
Manasseh, tribe of, 16
Manes, 252
Manishtusu, king of Kish, 123
Mannu-dannu, king of Magan, 48
Marad, 91, 96
Marduk, son of Ea, chief god of Babylon, 44, 48, 55, 73, 87, 92 ff.; 133 f., 137
Marduk - - - king of Babylonia (Dynasty D), 28, 63
Marduk-akbê-erba, king of Babylonia (Dynasty D), 28, 62
Marduk-apil-iddin, king of Babylonia (Dynasty C), 28, 66
Marduk-balatsu-iqbi, 57
Marduk-bêl-ushate, 57
Marduk-nâdin-akhê, king of Babylonia (Dynasty D), 28, 38, 60, 62 f.
Marduk-shâkin-shum, 57
Marduk-shâpik-zêr-mâti, king of Babylonia (Dynasty D), 28, 38, 53, 62, 135
Marduk-zâkir-shum, 57
Mârê-Amurrum, 103
Marriti, 38
Martu, 96, 97, 99, 109, 115
Mash, mountain of Mesopotamia, 105
Masius, 105 f.
Mastabas, Egyptian, 127, 258
Matriarchate, 104
Mechir, sixth Egyptian month, 180, 182 ff.
Medes, 158
Media, 145
Median usurpers, 77 f.
Medinet Habu, 193
Mediterranean Sea, 104; period 261
Melam-kurkura, king of Sea-Land (Dynasty B), 24, 26, 82

Meli-Shipak, king of Babylonia (Dynasty C), 28, 66
Memnonion, 198
Memphis, 154, 163, 175, 240 ff., 245, 247, 252, 254
Menus, king of Egypt, (Dynasty I), 169, 246 ff., 254 f., 264
Menkauhor, king of Egypt (Dynasty V), 245
Menmare (=Seti I), 222
Menophris (=Ramses I), era of, 177 f., 204
Menpeh(ti)re (=Ramses I), 204
Mentuhotep I, king of Egypt (Dynasty XI), 229, 231 ff.
Mentuhotep II, king of Egypt (Dynasty XI), 234 ff.
Mentuhotep III, king of Egypt (Dynasty XI), 231 ff.
Mentuhotep IV king of Egypt (Dynasty XI), 216, 231 ff.
Mephramuthosis (=Amenhotep II), 157
Mephres (=Thutmose III), 157
Merneptah, king of Egypt (Dynasty XIX), 207 f.
Mernere I, king of Egypt (Dynasty VI), 169, 244
Mernere II, king of Egypt (Dynasty VI), 244
Mesha, mountain of, 105
Mesilim, king of Kish, 123
Mesniu, 261
Mesopotamia, 20, 89, 103, 105 f., 115
Mestraeans, 251, 260, 264
Midian 20; oppression of Israel by, 18; Moses' flight to, 10
Miebis, king of Egypt (Dynasty I), 171, 249
Milkipal, king of Sea-Land (Dynasty B), 24, 26, 82
Min, Egyptian divinity, 263 f.
Minean dialect, 101
Mininum dates, of Babylonian kings, 31 f.; of Egyptian kings, 168, 174
Mitani, kingdom of, 104, 106 f., 117, 209
Mizpeh, 17
Mizraim, 251, 260
Moab, 18
Months, Egyptian, 180
Mortuary customs, 258
Moses, 10 f., 152
Muballitat-Sheruâ, 34, 40, 69 f., 131
Mummifying, 263
Muru, 91, 96

Mussian, 262
Mutakkil-Nusku, king of Assyria, 59, 135 f.
Mutemuya, 198
Mutnofret, 190
Muzazir, 262
Mycenae, 255

N

Nabonassar, king of Babylonia, 1, 2, 77, 112 f.
Nabonidus, king of Babylonia, 67 f., 74, 78, 80, 108 f., 111 ff.
Nabshemea, 82, 121
Nabû-apil-iddin, king of Babylonia, 55
Nabû-dâni, king of Assyria, 64, 131
Nabû-mukîn-apli, king of Babylonia, 55
Nabû-nâdin, king of Babylonia (Dynasty D), 28, 62; was called Adad-apil-iddin before his usurpation of the throne, 38
Nabû-nâzir, king of Babylonia, 57
Nabû-shum-ukin, king of Babylonia, 55
Nabû-ushabshi, 118
Nadab, king of Israel, 6
Naharina, 192, 196
Nahor, 11 f.
Nakhtnebtepnofer (=Intef II), 236
Nakht-set, king of Egypt (Dynasty XX), 210 f.
Nammakhni, patesi of Telloh, 114, 123
Nannar (=moon-god of Ur), 97
Narâm-sin, king of Agade, 48, 108 ff., 123
Nazibugash, usurper, 32, 34, 65, 69
Nazi-Maraddash, king of Babylonia (Dynasty C), 31, 36, 40, 66, 70, 132 f.
Nebhepetre (=Mentuhotep III), 232
Nebtawire (=Mentuhotep II), 232
Nebtepnofer (=Intef III), 233
Nebuchadrezzar I, king of Babylonia (Dynasty D), 36, 38, 62, 82 ff.
Neferirkare, king of Egypt, (Dynasty V), 245
Neheb, pre-dynastic king of Lower Egypt, 172
Nekhbet, Egyptian goddess, 259 f., 262
Nema(t)re (=Amenemhet III), 216
Neo-Bablyonian period, 151
Neolithic age, 257 f., 262
New-moon dates, 168, 175, 182 ff.
New-year's day, 2, 175
Ni, god of Kish, 91

Nibhotep, (=Mentuhotep I), 233
Nibma(t)re (=Amenhotep III), 198
Nile, 161, 256 ff.
Nimmuria (=Amenhotep III), 198
Nimrod, 118
Ninâ, city of Southern Babylonia, 117
Nine Bows, 234
Nineveh, 3, 60, 117
Ninib, Babylonian god, 44, 144, 146 f.
Ninib-apil-Ekur, king of Assyria, 36, 59, 134 ff., 138, 209
Ninib-kudurru-uzur, king of Babylonia (Dynasty F), 47
Ninmakh, 87, 89
Ninus, 144, 146 f.
Nippur, capital of Ki-en-gi, 44, 92, 94 ff., 111, 116 ff., 124, 129
Nisan, first month of the Babylonian year, 2
Nitokris, queen of Egypt (Dynasty VI), 243 f.
Nomes of Egypt, 154, 257
Northerners, 208
Northland, 254
Nubia, 192 ff., 199 f, 205; Nubians, 234
Nubkheperre (=Intef IV), 230
Nûr-Adad, king of Larsa, 120
Nuserre, king of Egypt (Dynasty V), 245

O

Olympiad, the first, 145, 201
Okheperkare (=Thutmose I), 190
Omen-tablets of Sargon, 48, 108, 112
Omri, king of Israel, 4, 6
On (=Heliopolis), 127
Opeh(ti)set, era of, 221
Opis, 38
Orontes, river of, 196
Orus (=Ikhnaton), 157, 161
Osarsiph, 159, 161–64, 200, 207 ff.
Osiris, god of Abydos, 127, 208, 252 f., 263 f.; Osyris, 164
Othniel, Hebrew judge, 16, 18

P

Paddan-Aram, 10
Pakhnan, Hyksos king, 220
Pachon, ninth Egyptian month, 180, 182 ff.
Palaeolithic age, 256 ff., 261
Palermo stone, 168, 172, 250
Palestinè, 14 f., 89, 115, 192, 208, 254 f., 261
Papis, 161, 163

Papyri, *Ebers*, 180 f.; *Harris*, 208; *Westcar*, 245; *Kahun*, 179, 211
Parian Chronicle, 8
Pashe, dynasty of, 28
Patesi (=judge, ruler), of Babylonia, 114, 120 ff.; of Assyria, 136 ff.
Patriarchs, 255
Paul, St., 18 f.
Peleg, 11 f.
Pelusium, 158
Pentateuch, 14
Pepi I, king of Egypt (Dynasty VI), 144
Pepi II, king of Egypt (Dynasty VI), 169, 244
Persia, 1
Philistines, 18, 161, 208
Phiops, see Pepi
Phoenicia, 158
Pilasqi, 36
"Pillar of his mother," 194
Pituru, 105
Pius II, Roman consul, 177
Polybus, 209
Pottery, prehistoric, 257 f., 262
Predynastic kings of Egypt, 172, 250 ff., 256
Proto-Aryan language, 126
Ptah, Egyptian deity, 251 f.
Ptolemaic Canon, 1 ff., 21
Punt, 193, 263
Pur-Sagali, 3
Put, 263
Pyramids, 127; the pyramid-builders, 255

Q

Qadushshi, king of Sea-Land (Dynasty B), 24, 26, 82, 86, 88
Qarqar, 3, 5
Qedem, 105 f.
Qenites, 220, 261

R

Raid by the Ephraimites, 16
Ramesses (=Ramses I), 157 f.
Ramesses (=Ramses II), 157, 203
Ramesseum, 205
Ramessides, 211
Ramses I, king of Egypt, (Dynasty XIX), 171, 178, 185, 192, 200 ff.
Ramses II, king of Egypt (Dynasty XIX), 159, 171 f., 201 ff., 221 f.
Ramses III, king of Egypt (Dynasty XX), 208, 211

INDICES 299

Ramses IV, king of Egypt (Dynasty XX), 211
Ramses VI, king of Egypt (Dynasty XX), 211
Ramses IX, king of Egypt (Dynasty XX), 211
Ramses XII, king of Egypt (Dynasty XX), 211
Rapiqi, 38
Rapsakes (=Ramses III), 211
Rathotis (=Tutenkhamon), 157, 200
Re, Egyptian deity, 260, 265
Re-Atum, 265
Re-Harakhte, 268
Re-Sebek, 265
Red Sea, 259, 263
Regions, The Four, 94
Rehoboam, king of Judah, 6
Re-sekhem-Amen-tawi, king of Egypt, 169
Rêsh-Adad, king of Apirak, 48
Reu, 11 f.
Rhampses (=Ramses II), 160, 163
Rhampses (=Ramses III), 164
Rîm-Sin (=Eri-Aku), 97
Rome, founding of, 7; consular office of, 2
Royal titles, in Egypt, 259
Rubatum, 91, 96
"Ruler of Heliopolis," 197
"Ruler of Thebes," 197

S

Sꜣ-n-g-rꜣ, 20
Sabaean dialect, 101
Sabbath, motive for, 15
Sahure, king of Egypt (Dynasty V), 169, 245
Saite Nome, 154
Sakkara, 171 f.
Sakkara-list, 171
Salatis, Hyksos king, 154, 219
Samaritan, 11, 103
Samuel, 13, 17, 19
Samsi-Adad, see Shamshi-Adad I
Samson, judge of Israel, 19
Samsu-ditana, king of Babylonia (Dynasty A), 24, 30, 45, 53, 79 f., 88, 138
Samsu-iluna, king of Babylonia (Dynasty A), 24, 30 f., 45, 51, 53, 79 f., 86, 91, 138
Sanctuaries, pre-Mosaic, 14
Sand-dwellers, 192
Sangara, 20
Saniru (=Shenir), 4

Sankh(kare), 233
Sankhkare (=Mentuhotep IV), 232
Sar, the Babylonian, 78
Sarai, 9
Sa-Re, 129, 265
Sargon (I), king of Agade, 47, 108 ff., 147; omens of, 48, 112
Sargon (II), king of Assyria, 3, 151
Sarug, 115
Saul, king of Israel, 13, 17 ff.
Sea of the East (=Persian Gulf), 48, 115
Sea-Land (=^{mât} *Tamtim*), 48, 53, 86, 263; Dynasty B, of, 24, 26, 45, 51, 53, 81 ff., 86; Dynasty E of, 28, 45, 47
Seal of Shagarakti-Shuriash, 71 f.
Sebek, Egyptian deity, 265
Sebeknefrure, queen of Egypt (Dynasty XII), 171, 210 ff.
Seka, predynastic king of Lower Egypt, 172
Seleucidae, 21
Semiramis, 144
Sennacherib, king of Assyria, 60, 71 f.
Sephar, 105
Septuagint, 11 f.
Sequence-dates, 256
Serpent-worship, 262
Serug, 11 f.
Sesostris I, king of Egypt (Dynasty XII), 212 ff., 227, 229, 236
Sesostris II, king of Egypt (Dynasty XII), 212 ff.
Sesostris III, king of Egypt (Dynasty XII), 179, 211 ff.
Set (=Hebrew El Shaddai, Syrian Adad), god of Tanis, 220, 260
Sethos, Hyksos king, 221
Sethos (=Nakht-Set), 163
Sethos(is) (=Seti I), 157 f., 160, 203
Sethroite nome, 154
Seti I, king of Egypt (Dynasty XIX), 159, 169, 171 f., 201 ff., 221 f.
Seti II, king of Egypt (Dynasty XIX), 201 ff.
Setnakht, 210; see Nakht-Set
Sezerkare (=Amenhotep I), 180
Shades, 252
Shagarakti-Buriash, 67; sec. following
Shagarakti-Shuriash, king of Babylonia (Dynasty C), 28, 31, 67, 70 ff., 133
Shala, Assyrian goddess, 60
Shalmaneser I, king of Assyria, 59, 71, 133, 140 f., 148

Shalmaneser II, king of Assyria, 3, 4, 146
Shamash, sun-god of Sippara and Larsa, 74, 108
Shamash-mudammiq, king of Babylonia, 55
Shamgar, Hebrew judge, 16
Shamshi-Adad I, patesi of Ashur, 136 ff., 141 f., 148
Shamshi-Adad II, patesi of Ashur, 134, 136, 143
Shamshi-Adad III, king of Assyria, 59, 136
Shar-kenkâte-Ashir, patesi of Ashur 143, 148
Shar-ali (="City-king"), Babylonian royal title, 116
Shar Kish (=king of Kish), 124
Shashu, 193
Shatt-el-Haj, the river, 97, 117
Sha-ush-kas, goddess of Mitani, 105, 117
Shelah, 11 f.
Shem, 11 f., 114; as deified ancestor of the Semites, 103
Shemu, third Egyptian Season, 180
Shenir, mountain of Syria, 4
Shepherds (=Hyksos), 155 ff.
Shepseskare, king of Egypt (Dynasty V), 245
Shigiltu, 57
Shinar, biblical name of Middle Babylonia, 20, 117 f.
Shu, Egyptian deity, 252
Shubari, later Shubria, 36, 105
Shumir and Akkad, 86, 116 ff., 129
Shuzigash, Babylonian usurper, 32, 40, 65, 69
Sidon, 4
Simeon, tribe of, 14
Silanum-Shuqamuna, king of Babylonia (Dynasty F), 47
Simmah-Shipak, king of Sea-Land (Dynasty E), 28, 45, 55, 63
Simti-Shilkhak, 97
Sin, Moon god of Haran, 104
Sin (=Ura-imitti), King of Isin, 108
Sinaitic peninsula, 261
Sin-gâmil, king of Erech, 121
Sin-gâshid, king of Erech, 121
Sin-iddinanan, king of Larsa, 120
Sin-Mâgir, king of Isin, 108
Sin-muballit, king of Babylonia (Dynasty A), 24, 29 f., 45, 79 ff., 90 f. 196 ff., 104, 107, 116, 119, 139, 143, 148

Sippâ, 47
Sippara, 91 ff., 99 f., 108, 119
Sippara of Anuitum, 38, 67
Sippara of Shamash, 38, 74 f.
Siptah, king of Egypt (Dynasty XIX), 201 ff., 209
Sir-'-la-ai (=Isràel), 4
Sirius star, 175 ff., 184
Sivan (=June), third Babylonian month, 3
Siût, 234
Skemiophris, 216
Snofru, king of Egypt (Dynasty IV), 109, 255
Soleh, 199 f., 205
Solomon, king of Israel, 6 ff., 12 f., 18
Somali-land, 263
Sosis, Egyptian deity, 252 f.
Sothis-book, 165, 179, 203, 209, 219, 221
Sothic cycles, 176 ff., 204, 251
Sothic dates, 179 ff.
Sothic festivals, 168, 204
Sothic Star, 175
Speos Artemidos, 193
Spirits, worship of, 257
Stele of Vultures, 262
Stone implements, 258
Strangers, 15
Su-abu, 51, 138, 141
Subartu, 57, 115
Su-êdin, 48, 57
Suez, 262
Sugagi, 34, 40
Su-gir, 117
Sukhi, 38
Sulili, 138
Sumer and Akkad, 55
Sumerians, 124 ff., 262
Sumgir, 117, 124
Sumir, 117, 129
Sumu-abi, king of Babylonia (Dynasty A), 29 f., 79, 90 ff., 103, 138, 141 f., 147, f
Sumu-la-ilu, king of Babylonia (Dynasty A), 22, 30, 45, 79, 90 ff., 103, 119, 138, 142, 148
Sungir, 117
Sun-worshipers, 265
Susa, 263
Sutû, 40, 55
Synchronistic history, 32 ff., 63, 69 f., 89, 130 ff.
Syria, 5, 89, 103, 106, 115, 156, 164, 195

T

Tammuz, Babylonian deity, 263 f.
Tanis, 222
Tashzigurmash, king of Babylonia (Dynasty C), 26, 64 f.
Taurus, zodiacal sign of, 112; era of, 112
Te, king of, 121 f.
Tehenu, (=Libya), 233, 236
Telloh, 86, 114, 121, 129
Temple of Anu and Adad, 134 ff.
Temple of Ashur, 137 ff.
Temple of Solomon, 7 f., 12
Terah, 11 f.
Teshup, Mitanic deity, 105 f.
Tethmosis (=Thutmose I), 156, 162
Teti, king of Egypt (Dynasty VI), 244
Text of the Bible, 11
Thebais (=Thebes), 155
Thebes, 171, 200, 214, 228, 233 f., 240 f.
Thesh, predynastic king of Lower Egypt, 172
Thinis, 233, 235, 241, 247, 249, 252, 264
Thmosis (=Thutmose I), 160
Thmosis (=Thutmose IV), 157
Thospitis, lake of, 105
Thoth, Egyptian deity, 228
Thoth, first month of the Egyptian year, 175
Thouoris, 200, 209 f.
Thummosis, 156
Thutmose I, king of Egypt (Dynasty XVIII), 186 ff., 199 f., 227 f.
Thutmose II, king of Egypt (Dynasty XVIII), 186 ff., 193
Thutmose III, king of Egypt (Dynasty XVIII), 180, 182, 185 ff., 194 f.
Thutmose IV, king of Egypt (Dynasty XVIII), 186 ff., 197 f.
Thutmosids, feud of, 188 ff.
Tib, the river, 262
Tiglath-pileser I, king of Assyria, 38, 59, 60, 62, 134 ff., 209
Tiglath-pileser IV, king of Assyria, 55
Tigris, 44, 53, 89, 105 f., 117
Timaeus, 153
Tithoes, Egyptian deity, 253
Tiu, predynastic king of Lower Egypt, 172
Tola, judge of Israel, 18
Town-rulers, 208
Tribes of Israel, 13
Troja, city of Egypt, 127
Troy, city of Asia Minor, 8, 159, 201, 209
Tukulti-Ashur, king of Assyria, 44, 64, 134
Tukulti-Ninib I, king of Assyria, 36, 44, 59, 64, 71, 73, 133 f.
Tum, Egyptian deity, 265
Tumilat, Wady, 265
Tunroi, 171 f.
Turanian languages, 124
Turin Papyrus, 168 f., 171, 173 f., 213 ff., 243, 250, 253 ff.
Turkish language, 124
Turra, 127, 196
Turushpâ, 105
Tushpâ, 105
Two goddesses, 254, 259, 262, 264
Typhon, Egyptian deity, 162, 252 f.
Tyre, 4, 8, 129

U

Ud-unu (=Laisa), 127
Ukush, patesi of Gishkhu, 122
Ula-Burariash, king of Sea-Land, 87, 89
Ulam-Buriash, king of Sea-Land, 53, 87, 88
Unas, king of Egypt (Dynasty V), 245
Upper Eygpt, 172 ff.
Upper and Lower Egypt, 254, 260, 262, 264
Ur, 91 f., 96, 104, 114, 120; dynasty of, 29, 108
Uraeus, 260, 262
Uranus, Greek deity, 261
Ura-imitti, king of Isin, 51, 144
Urartu, 105
Ur-Baʾu, patesi of Telloh, 123
Ur-Ê, patesi of Telloh, 114, 123
Ur-En-gur, king of Ur, 48, 107, 116, 121
Ur-Gur, king of Ur, 107
Urkal, patesi of Telloh, 123
Urlumma, patesi of Gishkhu, 121
Urmia, sea of, 105
Urnesu, patesi of Gishkhu, 122
Ur-Ninâ, king of Telloh, 122, 129
Ur-nin-Gir-su, patesi of Telloh, 114, 123
Ur-Ninib, king of Isin, 107, 116, 146 f.
Urninsin, patesi of Telloh, 123
Ursaguddu, king of Kish, 123
Uru-azag, 24
Urukagina I, king of Telloh, 122
Urukagina II, patesi of Telloh

Uru-kha, dynasty of, 24, 26, 29, 81 ff.
Urumush, king of Kish, 123
Uru-Ninâ, 86
Userkaf, king of Egypt (Dynasty V), 245
Userkare, king of Egypt (Dynasty VI), 244
Ush, patesi of Gishkhu, 121
Ushpia, patesi of Ashur, 139 ff.
Usurpers, Median, 77 f.
Uzet, Egyptian deity, 259

V

Van, lake of, 105
Versions of the Bible, 11 f.
Votive inscriptions, 96 f.
Vulture, 260, 262; stela of, 262

W

Wahanekh (= Intef I), 235 ff., 238
Wazenez, predynastic king of Lower Egypt, 172
West-Land, 115; see Martu
Wilderness, wandering in, 17
Worship, irregular forms of, 16; see also Serpent-worship; Sun-worshipers.

Y

Yabnik-ilu, 102
Yadakhu-Nabû, 102
Yakhar-zêr-ili, 91
Yakhzar-ilu, 102
Yakub-ilu, 102
Year, Lydian, 8; Egyptian, 175; Gregorian, 175; Julian, 175; Lunar, 252

Z

Zab, the Lower, 38
Zâb, the Upper, 34, 40
Zaban, 36
Zabu, king of Babylonia (Dynasty A), 24, 30, 45, 79, 90 f., 103
Zakardada, 91, 96
Zalzallat, the river, 40; the name is a miswriting for *Zâb-i-lat*, "the Upper Zâb"
Zamama-shum-iddin, king of Babylonia (Dynasty C), 28, 36, 66, 135
Zame --, king of Isin, 108
Zamua, 64
Zanqi, 36
Zazai, king of Egypt (Dynasty I), 171
Zenjirli, 144
Zeus, Greek deity, 253
Zibir, king of Babylonia (Dynasty C), 64 f.
Zimri, king of Israel, 6
Zoan, 222
Zodiacal signs, 2, 112

www.ingramcontent.com/pod-product-compliance
Lightning Source LLC
Chambersburg PA
CBHW050849240426
43667CB00031B/2939